PLANNING & MANAGING

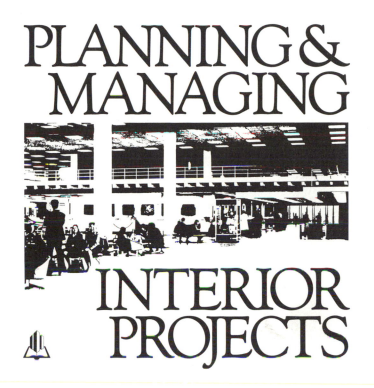

INTERIOR PROJECTS

CAROL E. FARREN

PLANNING & MANAGING
INTERIOR PROJECTS

C A R O L E. F A R R E N

R.S. MEANS COMPANY, INC.
CONSTRUCTION CONSULTANTS & PUBLISHERS
100 Construction Plaza
P.O. Box 800
Kingston, MA 02364-0800
(617) 585-7880

In keeping with the general policy of R.S. Means Company, Inc., its authors, editors, and engineers apply diligence and judgment in locating and using reliable sources for the information published. However, no guarantee or warranty can be given, and all responsibility and liability for loss or damage are hereby disclaimed by the authors, editors, engineers and publisher of this publication with respect to the accuracy, correctness, value and sufficiency of the data, methods and other information contained herein as applied for any particular purpose or use.

Printed in the United States of America

10   9   8   7   6   5   4

Library of Congress Catalog Card Number 88-151212

ISBN 0-87629-097-7

Dedication

This book is dedicated to my father, Merritt F. Farren, a beautiful person; the architect, designer, and artist who trained my first two on-the-job coaches.

TABLE OF CONTENTS

FOREWORD

Planning and managing interior design projects of any size requires considerable skill in coordinating people, furniture, equipment, and space, within typically stringent time and cost parameters. Sophisticated planning and organizational skills are essential. New information technologies, dynamic organizations experiencing rapid change, escalating space and property costs, and more educated, more professional office workers with higher expectations all contribute to new requirements of clients, and to new responsibilities for interior design and facility management professionals. The process of *implementing* the design—making sure that what is built actually corresponds to what the designers and clients intended—warrants as much attention as the design process itself.

Unfortunately, most interior design educational programs provide students with little practical advice on how to plan and manage a complex interior project. The process of managing an interior design project, from initial briefing to writing specifications to installation, is for many designers less glamorous than working with boards, colors, fabrics, lighting, and layout. Yet the aesthetics of design are what might be called the *visible spectrum*; the end, visible result of a complex process much of which is invisible to the end-user. The form of design catches our attention, but underlying this visible spectrum are all those aspects of the design process that transform ideas and concepts into three dimensional reality. This book addresses the *hidden spectrum* of design.

Drawing on years of experience working with projects from small office relocations to projects involving hundreds of thousands of square feet in multiple facilities, Carol Farren has provided in *Planning and Managing Interior Projects* a practical guide to help steer the interior designer, facility manager, architect, or contracts administrator through the intricacies of working with clients, contractors, and manufacturers to produce environments that enhance the ways in which people live and work on time and within budget. Farren also focuses on the *paying client*, the person(s) responsible for funding and administering an interior project.

Farren offers more than general concepts and ideas. A hallmark of *Planning and Managing Interior Projects* is that it provides copious illustrations of basic procedures based on actual working documents. The discussion of negotiating with landlords over tenant improvements, for example, is brought to life with an actual tenant work letter. Similarly, in sections dealing with topics such as furniture specification, budgeting, or identifying user needs, Farren provides sample forms, surveys, and contract documents that illustrate the kinds of points made in the text. These will be enormously useful to persons faced with planning or managing interior projects of any size.

In many cases, more than one approach is described so that the virtues of alternative procedures can be compared. Equally useful, the rationale for using different approaches is briefly described. One begins to get a feel for why one does certain things, not merely that they should be done. Considerable attention is also paid to details often overlooked in planning the overall design concept, such as budgeting for plants, accessories, artwork, and signage; making decisions about reusing or refinishing furniture; or handling change orders.

Planning and Managing Interior Projects covers implementation issues spanning the entire process from initial orientation meetings with clients through furniture specification, purchase, and delivery. Straightforward discussions of how to prepare budgets for different phases of an interior project, with many actual examples, presents the whole discussion in the "real world" financial context within which interiors projects live, die—or sometimes just shrivel. This book is a useful reference for anyone responsible for implementing an interior project.

Franklin Becker, Ph.D.

PREFACE

The job of any designer is to enhance space. His or her objective is to create an environment for improved living or working. To accomplish this requires not only artistic talent, but extensive design training both in school and on the job. The designer must also be a good manager and pseudo-psychologist in order to deal with the many parties involved in a design project. Clients can be capricious, unrealistic, dogmatic, or just plain difficult. In addition, there are building managers, construction contractors, furniture dealers, movers, telephone installers, and art consultants to work with and coordinate, all unique individuals who must be motivated and directed by the designer. By being familiar with all aspects of interior project management, the designer can speak with confidence to those individuals. This generates respect and leads to good working relationships with all parties.

This book deals with the areas of an interiors project that most design schools do not emphasize; in particular, the business aspect of medium and large commercial projects. Design schools teach the necessary basic design skills, techniques, concepts of good design, space planning, furniture layout, and color and material coordination, but this is not all one needs to become a successful designer or interior planner. The major portion of any project is composed of taking surveys, writing specifications, budgets, purchase orders, expediting deliveries, installing the furniture and furnishings, as well as other administrative matters. Whether the job is large or small, these steps are invariably involved.

Most students graduate from school thinking that they will be able to start designing glamorous spaces immediately. They are not aware that almost any client's first question is "How much will it cost?" But budgets were never of prime importance in design school. How does one write a budget, and more importantly, stay within it?

This book provides the tools necessary to perform a complete job for any client, from the first meeting to the final move. Included are sample forms, checklists, letters, and drawings. All the steps of interior project planning and management are spelled out in this book with examples. Those functions that are required are simplified and systematized so that the designer can spend more of his time doing the work he enjoys.

Any designer can commission one job, but unless he can perform the necessary administrative functions, he will not be able to retain repeat customers. The income of an individual designer and the success of a design firm (large or small) depends, in part, upon client referrals and repeat business. Thus, the designer's ability to perform necessary managerial functions greatly affects his success or failure. The designer must meet each client's individual functional and budget requirements, while also satisfying aesthetic needs and desires.

This book devotes little attention to space planning techniques, furniture selection, color coordination, drafting, or other interior design skills. Emphasized are coordination and communication with occupants, landlords, building managers, construction contractors, and interiors contractors, as well as the client.

Most designers, planners, and project managers become accomplished in the "business" aspects of the design field out of necessity and from experience. *Planning and Managing Interior Projects* attempts to make this experience more successful for all parties involved in an interior project.

Acknowledgments

The author wishes to express her appreciation for the creative and practical guidance she received from the following individuals: Dian Kaye, who originally collaborated on the book; Frank Otway and George Gaspar, her first two "on the job" trainers; Frank Becker, professor of facility management at Cornell University, who graciously critiqued the original efforts and contributed the foreword to this book; Eugene Boshes, designer, for insight into the book format; Georgie Thomas, Treasurer of New Hampshire, for her patience and support; and Elizabeth Winchester, interior designer, for her continued support.

For technical support, the author would like to ackowledge the following: Ida Wolecki, for editing; Tom Stauffer, for illustrations; and Fred Jackson, Judy Latzera, and Doris Williams, for word processing.

Editor's Note

The role of the individual or group responsible for an interior project is a versatile one, involving design, planning, budgeting, scheduling, and project management. The person who fills this role may be an interior designer, a facilities manager or planner, an architect, a building manager/owner, a contracts administrator, a furniture dealer, a design/build construction contractor, or an office manager. This person may be a self-employed individual or an architectural or design firm, a corporation or bank, a furniture dealer, a general contractor, a government agency, or a property manager.

For the purposes of this book, the terms "designer", "planner", and "project manager" refer to any or all of the above persons who may be involved in and responsible for interiors projects. Each term may be used, where appropriate, in discussions of the different phases of an interiors project as a description of the "role" at that stage. The processes, methods, and practices described herein pertain to all commercial interiors projects no matter who is performing the various functions.

C H A P T E R O N E

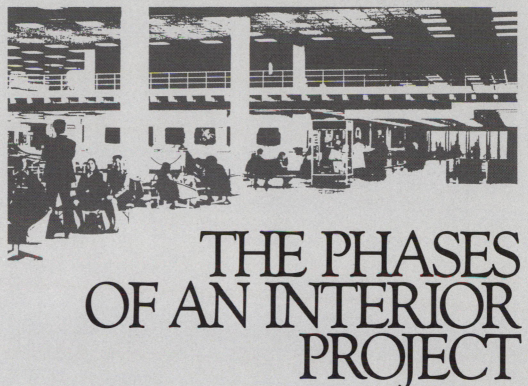

THE PHASES
OF AN INTERIOR
PROJECT

THE PHASES OF AN INTERIOR PROJECT

An interiors project is made up of several stages or phases. Whether a job is large or small, these same phases will always occur. Therefore, it is helpful to systematically consider every phase so that nothing will be omitted. The designer must be aware of his overall responsibility for each of these phases and the time frame in which he must operate. This chapter defines the phases and the roles of those involved in interiors projects.

The Orientation Meeting

Upon award of the design contract, the first objective is to get an overview of the client's needs: what he wants, how much he is willing to spend, and why the change is being considered. In order to accomplish this, the designer or project planner must meet with the client to discuss and conceptually analyze the project. The project planner must initially determine whether a change can be effected in the present facilities to accommodate existing and future space goals, or if new facilities and space are necessary. In order to evaluate the client's needs, the designer or project planner must determine the following:

- The client's goals and directions
- Future goals and directions
- Aesthetic needs and desires

Establish Goals and Directions

The designer must determine what the client has in mind—redecoration or renovation of current space, procurement of new space, or perhaps both. Some people consult a designer when their lease is almost up or when they have outgrown their present space, with no specific idea of what to do next. The planner begins in every case by determining how much money the client is willing to spend and whether or not additional space is required.

Determine Preliminary Budget

The client often has no idea of the cost of interiors projects and may be shocked when he discovers the potential costs. For this reason, an approximate budget should first be agreed upon, based on what the client intends to spend. This budget then serves as a guide for the designer's recommendations.

Occasionally, a client does not want to spend the money required to achieve necessary goals. In this case, the designer must persuade the client that the costs are justified. Or, a client might say he has no idea what he should spend to achieve the desired effect and asks the designer to recommend a budget based on the company's current needs. It is important, therefore, to be familiar with local current costs of new construction, renovation, new furniture, and rent for the proposed locality. Based on this knowledge and the size and type of the project, the designer is usually able to estimate an approximate cost per square foot for the project and thus determine a very preliminary budget.

Renovation

The client may simply want an improved appearance or upgraded image. The designer may suggest rearrangement and redecoration of the existing space, with little or no construction while at the same time improving the office environment. Noise reduction, improved lighting, and refurbished heating and air conditioning are some other possible objectives. Such improvements could be made assuming these factors: the client has a long lease or an option to renew; that space utilization can be improved; and that the company including any anticipated growth will still fit appropriately into the space. On the other hand, the client may intend to implement an organizational change, which may require more extensive renovation to better utilize the existing space.

Relocation

A firm may have already decided to relocate. If this is the case, the client and the project planner must determine whether to lease space or build new space. This decision must be made early, as there are very different cost and scheduling requirements involved for each alternative. If the client decides to lease space, the project planner may participate in the client's search for an appropriate space. The planner may even perform feasibility studies before the new location is selected.

The client may be involved in a consolidation due to past expansion which left the offices scattered. A new corporate headquarters may be desired. Or, a firm may be consolidating due to a reduction in forces. If this is the case, there are often serious personnel problems to consider. Another concern is the disposal or sale of excess furniture. The designer must be prepared to handle or assist with such concerns as an auxiliary, if not contractual, responsibility to the client.

Tax Ramifications

The project planner should be aware of possible tax ramifications of the various choices available and should discuss them with the client. The ever-changing tax climate can have a significant impact on the client's choice of options. Construction costs may be capitalized over the life of the facility. For example, movable walls, as well as furniture, can depreciate at a faster rate and over a shorter period of time than permanent walls. This faster depreciation may have a major impact on the firm's "bottom line" decision. In all cases, the designer should recommend that the client seek competent, professional tax advice.

Schedule of Completion

The time frame that the client has in mind will ultimately influence the interior design plan. If parameters are set by the imminent expiration of a lease, this may not allow for much flexibility. The project planner should be sure that the client is being realistic about the project completion date; projects often take longer than expected. The planner should be aware of the time schedules for new construction, renovation, and delivery or manufacture of furniture in the desired locality. With this knowledge, the planner will be able to offer informed advice about realistic completion schedules and, therefore, recommendations for the proper scope and size of a project.

Future Goals and Directions

The decision to redecorate, renovate, move, or build should, as much for other reasons, be based on the the company's future growth expectations. If a company is expanding rapidly and forecasts that the expansion will continue, the planner may suggest that the firm lease more space than is currently needed. The excess space can be sub-let on a short-term basis. Extra space is thus available for future expansion, saving the expense of moving again. Or, a company may wish to renovate and refurbish on a minimal basis now and save its capital for an expected relocation in the near future. A firm with an unknown future may need a space with maximum flexibility. Keeping in mind the many possibilities for expansion, the planner should encourage the client to look to the future in making the decision for today.

Determine Aesthetic Needs and Desires

The designer will need to know the client's aesthetic preferences. Some clients have specific ideas; others initially have no idea what they want. It is always a bonus if the client knows exactly what he wants. The most difficult clients are those who cannot make up their minds, or who don't know what they like. Actually, after working with these clients long enough, both the designer and the client usually discovers that they really do have very specific preferences. Unfortunately, this takes time, which is often a luxury.

Style

Styles are classified in three main categories: Traditional, Contemporary, and Modern. When selecting a traditional scheme, it is important to decide whether antiques or reproductions will be utilized. The cost difference between antiques and reproductions can be significant.

The choice of style is dependent on the type of atmosphere the client wants to convey. A client who wishes to appear very stable, as if he's been successfully in business for many years, may want a traditional look. A client who is in the recording business, however, may want an ultra modern look. The problem with wanting an ultra modern office is that what is current today is outdated tomorrow. A client wishing a modern image almost has to commit to refurbishing the space every two to three years to keep up with the latest style.

The vast majority of clients select a contemporary look which is classic in design and is essentially timeless. Only the color scheme, in this case, would date the interior. It is easier to change the color scheme (buying new carpet and upholstery) than to redesign the entire office and purchase new furniture.

Interior Palette

After the style has been selected, the basic interior palette must be chosen. The initial decision is usually between warm or cool colors.

Usually the background, or envelope, is kept rather neutral with shades of one hue or a patterned carpet with walls in tones from the carpet. The upholstery is often in an accent color or pattern to add interest. In addition, upholstery is the least expensive and least disruptive item to change should the client want to vary the appearance of the space in a few years.

It is at this stage that the designer and the client decide whether or not to purchase all new furniture or to retain any existing furniture in good condition and supplement with new only as required.

Feasibility Studies

The choice of a location is based on space requirements, budget restrictions, projected growth rate of the company, organizational goals, and tax ramifications. The designer should perform feasibility studies considering the above criteria. Spaces being considered are analyzed to determine how the firm would fit into these spaces and how much renovation would be involved with each one. Subsequently, preliminary budgets can be developed from the feasibility studies to determine rough costs.

For example, a client's primary goal for a project might be maximum flexibility. In this case, the designer would probably recommend an open office space. An open space allows for minimal construction and maximum flexibility of the space because there are fewer interior walls.

In order to perform a feasibility study, the following facts should be determined:

- The number and type of departments
- The number of people and functions of the individuals within each department
- The relationship of the various individuals and departments to each other

This information can usually be easily obtained from department managers. Planners may prefer to use a broad square foot method based on population for their feasibility studies (see below) because this method takes a minimal amount of time to complete. Realtors are often anxious to get the space rented and time may be limited. The square foot method gives the client a rough idea of the adequacy of a particular space. In addition, a preliminary budget can be estimated from the feasibility study. As more specific requirements are obtained from the client, they are incorporated into the preliminary design layout plans.

Population Projection

When performing a feasibility study, the project planner should be planning for future as well as present needs. Planning should include expansion based on the company's current growth pace and should consider anticipated variations. For this reason, the designer and the client must project personnel requirements for the next three, five, and ten years. To accomplish this, each manager is asked to project departmental personnel needs for the future. When the overall plan is then approved by top management, this information can be tabulated using the format shown in Figures 1.1 and 1.2. Future space

XYZ Company
Chicago, Illinois

	S.F. Req'd. x	Total Population =	Total S.F. Req'd.

Legal Department

General Open Area	90	16	1,440
10' x 15' Office	150	6	900
10' x 15' Interior Office	150	5	750
15' x 15' Office	225	9	2,025
Special Areas:			
(must be enumerated)			
Conference Room 3 x 5 module (seats 14)	375		375
Conference Room 3 x 3 module (seats 10)	225		225
Law Dept. Patent Search Library 3 x 3 module (seats 2)	225		225
Total Legal Dept.		36	5,940

Executive

Open Area	100	15	160
15' x 20' Office	300	13	3,900
20' x 20' Office	400	3	1,200
20' x 25' Office	500	1	500
Special Areas:			
(must be enumerated)			
Conference Room 12' x 24' (seats 10)	288		288
Board Room, Projection, Lounge & Pantry (seats 22)	1,000		1,000
Reception (seats 6)	300	1	300
Total Executive		33	7,348
Total Legal Dept. & Executive		69	13,288
Add 15% for circulation			1,993
Total square feet required			15,281

Figure 1.1

All Departments
XYZ Company
Chicago, Illinois

Space Type	Present	Additional Personnel			Total	Percent Increase
		3 Yrs.	5 Yrs.	10 Yrs.		
General Open Area	95	6	9	5	115	20%
10' x 15' office perimeter and interior	49	5	7	5	66	35%
15' x 15' office	20		1		21	5%
15' x 17'-6" office	2				2	0%
15' x 20' office	2				2	0%
Special Areas	86	2	2	1	91	5%
Executive	30	1	1	1	33	10%
Total	284	14	20	12	330	16%

Figure 1.2

needs can then be determined. For a firm which is expanding 15 to 20 percent per year, a considerable amount of extra space must be included when contemplating, for example, a ten-year lease. Portions of the extra space can be sublet over various intervals so that it will be available as the company grows. Conversely, for a stable firm signing a 10 year lease, a *total* of 20 percent expansion space may be sufficient.

It is harder to estimate space for an unknown expansion rate than if there is a known expansion rate. For example, if a company has a predicted 30 percent expansion for the next ten years, the designer can readily calculate the square footage required in the new location. On the other hand, the space requirements for a company which requires 50 percent more space now and is rapidly expanding are much more difficult to project.

Various contingencies for taking extra space or building expansion space at a later date should be contemplated. If the company growth rate is uneven, assigning square feet to functions can help forecast the overall space necessary, including future growth and expansion. Figure 1.3 illustrates a typical "space needs" calculation. Figure 1.4 is an example of a form which can be used to gather and tabulate such data.

Speculation

A client may ask the designer to perform one or more feasibility studies with the implication that the designer will be hired for the project. Many times, however, the client takes the final, accepted study to another designer, or designs the project himself. The designer is left out in the cold having done a lot of work with no compensation. For this reason, a designer should never perform feasibility studies for free on the speculation that he will be hired for the actual project. If a client feels comfortable working with a designer, he will hire that person for the project regardless of whether or not the feasibility studies were free. No one really expects to get something for nothing, and if he does, it is not regarded highly. The designer should always charge for services. If a client does not want to pay, the designer should walk away. This policy will prevent countless headaches and hours of deliberation over lost time and money.

Interior Project Overview

The phases of an interior project include work letter negotiation, determining existing conditions, survey of client requirements, space planning, layout, and design, dealing with existing furniture, determining the budget, writing the specifications, bidding and purchasing, scheduling installation and deliveries, supervising installation and move-in, and follow-up procedures. The following sections contain descriptions of these phases. Each phase is described in more detail in its respective chapter.

Legal and Executive Departments
XYZ Company
Chicago, Illinois

| Space Type | Present | Additional Personnel | | | Total | Percent Increase |
		3 Yrs.	5 Yrs.	10 Yrs.		
Legal Department						
General Open Area	13	1	1	1	16	
10' x 15' office	5		1		6	
10' x 15' interior office	2	1	1	1	5	
15' x 15' office	8		1		9	
Special Areas:						
Conference Room 3 x 5 module (seats 14)						
Conference Room 3 x 3 module (seats 10)						
Law Dept. Patent Search Library 3 x 3 module (seats 2)						
Total Population Legal Department	28	2	4	2	36	30%
Executive						
Open Area	15				15	
15' x 20' office	10	1	1	1	13	
20' x 20' office	3				3	
20' x 25' office	1				1	
Special Areas:						
Conference Room 12' x 24' (seats 10)						
Board Room, Projection Lounge & Pantry (seats 22)						
Reception (seats 6)	1				1	
Total population Executive	30	1	1	1	33	10%
Total Population*	284*	14*	20*	12*	330*	16%*

*Including other departments not shown

Figure 1.3

Building Space Allocation

Client _____ Location _____

Department _____ Division _____

Space Required for Officers/Employees	Number of Persons				Standard Square Feet Per Person	Total Square Feet Required			
	1988	1991	1993	1998		1988	1991	1993	1998
1. Chief Executive Officers					640				
2. Executive & Senior Vice President					485				
3. Regional Vice President					400				
4. Vice President Group V.P.					275–300				
5. Division Manager AVP, Grades 17 to 20					175–200				
6. District Manager Assistant Division Manager Associate Division Manager Group Manager, Grades 12 to 16					130–150				
7. Group Administration Personnel, Group Representatives Agency & Division Leaders Grades 6 to 11					75–100				
8. Grades 1 to 5					42				
9. Total Space Required for Officers/Employees (lines 1–8)									

Figure 1.4

	Number of Areas Required				Standard Square Feet Per Area	Total Square Feet Required			
Support Areas	1988	1991	1993	1998		1988	1991	1993	1998
10. Reception									
11. Conference									
12. Lounge									
13. Storage									
14. Terminal/Computer Equipment Room					Per Mfg. Spec.				
15. Other									

	Number of Units Required				Standard Square Feet Per Unit	Total Square Feet Required			
Equipment	(1)	(2)	(3)	(4)		1988	1991	1993	1998
16. Files					9				
17. Storage Units					18				
18. Coat Units					18				
19. Work Tables					42				
20. Open Shelving					18				
21. Copiers					Per Mfg. Spec.				
22. Computers									
23. Printers									
24. Other									
25. Total Usable Space Required (Add Lines 9 thru 22)									
26. Total Rentable Space Required — Line 23 x Bldg. Usable/Rentable Factor									
27. Total Rentable Space Assigned									
28. Occupancy Ratio (Line 26 + Line 27)									

Figure 1.4 (continued)

Work Letter Negotiation

If the client has not yet leased new space, the designer should help negotiate a work letter with the landlord to get the most for the rental dollar. A "building standard" work letter lists those construction items that come with the lease, which almost never provide for enough partitions, electrical outlets, telephone outlets, lighting fixtures, carpet, etc., to complete all the work required (see Figure 1.5). The work letter for a landlord "build-to-suit" job can often be improved using the designer's recommendations. Any greater allowances that can be negotiated into the work letter will benefit the client, saving a great deal of money in unanticipated construction costs or "extras".

Determine Existing Conditions

The first thing the project planner must do in order to perform a feasibility study or produce a preliminary plan is to obtain the drawings of the existing space, if there are any, from the landlord or building architect. If the project is new construction or a large renovation, there is usually an architect involved and the planner should be able to obtain good quality, accurate drawings. In many cases, however, the drawings, if available, may be of poor quality and out of date. In either case, the drawings must be checked against the actual space in great detail; changes are often made during the "life" of a space without updating the original drawings.

Should the "as-built" drawings be unavailable, it will be necessary to create them. In this case, all spaces must be field-measured in great detail. This entails measuring all partitions, doors, columns, and windows. It also means determining the accurate location of all telephone and electrical outlets, lighting fixtures, and their switches and circuitry. In addition, note all diffusers, air return grilles, convectors, sprinkler heads, all plumbing fixtures and pipes, exit lights, smoke detectors, existing wallcovering, carpet, and built-in cabinetry. Any special conditions and all miscellaneous items such as fire hoses and extinguishers, public address systems, and emergency lights should be noted.

After all of the necessary information has been compiled, Existing Conditions drawings are prepared. If the project is redecoration and refurbishing, plans for furniture layouts, carpet, window treatment, and wallcovering will be developed. If, on the other hand, the project is a renovation, a whole complement of plans is needed, including construction and demolition, reflected ceiling, and telephone and electric circuity. In order to obtain accurate bid prices, the project planner must provide the contractor with information about removal and relocation, along with plans for new construction.

Survey of Client Requirements

The designer must determine all of the client's requirements in detail before beginning work on a space plan. This includes a complete inventory of the present space and its use, existing and required furniture, and a projection for the future so that the space does not become obsolete shortly after the move-in. The detailed survey of client's requirements is an integral part of planning a design and is covered in more detail in Chapter 3.

TENANT WORK LETTER

ARTICLE TWENTY-SEVENTH. Layout and Finish. On or before ___(date)___, the Tenant shall submit to the Landlord, for the Landlord's approval, complete architectural working drawings and specifications showing the proposed subdivision, layout, and finish of the premises (hereinafter in this Article sometimes called "the Work Area") desired by the tenant. The work shown on all of said drawings and specifications must be consistent with the design, construction, and equipment of the Building and in conformity with its standards, and all in such form and detail (including layout for lighting and electrical work) as may be required for the use of the Landlord and/or Overlandlord and its or their contractor(s) except that, with respect to such part of the work in connection with the subdivision, layout, and finish of the Work Area for the execution of which engineering drawings and specifications are to be prepared by the Landlord or Overlandlord as hereinafter provided, said architectural working drawings and specifications shall contain such necessary information as may be required for use by the Landlord or Overlandlord in preparation of said engineering drawings and specifications. Said drawings and specifications to be submitted to the Landlord as aforesaid shall be prepared (in consultation with a competent engineer designated by Landlord where required by the nature of the work) by any competent architect, reasonably satisfactory to the Landlord, who shall be engaged by the Tenant and who, at the Tenant's expense, shall furnish all architectural services necessary for the preparation of said drawings and specifications and in connection with securing the aforesaid approval thereof by the Landlord or Overlandlord and with the securing by the Tenant of such approvals as by reason of the nature of the work shown on said drawings and specifications, may be required from the Department of Buildings of The City of New York and any other governmental authorities and shall perform such other services as may be necessary or desirable to the execution of said work and the letting of contract therefor. It is understood that the Tenant shall be under no obligation to furnish any engineering services with respect to any electric circuiting, heating, ventilating, or air conditioning work to be shown on the engineering drawings and specifications to be prepared by the Landlord or Overlandlord as hereinafter provided.

If the Landlord and/or Overlandlord shall not approve any drawing or specification as submitted by the Tenant, the Landlord shall notify the Tenant thereof and of the particulars of such revisions therein as are required by the Landlord and/or Overlandlord for the purpose of obtaining said approval and within 15 days after being so informed by the Landlord, the Tenant shall submit to the Landlord, for the Landlord's and/or Overlandlord's approval, a drawing or specification, as the case may be, incorporating such revisions or incorporating such modifications thereof as are suggested by the Tenant and approved by the Landlord and/or Overlandlord. Any such approval by the Landlord and/or Overlandlord shall not be deemed to be representation or warranty that the same is properly designed to perform the function for which it is intended or complies with any applicable law, ordinance, rule, order, or regulation of any governmental authority or insurance body, but only that the work required

Figure 1.5

thereby will not interfere with the systems of the Building and is compatible with the design and structure of the Building.

Upon receipt of said architectural working drawings and specifications to be submitted by the Tenant as aforesaid and based upon the information set forth therein, and such additional information which the Tenant shall furnish if requested by the Landlord for such purpose (expressly including details required for determining the location of electrical outlets, telephone outlets, and lighting fixtures), the Landlord and/or Overlandlord will prepare and submit to the Tenant such engineering drawings and specifications as may be required in executing that part of the work in connection with the subdivision, layout, and finish of the premises which consists of electric circuiting, heating, ventilating, and air conditioning. Within a reasonable time, but as promptly as possible after submission to it of said engineering drawings and specifications, the Tenant will approve the same as submitted to it or as modified at the request of the Tenant and with the approval of the Landlord and/or Overlandlord (all of said architectural working drawings and specification and said engineering drawings and specifications hereinabove mentioned in this Article as approved as provided herein, being herein called "the Working Drawings").

Following such approval of the Working Drawings, the Landlord, through a contractor or contractors to be engaged by it and/or by the Overlandlord for such purpose, will proceed to do (or will cause the Overlandlord to proceed to do) all of the work shown on the Working Drawings (said work being herein called "the Work") in accordance with ARTICLE SECOND hereof.

The Landlord will bear the cost of the Work to the extent that it constitutes Building Standard Work and the Tenant will pay to the Landlord the Work Cost of all that part, if any, of the Work which is not Building Standard Work ("Special Work"). If any changes or additions in or to the Work shall be made at the request of the Tenant or shall be due to any other act or omission on its part, such changes and additions shall be deemed to be Special Work and the Tenant will pay to the Landlord the Work Cost therefor. No allowance shall be made for the omission of any Building Standard Work except in the case where, at the request of the Tenant and with the approval of the Landlord, part of the Building Standard Work is omitted and Special Work of a similar nature and for a similar use is substituted therefor and incorporated in the Work, in which event an allowance shall be made by the Landlord to the Tenant applicable against the Work Cost of said Special Work in an amount up to but not exceeding the saving in Work Cost by reason of such omission of said Building Standard Work.

Before proceeding with any Special Work, the Landlord will submit to the Tenant an estimate of the Work Cost thereof and a statement of the terms and conditions on which such Special Work is to be performed and, unless and until the Tenant shall approve such estimate and such terms and conditions in writing, the Landlord and/or Overlandlord shall not proceed with the performance of such Special Work or with any other part of the Work which, in the Landlord's reasonable judgment, would be affected

Figure 1.5 (*continued*)

thereby. Notwithstanding any such estimate, the Tenant shall nevertheless pay the actual Work Cost of the Special Work. Bills for any amount payable by the Tenant under this Article may be rendered by the Landlord to the Tenant as the Work progresses and such bills shall be due and payable by the tenant in accordance with their terms.

The Landlord will (subject to all of the covenants, agreement, terms, provisions, and conditions of this Lease including, without limitation, subparagraph (e) of ARTICLE SIXTH hereof) give or cause to be given access to the Work Area to decorators and other contractors employed by the Tenant for the purpose of making improvements therein when and so long as, in the Landlord's and/or Overlandlord's reasonable judgment, the Work to be done in the Work Area by the Landlord and/or Overlandlord as provided herein shall have been completed to such an extent that the making of such improvements will not interfere with or delay the Landlord and/or Overlandlord's performance of the remaining portion of the Work; it being understood that the Tenant shall not be deemed to have entered into occupancy of the Work Area for the purposes of ARTICLE FIRST hereof by reason of the presence in the Work Area of any decorator or other contractor given access thereto as aforesaid.

The term "Work Cost", as used herein with respect to any part of the Special Work, shall mean the actual costs and charges incurred by the Landlord or Overlandlord in doing such part of the Work itself and/or in having it done by a contractor or contractors under the supervision of the Landlord or Overlandlord (including in such costs and charges the reasonable fees of any engineers whose services may be required because of the nature of the Work), plus 10% of all such costs and charges for the Landlord's or Overlandlord's (depending on which one of them is responsible for performance of the Special Work in question) servicing and overhead.

The term "Building Standard Work", as used herein, shall mean the following Work (which unless otherwise specifically provided herein, shall be of material, manufacture, design, capacity, quality, finish, and color of the standard adopted by the Overlandlord for the Building, and where quantities are hereinafter specified, such quantities shall include any existing installation to the extent usable and used in the performance of the Work), namely:

(a) partitioning of gypsum board or similar dry wall material to provide for the reasonable subdivision of the premises at the rate of not exceeding 10 linear feet of such partitions per square feet of floor area of the premises, with doors at the rate of not exceeding one door per 20 linear feet of such partitions; which doors shall be of metal;

(b) air conditioning duct work and outlets, including not exceeding one thermostatic control per 600 square feet of floor area of the premises, to provide for distribution of air conditioning to the area of the premises subdivided to the extent provided in the foregoing subparagraph (a);

Figure 1.5 (*continued*)

(c) concealed spline fissured tile-type acoustic ceilings;

(d) recessed flush type fluorescent lighting fixtures (including the initial lamping) in ceiling outlets at locations in the premises selected by the Tenant and approved by the Landlord so as to provide lighting of an average of 60 foot candles at desk level in the premises, including controlling light switches in the premises selected by the Tenant and approved by the Landlord at the rate of not exceeding one switch per office and one switch per 400 square feet of floor area of other areas in the premises subdivided to the extent provided in the foregoing subparagraph (a);

(e) duplex electrical convenience base receptacles at locations in the premises selected by the Tenant and approved by the Landlord, at the rate of not exceeding one such base receptacle per 125 square feet of floor area of the premises for use in operation of the Tenant's business equipment which requires neither more than 120 volts nor a separate electric circuit;

(f) telephone outlets (exclusive of wiring) on walls or on existing underfloor ducts at locations in the premises selected by the Tenant and approved by the Landlord at the rate of not exceeding one outlet per 100 square feet of floor area of the premises;

(g) vinyl floor tiling (Group "C"), except in areas, if any, to be carpeted by the Tenant;

(h) Venetian blinds on exterior windows; and

(i) painting the partitioning of gypsum board and similar dry wall material and the metal trim of the premises subdivided to the extent provided in the foregoing subparagraph (a) with not exceeding 3 coats of paint on newly constructed partitioning, and 1 coat of paint on metal trim, in not more than four Building Standard colors as shall be selected by the Tenant, provided, however, that the Tenant may not have more than two vertical color breaks in any one room area.

Figure 1.5 (*continued*)

Space Planning, Layout, and Design

The space planning, layout, and design phases involve planning meetings to review the requirements, creation of bubble diagrams, adjacency matrixes, stack plans of a building and preliminary space plans, and establishment of standards for space, furniture, and materials. The number of meetings leading up to an approved space plan will be determined by the size of the project and the attitude of the client. Some clients like to be very involved, while others prefer that the designer do everything and then present them with the results.

After the client approves the space plan, the designer can proceed with renovation drawings, furniture and materials selections, and finalizing the design scheme. This topic is discussed in more detail in Chapter 4.

Existing Furniture

In almost all cases, a client has existing furniture. Whether he intends to reuse it in the new space or to sell it, an inventory must be taken. If everything is to be sold, the client may prefer to take the inventory. Usually, however, at least some of the furniture will be reused; in which case the designer must take the inventory immediately in order to determine how much new furniture will be required. There are many methods of taking an inventory. Examples are discussed in Chapter 5.

Budget

One of the client's most important concerns is how much the project will cost. The budgeting phase of any project is, therefore, crucial. A reasonably accurate budget cannot be compiled until there are some approved drawings and a design concept in place. Prior to this, only a "guesstimate", or square foot estimate, can be given. The square foot estimate does, however, get the project rolling. The specifics of writing a budget are discussed in more detail in Chapter 6.

Specifications

One of the hardest tasks for many designers is the translation of what has been selected at the presentation into reality within the new space. Specifications, a detailed description with catalog numbers and other manufacturer's information, cannot be written until the designer knows how much money the client is willing to spend. Thus, the specifications cannot be written until the preliminary budget and design have been approved. Formulas and charts to aid in writing the specifications are presented in Chapter 7.

Bidding and Purchasing

Once the specifications are written, the client may wish to compare alternate quotations on various interiors items (i.e., furniture, window treatment, carpet, and wallcovering). Another common concern during bidding and purchasing is the verification that each bidder is quoting a price on the same items and services. These concerns are addressed in detail in Chapter 8. Purchasing methods and sample purchase orders are also included.

Scheduling Installation and Deliveries

This phase of the project can be frustrating as last-minute changes and time constraints frequently arise. Therefore, after the purchase orders are issued to the various vendors, the project manager cannot just sit back and wait. He must follow up with all vendors and expedite the delivery of all items. Manufacturers often change their schedules without notifying anyone. If orders are not confirmed, the project manager may not find out about a problem until it is too late. This topic is discussed in more detail in Chapter 12.

Supervising Installation and Move-in

Ideally, installation of all interiors items should be complete before the client occupies the space. However, this is not always possible. Problems often arise at this point such as the acquisition of temporary furniture because the new furniture is late. Solutions and ways to avoid such situations are discussed in Chapters 12 and 13.

Follow Up

A punch list of incomplete, or damaged items which must be repaired or replaced, should be compiled when construction is 80 to 90 percent complete. The punch list is given to the contractor or to vendors, who must complete these items in order to receive final payment. Most clients are unwilling to pay any vendor or contractor unless the project manager confirms that everything is complete and acceptable. This means that the designer has to check and approve all invoices and follow up on the punch list. For a large project, this can be a monstrous paperwork task. However, this is a relatively small "pain-in-the-neck" when compared to the problems that can arise if this task is neglected. Chapter 14 suggests methods for handling finalization of the project.

These phases pertain to virtually all interiors projects. Each phase is discussed in greater detail in the following chapters. It should be noted, however, that certain phases, such as the space planning design and budget analysis, are in progress simultaneously, although in this text they are covered in separate chapters.

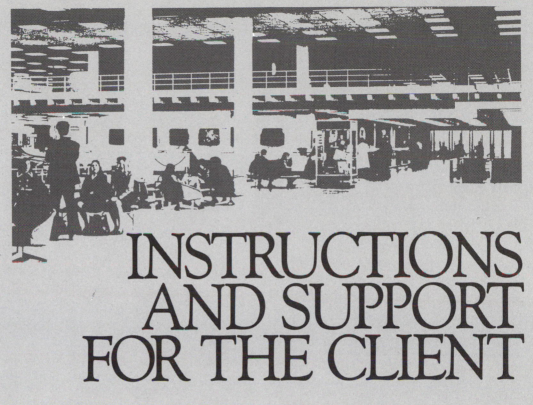

CHAPTER TWO

INSTRUCTIONS AND SUPPORT FOR THE CLIENT

INSTRUCTIONS AND SUPPORT FOR THE CLIENT

It is quite possible that the client has never been involved in any kind of interior design or renovation other than painting his apartment or selecting a sofa. However, the client undoubtedly knows of at least a few "horror stories" from assorted sources, or from past experience, about the happenings on an interiors project. For this reason, it is important that the client has confidence in the designer's abilities. Part of the designer's job involves playing the part of the "pseudo-psychologist", allaying the client's fears and misgivings. The best way to gain the client's confidence is to explain what is supposed to happen every step of the way, and approximately how long each phase will take. After feasibility studies are complete, the designer has a general idea of the amount and type of work necessary for this job and can give the client a reasonable estimate of the duration of the project.

As the survey of client's requirements progresses, the client should firm up the details of any planned operational changes. The client should bring these changes to the attention of the employees involved in their implementation and functioning. The staff must be adequately prepared for the changes and, hopefully, will be enthusiastic about them.

Methods and Practices

The designer should educate the client about the responsibilities and operating methods of each party. The designer, whether from a one man firm or a 100 person firm, still has the same responsibilities. This will ensure a good working relationship with the client.

Explanation of Methods and Practices

The designer should explain his basic working format to the client. The phases of a design project discussed in Chapter 1 should be reviewed. This will give the client an idea of the overall sequence of events and allow him to keep track of the project schedule.

The designer should specifically explain every document that the client will be asked to sign during the project. The client must understand that work cannot be implemented or orders issued without his signature. This primarily protects the client from having money spent without authorization. Procedures for changes should also be discussed in depth. The designer should make sure that the client truly understands that changes invariably cost money and delay the project. (Refer to Chapter 13 for further details on documents to be signed and change procedures.)

Reassuring the Client

At all times during the course of the project, the client must be assured that the project manager is capable of handling any unforeseen problems or difficulties. To accomplish this, the manager must always be precise, definitive, and professional. This can be augmented by a clear definition of the responsibilities of each party.

Some clients perceive a problem arising out of every trivial occurrence. Though it may, indeed, be a real problem, the project manager must reassure the client not to worry and that it will be solved. As problems disappear under the manager's able direction, the client's confidence in him increases.

It may be helpful to "predict" possible scenarios that could occur, including successful resolutions. The designer can relate happenings on other projects that seemed disastrous at the time, pointing out that everything worked out in the end. For example, the designer might tell the client that if any furniture gets lost or damaged, it will undoubtedly be the chairman's or president's! The designer might also warn the client that when the employees begin to work in their new offices, they will invariably dislike certain color chairs and begin switching the furniture around.

When forewarned, the client will realize that these happenings are normal adjustments and not catastrophes, if they do occur. The designer should always remind the client that it is the final result that really counts and that any problems during the project will be resolved. In order to convey the atmosphere of trust in the designer's ability to handle mishaps, his confidence in his expertise as a problem-solver is important.

Project Schedule

The project schedule agreed upon by the project planner and the client must be realistic. If a client's lease is due to expire in a few months and he isn't being given the option to renew, it is already too late to look for new space. It takes a considerable amount of time to find, plan, and renovate a new space. This time frame is usually dependent on the size of the space as well as the scope of the work. For example, a 10,000 square foot renovation should take a minimum of seven months to properly plan, construct, obtain the furniture, and move in. Even seven months is a tight time frame in which to complete a project. It would require total client cooperation assuming that nothing will go wrong. The planner should never commit to an unrealistic schedule.

New construction takes even longer than renovation of existing space. Once again, the actual time frame depends on the size and scope of the project, however, ideally, planning should commence at least one and a half years prior to expected occupancy.

Planning Operational Changes

A client often plans for an organizational or operational change in conjunction with relocation. The planner must work very closely with the client to iron out every aspect of the change as it pertains to the design. Some changes may appear to be simple, but are actually quite involved. For example, a change from typewriters to word processors for all secretaries creates the following concerns:

- What are the wiring requirements?
- How many printers are needed?
- Is there a need for an envelope or label printer? If so, one or both? If not, should some typewriters be retained for typing the envelopes and labels?
- Where should the printers go—general office or a separate room? (Noise and disruption factors.)
- Do the printers require sound hoods or other acoustical treatment?
- Will the existing furniture fit the new equipment or is new furniture required?
- Where is the mainframe and how do we connect with it?
- Should some of the managers have terminals for reference purposes?
- How will this affect the functioning of the department or firm?
- Should central word processing be pursued instead?

Another organizational change might be the decentralization of an accounting, purchasing, legal, or tax department. This type of change requires new methods of communication and paper flow. It also means changes in level of efficiency, employee relocation, and document storage. If a company is consolidating its forces to one office from numerous locations, certain receptionists, switchboard operators, mail room workers, office managers, conference rooms, and copiers may no longer be needed. Unique questions arise with this kind of change, especially in the area of human resources. A number of brainstorming sessions with all the people involved can serve to get all the questions "on the table", so that decisions can be made as to how to implement the change.

All of these possible scenarios can have a significant effect on how the space is designed and how the project is managed. The project planner must keep in mind that each situation is different and must be handled individually.

Summary of Responsibilities

The designer must:
1. Assume full project responsibility.
2. Utilize the tools of his organization as well as his own talents to effect the success of the project.
3. Effectuate a smooth transition from the salesperson and establish liaison with the client.
4. Alert the design and/or production departments so project time can be scheduled.
5. Schedule the necessary surveys and inventories.
6. Obtain all necessary 'as-built' drawings.
7. Arrange all necessary meetings with department heads, managers, and other decision-makers; attend these meetings and record the minutes.
8. Determine if engineering drawings will be required and hire an engineer if necessary.

9. Obtain forms and file the necessary documents with the local government authorities (re: zoning, building code, fire code, etc.).
10. Meet with the landlord or building manager to determine any restrictions the building may have.
11. Prepare preliminary space studies, block plans, and bubble diagrams for client approval.
12. Prepare a preliminary budget for client approval.
13. Sketch concepts for renderer if renderings are desired.
14. Prepare a complete design presentation of furniture and materials based on approved space plans and budget.
15. Make adjustments to design as dictated by outcome of design presentation.
16. Give proper instructions to the interior and/or production departments so they can prepare interior and working drawings.
17. Sketch cabinetry so it can be detailed.
18. Check and coordinate all drawings prepared by the interiors and/or production departments, including detailed drawings.
19. Check and coordinate all drawings prepared by others with the working drawings (i.e., engineering drawings and vendor shop drawings).
20. Arrange to have furniture shown as required in the showroom or have actual samples sent to the client's office for him to approve or disapprove.
21. Have all drawings approved by the landlord.
22. Observe the project in the field and communicate any defects or problems for remedial action.
23. Write all specifications and establish codes.
24. Perform any required product research.
25. Obtain bids for all design items (i.e., furniture, cabinetry, carpet).
26. Order new items required if the client does not wish to place the orders himself.
27. Expedite changes and revisions due to field conditions and new client requests.
28. Coordinate with the architect, engineers, and general contractor.
29. Select plants, artwork, and accessories.
30. Supervise new furniture and furnishings installations.
31. Assist in selecting a mover.
32. Assist in tagging and scheduling the move.
33. Assist in installation of plants, signage, accessories, and artwork.
34. Be present at the move.
35. Follow up on any items pending after the move.
36. Complete punch list.

The client must:
1. Provide the designer with information necessary to do the job properly (i.e., organizational charts, current plans, if available; personnel lists, population projections, etc.).
2. Provide the designer with access to present work space.
3. Obtain the cooperation of his department managers and other key personnel.
4. Define his priorities and desires for the project.
5. Communicate reactions to presentations clearly.
6. Be available for consultation on an as-needed basis.
7. Attend meetings and make decisions.

8. Sign documents expeditiously (i.e., purchase orders, plans, shop drawings, change orders, etc.).
9. Spend whatever time is necessary in the planning phase to avoid major changes later in the project.
10. Be specific and accurate regarding special equipment requirements (i.e., computers, copiers, word processors, etc.).
11. Give the designer a realistic time frame in which to work.
12. Pay all invoices in a timely fashion.
13. Order telephones.
14. Order stationery and move notice cards.

CHAPTER THREE

SURVEY OF CLIENT REQUIREMENTS

SURVEY OF CLIENT REQUIREMENTS

In creating a workable building design, the designer is serving the needs of two very different clients. The first is the "paying" client: the organization and its formal representatives who interact with the design professional. The other is the "non-paying" client: the actual user of the finished facility. In general, this book refers to the "paying" client who is the decision-maker and main liaison with the designer. This client may be a building committee, an office manager, or a Vice President of Facilities Planning. The "non-paying" client, on the other hand, may be an accountant, clerk, secretary, programmer, manager, or executive. The requirements of both clients are usually different and may conflict.

Working with each of these two "clients" is different, as both are distinct, complex, and deserving of special attention. The designer's talents are necessary to balance effectively their competing goals. This chapter addresses these issues and demonstrates the interplay between the designer and the different types of clients. Hereafter, the "paying" client will be referred to solely as the "client." The non-paying client is referred to as the employee or the user.

Parameters and the Needs Analysis

At this stage, a generalized *needs analysis* must be performed. From this analysis, decisions are made concerning the overall framework of the project. The client must provide some direction regarding expansion/contraction of space, reuse of existing furniture, use of open office systems, addition of a training center (for management training) and type of project (expensive, moderate, or inexpensive). This is a time for negotiation, to balance the client's needs and desires with the budget and to establish the scope of the planner's vote. At this stage, it is important to obtain all of the necessary information. No detail should be overlooked.

The designer begins with a tour of the existing facility, guided by the client. This gives the designer a general "feel" of the working environment. The designer should note population density, condition of the existing furniture, noise level, and ambiance. If, for example, the client wishes to reuse all existing furniture, the designer may discover on his tour that a good portion of it is in poor condition and not worthy of being refurbished and moved. The client, in this case, must revise the budget if he agrees to purchase more new furniture. This is a give and take process in which the designer should recommend the best possible parameters for the project within the client's financial capacity.

Establish Authority

Often department managers and other employees, the non-paying "clients", request changes in project design. Many of these changes cannot be done within the budget. Such requests can create "touchy" situations. For this reason, it is necessary for the client to define the designer's level of authority when dealing with the firm's employees. This should be done as soon as the design process begins. The client usually prefers to be notified every time an employee makes a suggestion, realizing that there are exceptions to every rule. The client will then make a decision, and ask the designer to notify the user who requested the change that it is, or is not, authorized.

In other cases, the decision to tell the client of the request is left to the designer's discretion. If he feels the request is justified and may be meritorious to the project, the designer may tell the individual that he will present the idea to the client. In either case, the client is ultimately responsible for any decision to make a change in the design or scope of the project.

Determine Organizational Structure

In the process of defining a firm's space needs, the planner reviews the organizational structure of the company, departmental proximity needs, work flow and traffic patterns, existing space standards, interpersonal contact, and frequency of visitors to the building. The planner begins this process by gaining an overview of the firm, its functions, and its organization.

Company Organization
The planner can usually obtain an organizational chart from the client. This should include names, titles, and positions within the company. If such a chart does not exist, the planner should draft one, listing the names, titles, and positions, as suggested above.

Departmental Proximity
The relationships between various individuals and departments within a firm will dictate the placement of offices in the new space. For example, in one firm, the accounting and finance departments may work very closely together, thus requiring close proximity to each other. In another firm, accounting, purchasing, and data processing may work together, requiring that they be adjacent to each other. (This topic is discussed in more detail in Chapter 4.)

Work Flow and Traffic Patterns
The designer must obtain a general understanding of work flow patterns from the various department managers (i.e., purchasing approves invoices and sends them to the accounting department for payment); and traffic patterns (i.e., who speaks with whom, how often, in what direction do they walk, and how long is the walk?). Too much distance between co-workers can sometimes diminish company efficiency. Questions asked of employees and objective observation are helpful to determine work flow and traffic patterns.

Existing Standards

The designer should determine whether the client is utilizing any existing space, furniture, or material design standards. For example, there may be carpet and landscape furniture standards that the client may insist be followed in the new space. However, a new space can sometimes dictate different space or furniture design standards. Or, the client may wish to upgrade a materials standard, for example, from paint to vinyl wallcovering. In any case, it is imperative that these parameters be identified before any decisions are made concerning standards for the new space.

Interpersonal Contact

A firm's interpersonal contact policy can help determine the amount of space required for each office. Some firms are very formal and have closed-door policies. No meetings are held unless scheduled, and secretaries prevent employees from dropping in to see the boss. Other firms are very informal and have complete open-door policies where anyone can stop in as long as the door is open. There are obviously many variations along the continuum. Interpersonal contact policies must be clearly understood by the planner, as well as defined by the client, in order to plan a usuable space for the firm.

Visitors

The number of visitors to the company and to each department must be determined. Reception areas are sized according to the number and frequency of outside visitors. Conference rooms are another important consideration if outside visitors arrive in groups for meetings or other functions. Some departments may have a lot of inter-office traffic, necessitating seating areas, while other departments may have little or none.

Conference Rooms

The frequency of inter- and intra-departmental meetings should be taken into consideration when planning the space needs of each department. Some departments have weekly staff meetings, while others only have them monthly. A firm will need certain numbers of small, medium, and large conference rooms. Large conference rooms are usually shared by two or three departments, but this isn't always feasible. The designer must first determine the frequency of conference room usage for each department by asking questions of each department manager.

Inventory of Existing Space

In order to have a broad understanding of a firm's current usage of space, the designer should draw or obtain a rough plan of the existing space. This plan should be broken down by department, job, or function. This will give the designer a better viewpoint on the overall sizes of departments and their relative relationships. This section describes methods for evaluating an existing space.

Once the inventory of existing space is completed, the designer can evaluate each space for overall efficiency. There is often excess space in one location, and overcrowding in another. Books or computer printouts piled up on the floor of an office indicate poor utilization of space. An office in disarray may indicate a disorganized individual, but a trained eye can often differentiate between sloppiness and lack of appropriate storage, filing facilities, and/or work surface.

Department Requirements

The designer now must determine intra-departmental space requirements in more detail. The client should introduce the designer to all department managers, to continue research with them directly. For each department, the designer will need to know the numbers of each type of the following positions:

- Executives
- Senior/middle managers
- Junior managers/trainees
- Professionals
- Secretaries
- Clerks

Any available organizational charts at this point can be extremely helpful.

For each department, current square footage occupied and the projected space needed within one to three and three to five years must be determined. The department manager may not have this information and the designer may have to calculate it as a "best guess".

A *Departmental Information Form* should be developed to aid the designer in collecting all the necessary information. Figure 3.1 is a sample Departmental Information Form. The designer should preferably interview each department manager personally and fill out the form himself. If time, fee restrictions, or overall size of the project do not allow personal interviews, the forms can be given to the department managers to be filled out individually. The client should accompany this with a memo requesting everyone's cooperation and the completion of the forms in a timely fashion (i.e., one to two weeks).

Individual Offices and Work Stations

For each office or work station, the designer must have a complete listing of all items required for the effective functioning of the individual. It is easy to leave something off a plan if there is no checklist with all necessary items. A sample *Departmental Requirements Form*, which can be used as such a checklist, is illustrated in Figure 3.2. For each individual, the the following information should be tabulated:

- Space type and size (see Legend in DR-2 form)
- Desk type (see Legend in DR-2 form)
- File drawer
- Credenza
- Seating type
- Storage
- Visitors' chairs
- Sofa
- Conference table
- Work table
- End table
- Lounge table
- Lineal feet of shelving
- Files in the department
- Storage in the department
- Equipment
- Specialty items

Company: _____

Department: _____   Section: _____

Prepared by: _____   Date: _____

Present location of section: _____

Note: If insufficient space has been provided under any question, mark
           question with an asterisk and give information on an attached
           sheet. Heading of the sheet should be the question to be
           answered.

1.   Departmental requirements: Prepare form DR-1, indicating individual

     requirements, per attached sample.

2.   Working relationship: With what other departments or sections does

     this section have the most contact? Is this contact primarily by

     telephone or in person? List by order of most contact with type of

     contact.

     a.   _____

     b.   _____

     c.   _____

     d.   _____

     Under ideal conditions, what other departments or sections should be

     physically located near this section? List by order of importance.

     a.   _____

     b.   _____

     c.   _____

     d.   _____

Figure 3.1

3. <u>Overall departmental requirements</u>: Check applicable items and fill

    in information required.

    a. Number of visitors daily:

       1. From outside company, usual _____, maximum _____

       2. From inside company, usual _____, maximum _____

    b. Meetings with staff _____, outsiders _____

       Number attending, usual _____, maximum _____

       Frequency of meetings _____

    Type of meetings held, give description:

    _____

    _____

    c. Office or desk space for outside consultants, auditors,

       engineers, etc. List these requirements with regular personnel

       on form DR-1.

    d. Departmental library: _____; if so, state average

       and maximum size books. _____

       _____

       Lineal feet of shelves _____; located centrally

       _____; located near

       which specific area _____

       _____

       Remarks: _____

       _____

       _____

    e. Catalog or reference material storage, size, and

       quantities:

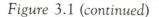

Figure 3.1 (*continued*)

_____

_____

_____

Can this be pooled with library? _____

Remarks: _____

_____

_____

f. Special material storage, size, and quantities: _____

_____

Where located? _____

Remarks: _____

_____

_____

g. Sample storage: _____; if so, indicate size and

quantities and preferred location _____

_____

_____

Remarks: _____

_____

_____

h. Departmental stationery storage: _____; supply

sample of all forms and indicate quantities stored.

Stationery stored in offices _____

Remarks: _____

_____

i. Other departmental storage: _____

Figure 3.1 (continued)

j. Indicate type and measurement of special size file drawers and units, such as jumbo, plan files, fireproof or card files, indicated on DR-1 form:

_____

_____

_____

k. How frequently are files closed out to semiactive or dead storage? _____

Remarks: _____

_____

l. Safe(s) _____; make, model number, size, weight, and location

_____

_____

Check security required: fireproof ____; burglarproof____

m. Vault(s) _____; indicate use, size, location(s): _____

_____

_____

Check security required: fireproof ____; burglarproof____

_____

n. Equipment other than typewriters, adding, or calculating machines:

Copiers _____; make, model number, size _____

_____

Used by _____

Word processors _____; make, model number, size ____

Figure 3.1 *(continued)*

_____

Used by _____

Computers _____; make, model number, size _____

_____

Used by _____

Other: _____

4.   Special outside communication equipment, such as telephone tie
     line, data line, videoconferencing, teletype, telefax, Western
     Union call bell, etc. State type, model number, size, by whom
     used or operated, present or desired. _____

_____

_____

_____

_____

5.   Special inter-office communication equipment, such as
     annunciator system, electronic mail, dumbwaiter, pneumatic
     system, etc. State type, model number, size, by whom used or
     operated, present or desired. _____

_____

_____

_____

6.   Special power outlet requirements. State purpose, voltage, and
     location. _____

_____

_____

_____

Figure 3.1 (*continued*)

7.   Utility or storage room requirements: _____; indicate

      type of storage, floor area, shelf requirements (linear feet, depth,

      and height): _____

      _____

      _____

8.   Other equipment, not otherwise listed above: _____

      _____

      _____

      _____

      _____

9.   Describe any unusual sound control problems of this section due to

      high concentration of mechanical equipment or the use of particular

      noisy equipment (graphotype, addressograph, printers, etc.).

      _____

      _____

      _____

      _____

10.   Additional comments: _____

      _____

      _____

      _____

      _____

Figure 3.1 *(continued)*

Departmental Requirements

Doe Interiors, Inc.

	Client	Division	Dept.	Job No.	Date	Page of	Remarks
Name							
Title							
Reports To							
Space Type/Size							
Desk (Type)							
Seating (Type)							
Credenza							
File Drawers Adjacent							
File Drawers Department							
Lin. Ft. Storage Dept.							
Additional Chair(s)							
Lounge Chair(s)							
Sofa							
Conference Table							
Work Table							
End Table							
Lounge Table							
Lin. Ft. Shelving							
Typewriter							
Word Processor							
Computer (Type)							
Calculator							
Printer (Type)							
Other							

Legend

Space Types

Private offices with Ceiling-High Partition

A _____ X
B _____ X
C _____ X
D _____ X

Semi-Private Offices without Ceiling-High Partition

E _____ X
F _____ X

Special Areas:
SPL – Mailroom Reception, Conf., Library, Etc.
General Office Area
OA – Open Area
Not Immediately enclosed by partitions

Desk Types:
D-1R – Right-hand secretary
D-1L – Left-hand secretary
D-2 Double pedestal

Seat Types:
1. Secretary
2. Clerical
3. Junior Manager
4. Manager
5. Executive

Figure 3.2

It is also useful to know the particular person's title and the name of the person to whom he/she reports.

Special Areas

There are numerous special areas which require individual attention and sometimes outside consultation. Some of these, such as conference rooms and reception areas, may warrant special design effects as they are the areas most often seen by outsiders and can influence the company image in the minds of visitors. There are other special areas which may require a consultant and/or special consideration. Some of these are listed below:

- Mail room
- Central file room
- Library
- Kitchen
- Cafeteria
- Duplicating/print shop
- Medical facility
- Special storage/vault
- Supply storage
- Workshop
- Laboratory
- Toilets
- Computer room
- Screening room

In small firms, the mail room may be a simple counter with a scale and postage meter with sorting racks on the wall. On the other hand, the mail room of a large company or a company that sends out mass mailings is much more complex. Sales representatives who work for mail room equipment companies can assist and advise the designer in defining a firm's requirements, based on volume. The representative will often prepare a plan, if requested, as will representatives of most specialty manufacturers.

For central file rooms a mobile system may be desirable. Three or more vendors or a specialist should be consulted. Each vendor makes a presentation to the designer who, in turn, advises the client of the best system for the lowest possible price. The designer should also check the weight per square foot of such a system against the load-bearing capacity of the floor. If the weight is greater than the floor's capacity, the designer should seek advice from a structural engineer. If supporting steel is too complex and costly, the idea of a mobile system may have to be abandoned.

The thorough planner must do all the necessary footwork and research to fully understand what makes the present space function and what will make the new space function better. This information is not always readily available. Sometimes it must be ferreted out with great difficulty. No one individual is expected to be an expert in all specialized areas. Consultations with manufacturer's representatives and other professionals can only enhance the designer's overall performance by helping to produce a more efficient space for the client.

Special Equipment

Any special equipment utilized in the building may require a certain amount of space, power, wiring, support equipment, and servicing/repair area. Typewriters and calculators are common items which do not require special power, however, an adequate number of outlets for each workstation must be included. Extension cords and three-way plugs are not acceptable in commercial space in many areas due to code restrictions. If a secretary has a typewriter, a calculator, and a pencil sharpener and only a duplex outlet, the designer has not done his job properly.

Each size copier from each manufacturer has different power and servicing requirements. These requirements are listed in the product's specifications, and the designer must make sure that all such requirements are met. Other reproduction equipment, such as microfilm printers, photostat machines, and printing presses, have individual requirements which must also be met. Certain equipment is becoming more and more common as offices become increasingly automated:

- Outside communications equipment (i.e., fax machines, telex, telecopier, etc.)
- Inter-office communication (i.e., pneumatic tubes, electronic mail)
- Word processors with printers
- Computer terminals with printers, and computers used with telephones attached to modems
- Cable television with computer mainframes and disc drives; related earth stations and dishes
- Microfiche and microfilm readers
- Video tape recorders and video cassette recorders

Manufacturers for this equipment are numerous and each has its own specific requirements.

One situation the designer may face is getting two or more systems to interface with each other. To accomplish this, the designer may have to consult with an electrical or electronics engineer. For any kind of sophisticated audio/video work, the designer should consult a specialist. A microphone system, projection system, video-conferencing, and remote controls for projectors and lights require certain electronics expertise. In order to build a darkroom, the designer should consult a photolab specialist on the purchase of enlargers, dryers, sinks, darkroom lights, etc.

Some special equipment requires special files or storage systems. Examples are computer printout files, tape and disc hanging storage, microfilm and microfiche storage, disc storage for word processors, check files for cancelled checks, record album storage, tape and cassette storage, or slide tray storage. The designer must suggest appropriate amounts of the proper storage for all such items.

For example, when designing a sound studio, broadcast station, or other area that requires special acoustics, the designer should hire an acoustical engineer. This is a very specialized field and a knowledgeable consultant is essential to the success of the project. Similarly, any special lighting effects might require a consultation with a lighting specialist. Art galleries need special changeable display lighting effects, therefore, flexibility should be built into an art gallery lighting system. Theaters and screening rooms also require special lighting.

The designer will discover that one of the most knowledgeable sources of information regarding special areas is the executive in charge of the function. This person frequently has the information the designer needs or, at least, knows how to find it.

The designer may have to do some product research on a new item that the executive would like, has never used before, and has only heard about it "somewhere." This might be a training center, a theater, an executive dining room, a squash court, or teleconferencing system. The designer can research the item by viewing various completed areas of this type at other companies. Manufacturer's representatives will often be happy to "show off" completed installations. The designer should ask the attendant manager how well the space functions. Another question that should be asked is if the facility were to be built again, what would the manager wish to change.

Future Requirements

In planning an office, the client should be asked to make personnel and equipment projections for three, five, and ten years. This is combined with and compared to projections made by each department manager. The present population count should be listed by space type or by department. A space might be classified as a secretarial area, clerical area, professional cubicle, manager's office, and executive office. The designer should then apply the space standards (existing and/or new) to these space types and provide an expansion projection for the next three, five, and ten years. This information, when carefully applied, produces a realistic plan regarding overall space. Future projections will give the designer a better idea of which areas will need flexibility in the future. Extra space may be sublet over three, five, and ten year terms until a department grows into it. (Refer to Figures 1.1, 1.2, and 1.3 in Chapter 1.)

Small Projects

If a job is relatively small, the designer may be able to gather all the information in two to three meetings with the client. Taking notes may be sufficient and the client may not have to fill out any forms. The designer may also develop some abbreviated forms or a customized check list for use in interviewing. Each designer must discover his own method for compiling forms. It does not necessarily matter which forms are used, as long as the information is complete and can be retrieved at a later date.

Some designers may feel that the acquisition of so much detail for large and small project alike is tedious, time consuming, and not worth the effort. This is, however, an essential part of any project. The larger and more complex a project, the better organized the designer needs to be to keep track of all the details. Proper planning and research in the initial stages can avoid difficulty due to lack of control later in the project.

SPACE PLANNING AND DESIGN

SPACE PLANNING AND DESIGN

The next step in interior project planning is to perform a detailed analysis of the existing office and its employees. This is an important step, as it will ultimately influence the end design. For this reason, the designer should not be rushed, and must take time to analyze and plan the project in great detail. This chapter contains suggested methods of accurately recording the detailed analysis, and implementing the findings into a workable design.

Detailed Analysis

It is at this point in the design that the designer must really get to know the client. In this phase, the designer asks scores of questions and analyzes the answers in depth. Using feedback from questions asked of management, supervisors, and employees, the designer discovers the company's major concerns. For example, on a large scale these concerns might include whether the current arrangement of space and furnishings helps people meet corporate objectives, or if it contributes to wasted time and effort.

The client will have ideas about what would make the workplace more efficient. For example, employees may feel that improved acoustics (sound proofing) and more privacy would increase concentration levels. Or, that the reduction of glare may increase the comfort level for people working at computer terminals.

From these questions and answers, a detailed analysis is made of the current work flow and space usage. All the flows of communication, documentation, and information are studied. Interpersonal contact and flows both within and between departments are identified. All current procedures are analyzed to determine what should be changed in the new location.

With top management, the designer relates procedural and informational flows to corporate objectives, end products, and services. Development of new procedures to simplify daily routines, consolidation of functions, rearrangment of cycles of activity, improvement of scheduling, and utilization of new equipment for better results are other tasks the client may wish to accomplish at this stage. Following are procedural suggestions which will aid the designer in making an accurate analysis.

Bubble Diagrams/Matrix Analyses

Many planners and designers draw bubble diagrams or adjacency matrixes to illustrate the relationships, both formal and informal, in a firm. Figure 4.1 is an example of a bubble diagram and Figure 4.2 is an example of an adjacency matrix. As can be seen in these examples, the diagrams show the formal reporting structure in a firm and indentify the groups that work closely together. "Weights" are assigned to each relationship to determine the importance of proximity in space. Incorporating these relationships into a space design will reduce travel time and improve communication between groups which work closely together.

Block Plans

Bubble diagrams and adjacency matrixes are translated into block plans. Block plans allocate square footage to the various departments and groups. This is done on the actual building plans. From the population projections previously established, the designer has a good idea of the square footage requirements for each department. Groups working closely together are situated adjacent to each other if possible. This may not always be possible due to limitations of the actual space, but compromises are kept to a minimum. An example of a block plan is shown in Figure 4.3.

Block plans are useful for feasibility studies because they show whether the proposed space would work for the size group in question, or whether different size floors would be more appropriate. If the floor sizes prove to be incorrect, groups may have to be split. If two groups working closely together are split, this may reduce efficiency of both departments.

Stack Plans

Departments working closely together in a multi-story building are sometimes situated vertically adjacent to each other. If one department is located on two floors, they may be connected by an interior staircase. This speeds travel time, even with elevators. Executive floors including offices, board rooms, dining rooms, health clubs, and barber shops are generally situated on the top floors. Corporate offices may be next followed by divisions or operations and, finally, staff. This kind of layout is planned on a stack plan (see Figure 4.4).

The stack plan can also be used to plan for the use of any future space. If, for example, a particular function currently occupies half a floor, but is expected to grow rapidly, the other half of the floor may be left unoccupied for the present to allow for future expansion. Or if the space is not going to be used for a known period of time, it can be sublet until needed.

Systems Analysis

Before finalizing any space plans, it is necessary to analyze all the present systems to see how they might be improved or changed in the new location. For example, it might be decided that a microfilm/microfiche system will be used instead of sending hard copies of documents to storage, or to have everyone use a central filing system instead of individuals retaining their own files. Another example is a change in the mail distribution system. The client may wish to implement automated mail delivery and/or electronic mail. The designer may suggest removal of physical barriers and planning

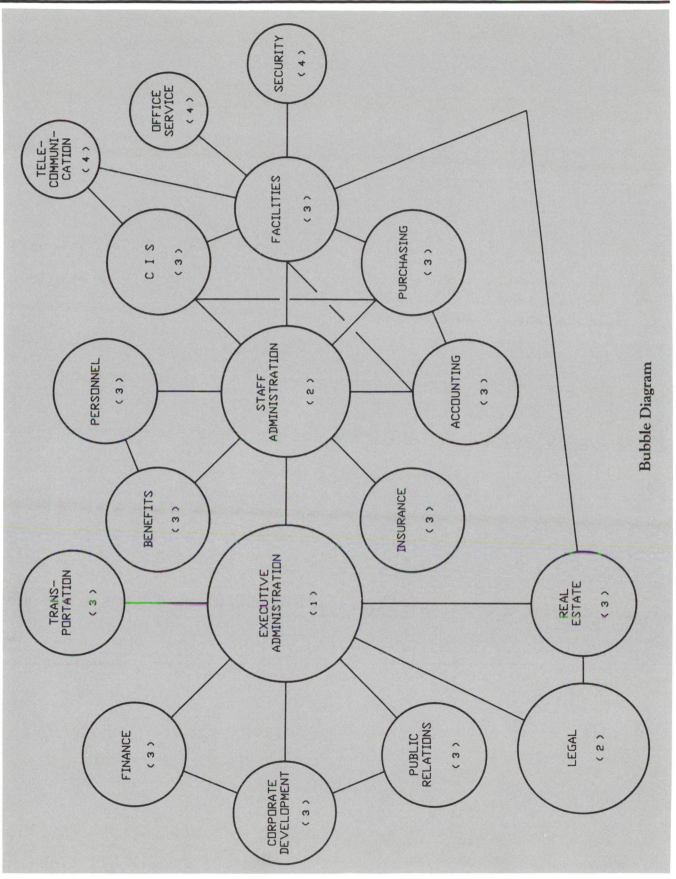

Bubble Diagram

Figure 4.1

49

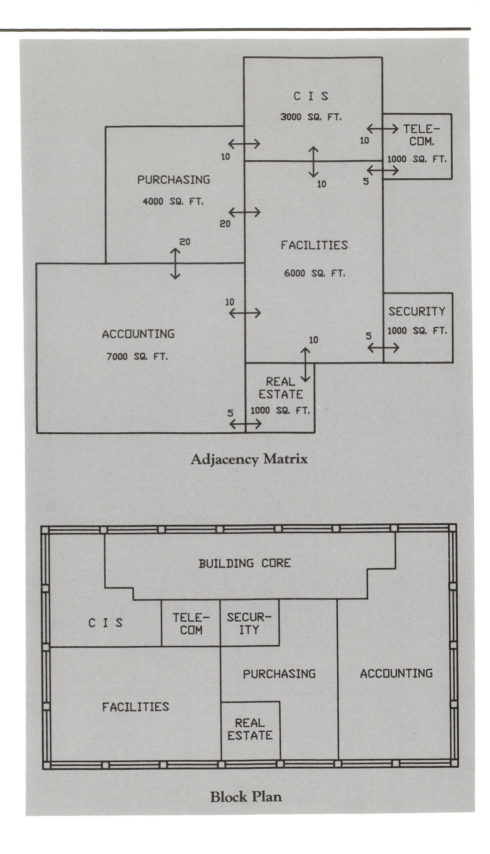

Adjacency Matrix

Figure 4.2

Block Plan

Figure 4.3

Stack Plan

16,000 S.F.	EXECUTIVE DINING ROOM			
	EXECUTIVE			
	EXECUTIVE			20TH
	LEGAL			19TH
	TAX	AUDIT		18TH
	FACILITIES	PURCH.	CIS.	RE.	17TH
	ACCOUNTING	FINANCE		16TH
	TRANS.	P.R.	INSURANCE	15TH
	BENEFITS	PERSONNEL		14TH
	INTERNATIONAL DIVISION			13TH
	MOVIE DIVISION			11TH
	SUB-TENANT TO 12/89			10TH
	VACANT			9TH
	SUB-TENANT TO 6/88			8TH
	SUB-TENANT TO 6/88			7TH

20,000 S.F.	PUBLISHING DIVISION			6TH
	PUBLISHING DIVISION			5TH
	SUB-TENANT TO 2/92			4TH
	SUB-TENANT TO 2/92			3RD
	RECORD DIVISION			2ND
	RECORD DIVISION			1ST
	LOBBY AND SHOPS			G
	DATA PROCESSING	CAFETERIA	SECURITY	STORAGE	B1
	MAIL ROOM	PRINT SHOP	STORAGE		B2

Figure 4.4

for the safety, comfort, and improved on-the-job efficiency of the handicapped. This requirement is often dictated by building codes.

Improvements raise many organizational issues and require changes in the way employees have been doing things, perhaps for years. For this reason, changes must be carefully considered and analyzed. For example, a change from a manual typewriter system to an automated computer/word processor system has a great impact on the employees. A host of considerations must be addressed to implement such a change. Work is performed differently with new equipment. The planner must ensure that all the old tasks can still be performed without great inconvenience to the employees. Has the client considered networking of its various types of computers? Is the client using a mainframe computer with remote terminals or is he using personal computers? What about communicating over distances with copy equipment hooked up to telephones, computers connected to data transmission lines via modems, teleconferencing, and videoconferencing?

Improvements must be carefully studied and researched. All the appropriate questions must be asked. No final decisions should be made until all existing and proposed systems are studied, and conclusions drawn regarding their implementation.

Square Footage Standards

Before preliminary space plans can be drawn up, square footage standards for employee workstations can be developed. These are based on information derived from Figure 1.4 as well as the basic building module of the space being designed. The standards organize the space according to job level, title, or function (refer to Figure 4.5). If new standards are set for the new quarters, there may be problems with some employees. Often, there are employees who currently have more space than they really require or to which they are entitled. In the move, they are located in smaller spaces. Or, an employee may be moving from a closed office to a cubicle. These instances are usually met with negative responses and must be handled tactfully by top management in order effect a smooth transition. On the other hand, moving from a crowded open space to a cubicle is usually met with a positive response.

Top management must review and approve the square foot standards developed by the designer. The client should understand that these standards, once set, must be adhered to. If one exception is made, it opens the way for many more and a certain degree of control is lost.

Office size is frequently referred to by the number of *modules* it holds. A module is a basic building block. For example, a building has a glass curtain wall with the mullions five feet on center, therefore, the building consists of five foot modules. In this case, a fifteen foot office would be a three module office.

Grade Level	Title	S.F.	Space Description
1-6	Secretarial/Clerical	54	Open Area
1-6	Clerk/Accountant	64	Cubicle
6	Supervisor/Professional	97	Cubicle
7-9	Manager	94-113	2 Module Office
10-12	Senior Manager	115-138	2 1/2 Module Office
13-14	Director	144-164	3 Module Office
15-18	AVP/Sr. Director	168-200	3 1/2 Module Office
15-18	Vice-President	189-225	4 Module Office
15-18	Senior Vice-President	250-280	4 1/2 Module Office
19-25	Group Senior VP	242	4 1/2 x 3 Module Corner Office
19-25	Executive VP/Pres	338	4 1/2 x 4 Module Corner Office

Figure 4.5

Preliminary Plans

The designer can now combine the information from the survey of client requirements with the block plans and square footage standards. These are used to produce a preliminary layout for client review and discussion. The designer, however, cannot usually accomplish, on the first plan, everything the client desires and needs. In planning a space, compromises in space plans, layout, and furnishings must inevitably be made. Anticipating this, the designer should develop a few alternate plans for review by the client as he may be willing to go along with some compromises but not others. This usually saves hours otherwise spent revising and reworking the drawings and may eliminate the need for more meetings and presentations.

Standard Furniture Layouts

The designer draws furniture layouts to accompany the square footage standards. It is good practice to draw several possible furniture layouts for each space type for the client's perusal, as clients often prefer to see many possible choices. Examples of typical furniture layout options are shown in Figure 4.6.

Materials and Furniture Standards

The designer has probably had a general design concept from the onset of the project; now he must establish the actual details. By now the designer is aware of how much new furniture will be purchased and what portion of the existing furniture will be refurbished and reused. With this information, the designer develops the materials standards by starting the selection process.

The general area materials for the project such as carpet, wallcovering, paint, furniture finishes, upholstery, and window treatment are selected first. Once the designer obtains preliminary approval of these main finishes, the working drawings can be started. This can be done even if the designer is still preparing the design for the executive offices and special areas.

Preliminary Presentation

In making a preliminary presentation, the designer is seeking approval to proceed with the working drawings, as the drawing phase of the project is very time-consuming and must begin as early as possible. At the preliminary presentation, the designer presents the preliminary layouts and ideas for general office materials and concepts. The cost of these items must remain within the limits set by the initial target budget. With approval of the preliminary design scheme, the designer can then begin to detail the drawings necessary for the final presentation.

Working Drawings

From the approved preliminary layout, a base partition plan is drafted from which sepias for all other plans are made. This process saves many hours of tedious drafting. The designer must work closely with the draftsmen and/or architect to coordinate and cross-check all drawings. The following working drawings are necessary for any renovation or new construction project:

- Construction/demolition plan
- Telephone/electric plan
- Reflected ceiling plan
- Architectural details plan
- Department of Buildings (for filing) plan

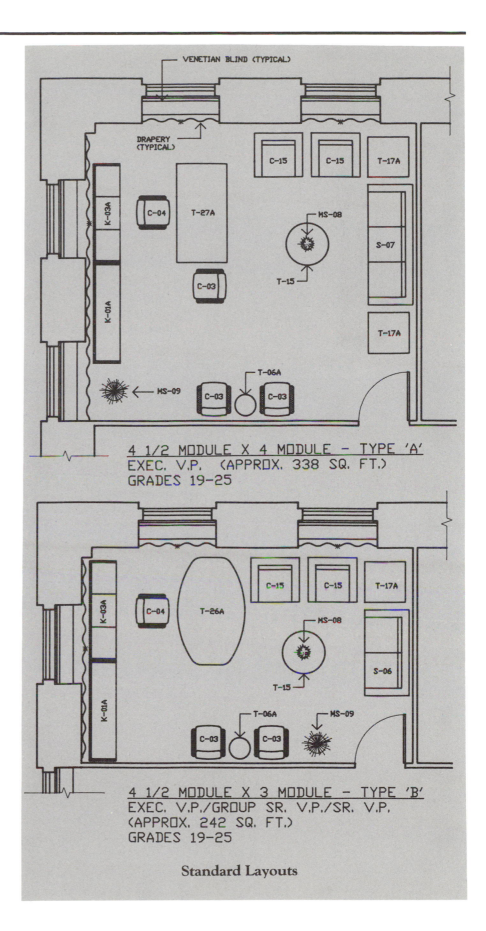

Standard Layouts

Figure 4.6

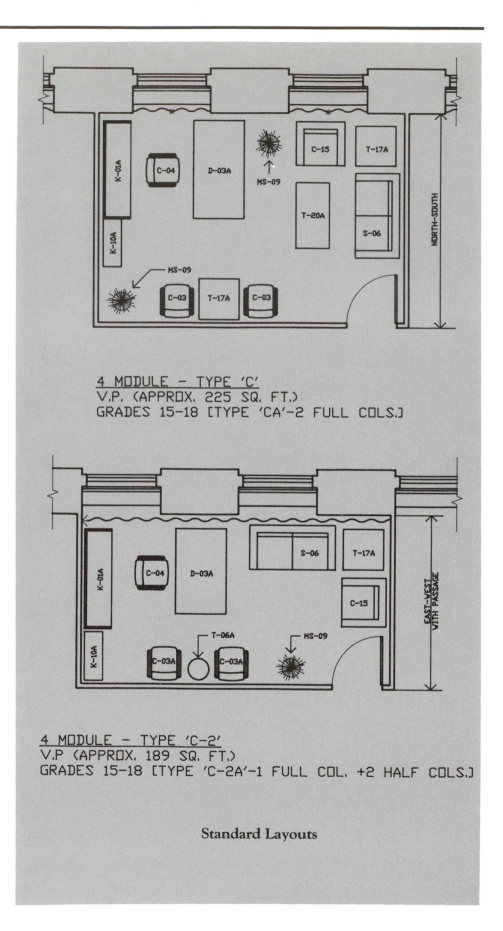

4 MODULE — TYPE 'C'
V.P. (APPROX. 225 SQ. FT.)
GRADES 15-18 [TYPE 'CA'-2 FULL COLS.]

4 MODULE — TYPE 'C-2'
V.P (APPROX. 189 SQ. FT.)
GRADES 15-18 [TYPE 'C-2A'-1 FULL COL. +2 HALF COLS.]

Standard Layouts

Figure 4.6 (continued)

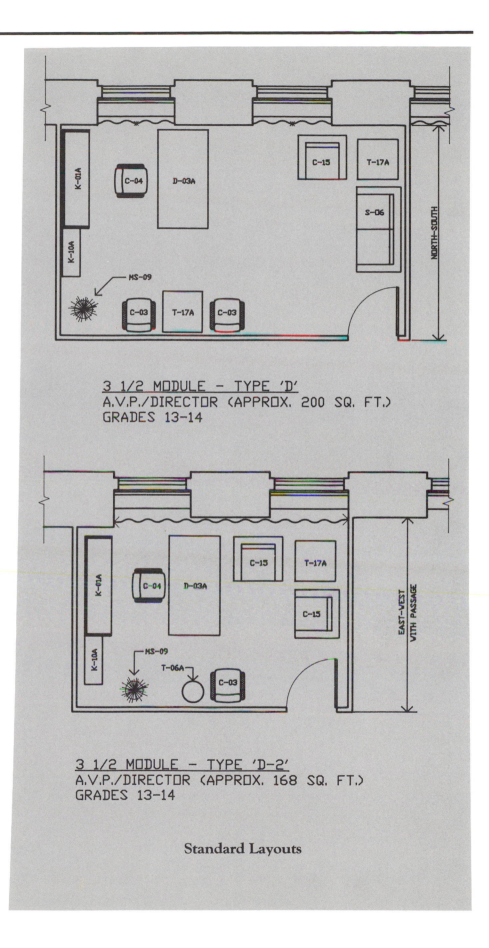

3 1/2 MODULE — TYPE 'D'
A.V.P./DIRECTOR (APPROX. 200 SQ. FT.)
GRADES 13–14

3 1/2 MODULE — TYPE 'D-2'
A.V.P./DIRECTOR (APPROX. 168 SQ. FT.)
GRADES 13–14

Standard Layouts

Figure 4.6 (continued)

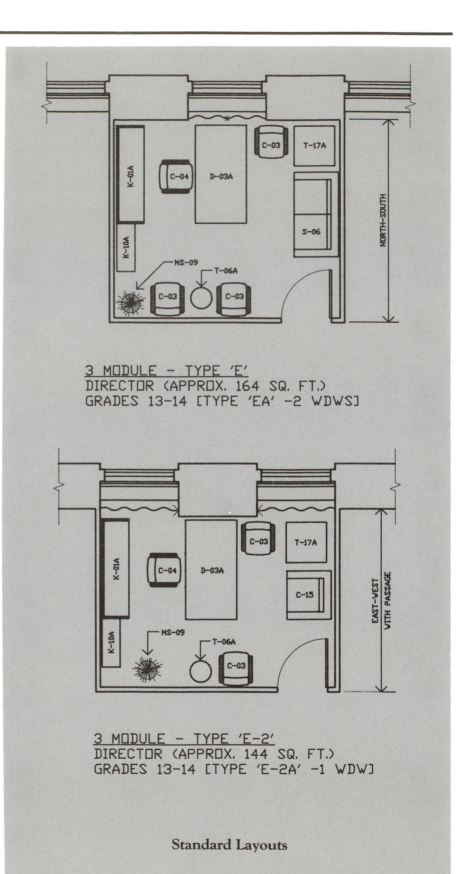

3 MODULE – TYPE 'E'
DIRECTOR (APPROX. 164 SQ. FT.)
GRADES 13-14 [TYPE 'EA' -2 WDWS]

3 MODULE – TYPE 'E-2'
DIRECTOR (APPROX. 144 SQ. FT.)
GRADES 13-14 [TYPE 'E-2A' -1 WDW]

Standard Layouts

Figure 4.6 (*continued*)

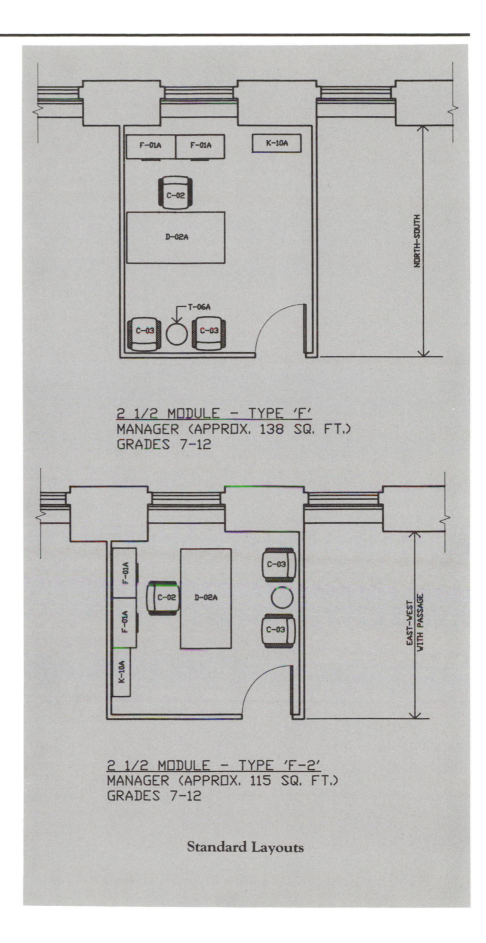

2 1/2 MODULE — TYPE 'F'
MANAGER (APPROX. 138 SQ. FT.)
GRADES 7-12

2 1/2 MODULE — TYPE 'F-2'
MANAGER (APPROX. 115 SQ. FT.)
GRADES 7-12

Standard Layouts

Figure 4.6 (continued)

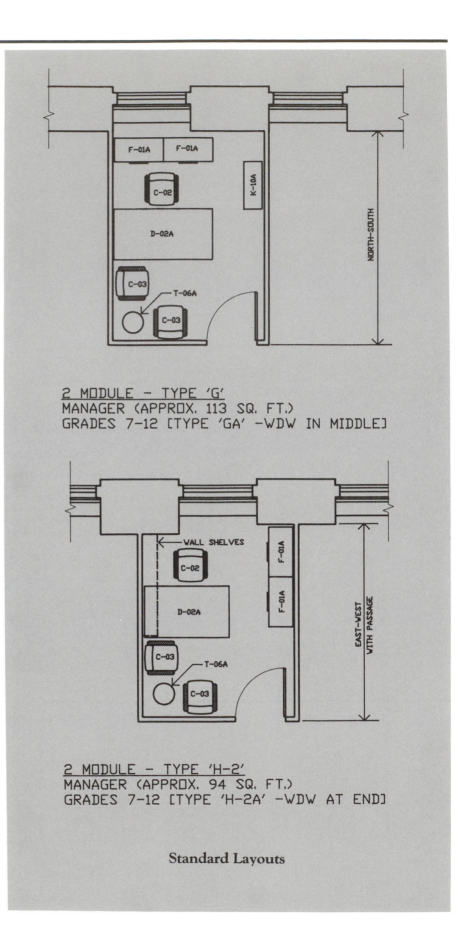

2 MODULE — TYPE 'G'
MANAGER (APPROX. 113 SQ. FT.)
GRADES 7-12 [TYPE 'GA' —WDW IN MIDDLE]

2 MODULE — TYPE 'H-2'
MANAGER (APPROX. 94 SQ. FT.)
GRADES 7-12 [TYPE 'H-2A' —WDW AT END]

Standard Layouts

Figure 4.6 (*continued*)

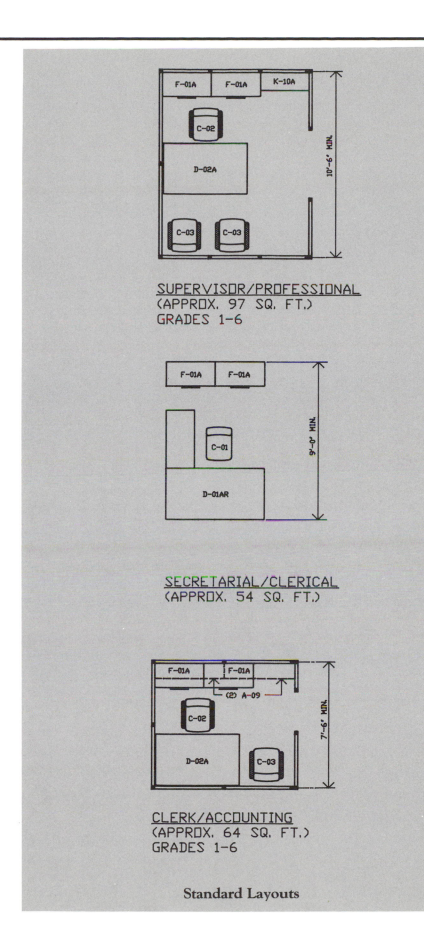

Standard Layouts

Figure 4.6 (*continued*)

For convenience, all other drawings which become part of the working drawings are referred to as the Interior Plans.

The designer/planner is the driving force of the project. He must meet with draftsmen daily to ensure that nothing is omitted and to resolve any problems or inconsistencies. Draftsmen must be instructed where to incorporate telephone, electrical, and special outlets, wall switches, lighting patterns, fire walls, and fire doors into the construction drawings. The designer may specially design the ceilings to accommodate special lighting effects. Indirect lighting in combination with task lighting and cove ceilings or other special lighting also deserves special attention.

Interior Plans

The necessary interior drawings are listed below:

- Furniture plan
- Floor finishes plan (carpet, vinyl tile, wood, quarry tile)
- Applied wall finishes plan (acoustical treatment, wallcovering, paint, stretch wall, wood)
- Window treatment plan (slim line blinds, draperies, vertical blinds, blackout shades)
- Open office panel layout
- Details (cabinetry, millwork)

The drawings listed above can be started, but cannot be finished until approval of the final design presentation. If renderings are to be part of the final presentation, the designer will make sketches, at this point, for the renderer to use. Any cabinetry or architectural details are sketched to obtain cost estimates and for approval at the final presentation.

Engineering Drawings

Depending on the scope of the work and building and fire code requirements, engineering drawings may be necessary. Generally, mechanical, electrical, and plumbing drawings are required for renovation. The building may also require sprinkler drawings for fire protection, or structural drawings for items such as new stairways. A professional architect or engineer should be consulted for such drawings.

Overall Design Concept

At this point, the final design concept can be developed from the information the designer has gathered. The general direction for the project has already been established and approved; now the designer must "fine tune" the details. The final design presentation will also require a final budget. This topic is discussed in more detail in Chapter 6. The budget is, however, as important as the actual design and must be developed as other design details are being formed.

Furniture and Materials Selection

The actual furniture selected is based on the initial budget discussions with the client, agreed upon materials standards, and the designer's understanding of what appeals to the client. If this includes reusing existing furniture, the designer will probably want to try to blend the old with the new. If new furniture is to be purchased, the designer selects the grade, or degree of quality, depending on the client's budget. The quality of material selected depends on the budget. More expensive fabrics and finishes are usually used in such areas as reception, the board room, and the chairman's office. The overall furniture budget divided by the square footage of the office indicates how much money can be spent per square foot, and thus, per workstation.

$$\frac{\text{Overall furniture budget}}{\text{Square footage of new office}} = \text{Average cost per S.F.}$$

$$\text{Avg. cost per S.F.} \times \text{S.F. of ea. workstation} = \text{Avg. cost per workstation}$$

The client will appreciate the designer who selects furniture and materials that are functional, practical, and easy to maintain. Maintenance headaches are created every day by people with good intentions but little foresight. The designer should always research and test every item and material thoroughly before recommending it.

Final Design Presentation and Approval

Necessary items for this presentation are:
- Final floor plan layout (rendered in black and white, or in color to indicate the various colors, materials, and finishes)
- Design budget
- Finish plans (rendered in color to indicate various wall finishes and colors on the floor plans)
- Ceiling design
- Cabinetry sketches
- Architectural detail sketches
- Renderings/models (only if necessary; they are very expensive)
- Presentation boards with:
  - Furniture photographs
  - Material Samples
  - Finish Samples

Methods of Presentation

Most designers use boards to illustrate the design presentation. Photographs and materials are carefully cut, pasted, and labeled onto these boards. The boards may then be covered with acetate for protection. One of the problems with this type of presentation is that incoporating any changes into this package can be time-consuming. Another drawback is that the small swatches of fabric used in this type of presentation often do not give a realistic representation of the same fabric in larger scale. Various fabrics cannot be juxtaposed for comparison because they cannot be readily removed from the board. Sometimes it is important to feel the texture of a particular item.

Alternately, some designers prefer to keep all items for the presentation "loose". This enables the use of large fabric samples, as opposed to small ones. Large fabric samples give the client a better idea of the overall appearance of the material. It also allows for juxtaposition of various samples, so that the client can compare them in different proximity and proportion. In addition, a few alternate choices can be included as possible substitutes if the client disapproves of a particular sample. The loose method can save time otherwise spent preparing a new presentation and rescheduling a meeting.

After the Presentation

After the presentation, any agreed upon adjustments to the design must be implemented. All information will then be turned over to the draftsmen to finalize the working and interior drawings. If the client wishes to see and try out some of the furniture, the designer may arrange for showroom visits. If a substantial quantity of furniture is to be ordered, manufacturers may even be willing to deliver sample items to the client's office.

The designer is now free to go on to the next project phase, which is furniture specifying and ordering. However, the client's existing furniture and budgeting should be addressed first. These tasks will, on an actual project, be developed simultaneously with space planning and design.

REUSE
OF EXISTING
FURNITURE

REUSE OF EXISTING FURNITURE

Rarely is a client willing to dispose of all the furniture he owns in order to buy new furniture. Depending on the budget and the condition of the existing furniture, he may wish to retain most or all of the items in good condition, or keep just a few pieces. Occasionally the existing furniture is not appropriate to the new design. For example, a new location may call for an open plan, when the old location consisted of closed offices. In this case, some of the existing furniture may be retained for closed office or conference room use, but most would be sold or given away.

Regardless of what the client's plans are for the existing furniture, an inventory must be taken. All furnishing items must be listed in order to sell, donate to charity, or integrate them into a new design. The client often has an existing furniture inventory, but it may not be detailed enough for the designer to visualize it for reuse in the new plan. An inventory should include finish, type, and color information, especially if the designer is to incorporate it into the new space.

This chapter contains descriptions of the inventory taking process, including methodologies, tagging procedures, rating the condition of items, refurbishing and repair advice, incorporation into new design, and disposal of existing furniture. If the designer is precise and follows the numbers exactly, the move-in will go smoothly. It is important that these procedures are considered, whether a client intends to retain, sell, or give away the furniture.

Taking Inventory

The furniture inventory can and should be taken as early as possible; this task is often independent of the design phase. Methods of taking inventory vary greatly with the size of the project. The methods considered here are primarily used for medium to large projects, but the concepts are applicable to projects of all sizes. Short cuts for small projects are discussed at the end of this chapter.

The main goal of any inventory is to be able to keep track of each item of furniture, from its present location to its final destination. The designer frequently performs the inventory, often in conjunction with the client's office manager or another person assigned to act as liaison between the client and the designer. If the project is large in scope and the time frame short, the client may hire a special contractor to take the inventory. It doesn't really matter who performs the inventory as long as all necessary information is listed. If the client intends to sell or donate the majority of the existing furniture, it might be preferable to have an appraiser perform the inventory and place a value on all items at the same time.

Different offices use varying formats to list the furnishings, but the necessary information is usually the same. Information that should be included in any inventory is listed below:

- Number or code
- Present location: division, department, room number, occupant/user's name
- Category of furniture: desk, chair, sofa, table, file, credenza, storage cabinet
- Description (by abbreviation, see Figure 5.1)
- Manufacturer (if known)
- Size: depth, width, height
- Material: top, base
- Color: top, base
- Finish
- Fabric
- Hardware
- Condition: excellent, good, fair, poor
- Lock(s)
- Remarks
- Disposition: remain, relocate, refinish, reupholster, sell, donate

If the new inventory is used in conjunction with a client's existing inventory, the following might be included:

- Purchase price
- Purchase date
- Depreciation rate

Inventory Methods

In order for the designer to place existing furniture on the floor plans, each item must be tagged with a number or a code and described fully on a central listing. Sequential numbering is probably the most common inventory method. Another method which works well if the client has a lot of standardized furniture is to inventory by category of furniture. One type of chair is coded C-1, the next C-2, and the next C-3. Desks are coded D-1, D-2, D-3, etc. Counts are taken of the total quantity of each type, per room or office.

Sequential Method

Using the sequential method, all items are numbered individually and the inventory is taken room by room. Figure 5.2 illustrates a format for this type of inventory. The sequential inventory can be computerized. Computerization allows all of one type of item to be grouped together for easier programming onto the drawings. If photographs are taken for future identification, the inventory numbers are written on the photographs which are then filed by inventory number.

Category Method

This method utilizes photographs affixed to the forms to identify the codes, and works well with large quantities of standardized furniture. The category method saves time, as the description is written in detail only once. The individual items are listed only by location each time they occur. See Figure 5.3 for an example of a format used for the category method.

Tagging

If an inventory is used only for the move, the type of tag is relatively unimportant. A memo should be issued, however, requesting that employees leave the tags on the furniture until after the move. (Frequently, employees peel the tags off as they believe they are unsightly and unnecessary.) If the inventory is to be retained as a permanent record (new furniture included) good quality tags should be acquired. Preprinted and numbered tags with lasting adhesive are necessary. Custom printed tags must be ordered in advance.

Listing of Inventory Abbreviations			
Abbreviation	Term	Abbreviation	Term
BC	Brushed chrome	PC	Polished chrome
BL	Black	PL	Plastic laminate
CONF	Conference	R	Refinish
DBL	Double	RET	Return
DP	Double pedestal	RH	Right hand
DWR	Drawer	SEC'Y	Secretarial
E	Excellent	SP	Single pedestal
EXEC	Executive	SS	Stainless steel
F	Fair	ST	Swivel tilt
G	Good	TBL	Table
LAT	Lateral	U	Reupholster
LH	Left hand	UPH	Upholstery
P	Poor	VERT	Vertical

Figure 5.1

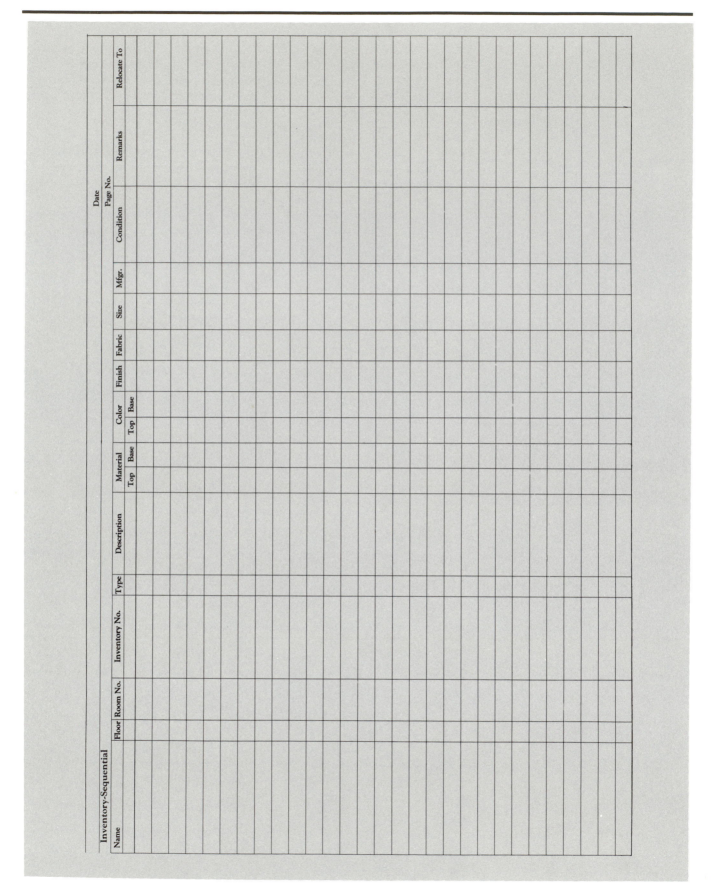

Figure 5.2

Inventory Category

		Page _____ of _____
(Photo)	Doe Interiors	Code
	Existing Furniture & Furnishings	
	Client	
	Date _____	

Item _____ Color _____ Top _____ Base _____

Mfg. _____ Top Material _____

Cat. No. _____ Base Material _____

Width _____ Depth _____ Height _____ Total Quantity _____

Present Space	Inventory No.	Quan.	Finish	Fabric	Cond.	Remarks	Relocate To

Figure 5.3

Another method of tagging utilizes bar codes. The bar codes can be read with a computerized laser reader, for both furniture and rooms. The laser can read the tag on each piece of furniture and on each door and update a computer automatically. For example, furniture is tagged in Room 1 and is on a print out. The same furniture is moved to Room 2 and the laser reads all furniture codes from the tags, as well as a tag on the back of the door which contains the room number. The computer now has the current information; the furniture that used to be in Room 1 is now in Room 2. Although this method does not save any time initially, it saves a lot of time later when items are relocated.

The cost of this type of system is generally moderate. Another advantage to using the bar code system is that the tags can be hidden since the laser can "read" through wood and fabric. If the employees can't see the labels, they'll be less likely to peel them off.

Rating of Items by Condition

The condition of each item is a subjective consideration. Some clients decide to retain only items in excellent or good condition. Others elect to keep those in fair condition as well, to be refurbished, since refurbishing is usually less expensive than buying new. In either case, the designer must record the condition of each piece of furniture in order to determine those pieces to be retained and those to be sold or given away. The following definitions are guidelines for labeling the condition of furnishing items:

- **Excellent:** New or virtually new.
- **Good:** In prime condition and reusable "as is" with minor touch-ups or polishing required to put it back in excellent condition.
- **Fair:** Needs work to get it into reusable condition. May need refinishing, reupholstering, or other repair.
- **Poor:** Should not be reused. Broken beyond repair or too extensive work required to upgrade to usable condition.

In a remarks column on the inventory, notes can be made such as "needs new casters", "broken chair base", "ripped seat or arms", etc. This will remind the designer later of the exact nature of the work to be done and eliminates the time it would take to go back and physically survey the item again.

Computerization

The use of a computer can significantly increase the efficiency of an inventory system. If the computer program is set up properly, it can be easily updated for the new space and future relocations. Deletions and additions can be readily handled. Although inputting every furnishing item into a computer does not save any time initially, it saves countless hours later when changes are made.

Refurbishing

Some designers prefer not to get involved in refurbishing work, as it requires time and expertise to accomplish. If the designer performs some or all of the refurbishing work, however, it does save the client money. This may be an option if the client is on a limited budget.

Refinishing/Respraying

Items in good condition may simply require polishing. On the other hand, some items will require refinishing. A skillful refinisher can work wonders with old, but good quality, desks, credenzas, tables, and chair frames. These items can be made to look almost brand new by stripping and refinishing. Refinishing, when possible, saves the client a great deal of money. It is not usually worthwhile, however, to refinish inexpensive furniture.

Metal files, desks, credenzas, and storage cabinets can be electrostatically resprayed to complement the new color scheme. These items can be made to look new, and this will accent the overall aesthetics of the new space.

Reupholstering

Some upholstered furniture that appears to be in terrible condition can be dramatically upgraded with a thorough cleaning. However, if items are permanently soiled, faded, or ripped, they must be reupholstered in order to be reused.

Wood frames, if structurally sound, can be refinished and will complement the new or cleaned fabric. Reupholstering is expensive due to the amount of labor involved and the cost of pick up, trucking, and redelivery. It is, however, usually less expensive than buying new furniture.

Repair

The designer should be able to discriminate between items that can be economically fixed and those which should be thrown out. He should know what can and what cannot be repaired. Broken chair bases can be replaced if they can be reordered. Detached chair arms can be secured, casters can be changed to operate on the new floor surface, and weak items can be braced. If a wood desk leg is broken off it usually cannot be repaired. Sometimes it can be ordered from the manufacturer and replaced, but that is dependent on the desk construction. Each situation must be judged independently.

Incorporate Existing Furniture onto Drawings

This phase of the project should be completed prior to the final design presentation if a great deal of existing furniture is being reused. If, on the other hand, the majority of the furniture will be new, both inventory and incorporation can wait until after approval of the final presentation.

The reusable furniture is indicated on the drawings by inventory number so that the designer can determine exactly what new furniture must be purchased. Only after this has been determined can an accurate budget be developed. This means that the inventory and incorporation into the plan are generally completed first.

Determine Upgrading Standards

There are several ways of upgrading the furniture in an office. A general upgrading of furniture can be accomplished by purchasing new furniture for the top executives and passing their present furniture down to the middle managers. The furniture of the middle managers will, in turn, be passed down to the lower managers. This technique keeps the top executives happy and is usually well received by the other managers. On the other hand, this method can cause complications. Certain items may not fit into the office of the person who has been promised another executive's furniture. In this case, substitutions have to be made. Another complication occurs when the same furniture is sought after by more than one person and is inadvertently promised to two people at the same time. The designer will have to find viable solutions to these kinds of problems.

Another technique that is often employed, if the existing furniture is relatively new, is that each individual retains his existing furniture. The furniture is then refurbished in whatever manner necessary. This is a much simpler plan for the designer to implement because office politics do not interfere with the plans. The only time switches are made is if something doesn't fit or is "wrong handed" for the space (i.e., a right-hand desk is needed when only a left-hand is available).

Code the Plan

Once an overall furniture plan is decided upon, the designer can begin to draft the furniture layout. Depending on the inventory numbering system selected, the plans will either be numbered or coded. Figure 5.4 is an example of a coded plan. For example, if the designer wants to use desk #BO11759 in Room 16-25, he will write the number, "BO11759", on the rectangular representation for the desk in room 16-25 on the plans (as shown in Figure 5.4). Items to be refinished can be coded with the suffix "R" added to the end of the inventory number. Similarly, the suffix "U" plus a fabric code is added to the inventory number for items to be reupholstered. The suffix "RU" indicates refinish and reupholster, while the suffix "RS" means respray (electrostatic). In addition to producing an organized tracking method, this technique helps illustrate the overall scheme of the design.

If the client has standardized furniture and the designer has utilized the alpha-numeric category inventory method, the plan will look more like Figure 5.5. If there is very little new furniture, it can be given the suffix "N", to differentiate new items from existing ones. This can be very helpful if, for example, the new furniture is late and temporary furniture must be provided.

Indicate New Room Numbers

While coding the plans, the designer should color in the item on the plans as he writes the new room number in a "relocate to" column on the inventory sheets. Figure 5.6 is a sample inventory sheet showing the use of the "relocate to" column. This process provides a double-check of the furniture plan, because sometimes numbers get transposed, or the same number gets inadvertently written on two items of furniture. By coloring in the plans as the items are assigned to rooms, such errors can be avoided.

If room numbers are correctly labeled, the designer can readily find out what any existing item on the plan is by looking up the inventory number. The inventory sheets will also indicate where this item is going to be placed in the new plan.

Professional movers work with this complete inventory when they tag the furniture for the physical move. The designer need only be available to answer questions. The coded plan alone can be confusing and, without a complete inventory, the designer would have to perform the relocation tagging with the movers. Completion of inventory sheets and plans is a tedious task, but can save the designer much time and expedite a smooth transition at the time of the actual move.

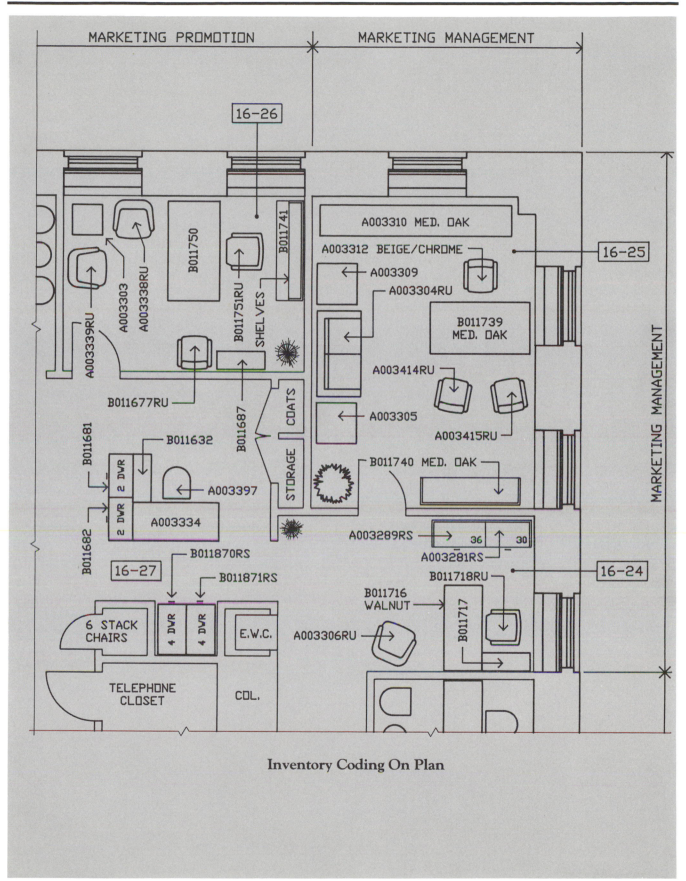

Inventory Coding On Plan

Figure 5.4

Disposal of Furniture

Discarding furniture entails hiring laborers and dumpsters to remove and cart items being thrown out. While laborers are not as expensive as carpenters or electricians, the designer must remember that it still costs money to throw things away. If there is a large quantity of furniture, this can become a significant cost factor in the project. It is, therefore, preferable to sell or donate any furniture the client does not want.

Sale of Furniture

Buyers of used furniture often quote a dollar amount per truck load. The amount they quote is usually insignificant in comparison to initial purchase or replacement costs. However, if someone carts the excess furniture away and is willing to pay for it on top of that, the cost of trucking or disposal is eliminated and the client has made money at the same time. If a complete inventory listing all the items to be sold and their condition has been taken, it is relatively easy to inform interested buyers of the amount and quality of the items. The items can then be readily bid and removed in conjunction with the move.

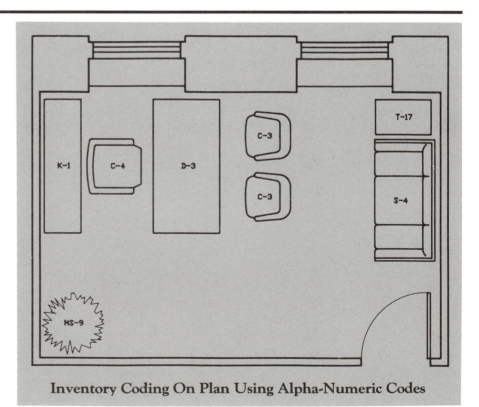

Inventory Coding On Plan Using Alpha-Numeric Codes

Figure 5.5

Inventory Category

| (Photo) | Doe Interiors | Page __1__ of __1__ |
| | | Code C-4 |

Existing Furniture & Furnishings

Client   X Y Z Co.

Date _____

Item DESK CHAIR	Color _____ Top CHAR-COAL Base _____
Mfg. STEELCASE	Top Material POLY SHELL
Cat. No. 451-322	Base Material POLISHED CHROME
Width 22" Depth 20"	Height 31" Total Quantity 8

Present Space	Inventory No.	Quan.	Finish	Fabric	Cond.	Remarks	Relocate To
17-02	001314	1	P.C.	BLACK	G		16-01
17-06	001352	1	"	"	G		16-03
17-09	001396	1	"	"	E		16-04
20-03	001983	1	"	"	F	REPLACE BROKEN CASTER	16-05
20-05	001944	1	"	"	G		16-06
20-08	001930	1	"	"	P	DISCARD	———
20-22	001811	1	"	"	F	REUPHOLSTER	16-11
23-11	002403	1	"	BROWN	G	REUPHOLSTER	16-23

Figure 5.6

Donation to Charity

In some cases it is more beneficial to donate excess furniture to charity because the client can claim a tax deduction based on the appraised value of the items (often higher than resale value). This value should be determined by an appraiser contracted early in the project. A representative of the client's tax/accounting department can usually determine whether it would be more beneficial to sell or donate the excess furniture.

Small Projects

Certain short cuts can be taken for relatively small projects. For example, any existing furniture might simply be coded "E," for existing, on the furniture plans. A list can then be made up for the movers stating that the furniture in, say, Room 9-46, goes to Room 11-32. The plans for the 11th Floor will indicate the layout for Room 32, using the existing furniture (from floor 9, room 46). This method saves time by eliminating the process of numbering and describing each furniture item.

Another technique used for very small projects with no lead time involves tagging the furniture for the new room number and checking the item off on the new plan as it is tagged. This is a very informal method and only works if very few people are involved. With this procedure, there is no documentation available with which to inform others. It is, however, quick, and in some cases, time is of the essence.

Now that the somewhat tedious task of taking inventory is complete, the project manager can go on to plan the budget. As previously stated, the inventory taking process proceeds simultaneously with the space planning and design phase of the project. So too does the budgeting phase. The design criteria and product selection are completely interwoven with the budget restrictions. The designer must constantly check back and forth, from budget to design, to insure that the selected items are within the budget.

CHAPTER SIX

PREPARING
A BUDGET

PREPARING A BUDGET

This chapter contains descriptions of suggested estimating methods and practices for all items that may be included in an interiors budget, as well as a description of the overall budget estimating process.

The division of labor for an interiors project often has many grey areas that are worked out on a project by project basis. For example, the project architect may be responsible for the construction budget or there may be a construction manager. In this case, the construction manager is responsible for everything that goes into the building envelope, including walls, plumbing, ceilings, floors, wallcovering, air conditioning, etc. The furniture, window treatment, art work, plants, and accessories are then the only "interiors" categories. Nothing is ever that simple, however. The project manager/designer may consider the entire project to be under his authority. There are no exact guidelines. Categories such as flooring and wallcovering are often claimed by the designer, due to the selection process and timing. If the designer is responsible for the entire project, there is no conflict. If there is a project architect or a construction manager, he may or may not budget the walls, outlets, lighting fixtures, etc., that the designer has planned to use.

It is not the intent of this book to teach the reader how to write a construction budget. There are many other good books written on this subject. It is, however, the intent to include any categories strictly falling into the "interiors" category or in the grey area between construction, architecture, and interior design.

An example of a construction budget for comparison purposes is shown in Figure 6.1. Construction budgets ordinarily do not include furniture or other interiors categories.

The interior project manager may prefer to work up a total project budget to include all construction and interior costs as well as costs for engineering, architectural services, permit fees, inspections, telephones, moving, and sales tax.

Each facilities department or design/architectural firm is set up differently so there will be many variations on the theme. The designer should use the type of budgeting process with which he is most comfortable.

<u>Accounting Department</u>
3500 S.F.

1. Minor demolition/labor/clean-up $ 4,000

2. Drywall construction, including hollow metal
        doors, taping, and spackling   12,000

3. New ceiling   8,000

4. Electrical work   30,000

5. HVAC work   20,000

6. Painting   10,000

7. New bathroom (including plumbing work)   10,000

8. New kitchenette with plumbing work   7,500

9. Carpet (including vinyl base)   12,000

10. Vinyl tile flooring   600
                                                          ─────────
                              Subtotal $114,100

                              10% Contingency   11,400
                                                          ─────────
                              Grand total $125,500

Items not included:
        Filing fee
        Wallcovering
        Telephones and cables
        Relocation
        Plants
        Engineering fees
        Finish carpentry
        Furniture
        Window treatment
        Art work

Figure 6.1

Furniture

To obtain prices for furniture, the designer should consult manufacturers' catalogs, or work directly with manufacturer's representatives. Representatives can provide helpful information and are always willing to assist potential clients. Furniture dealers can also be helpful at this stage. Figure 6.2 is a furniture budget worksheet. After developing a number of these types of estimates, the designer may be able to write a budget without such extensive use of these aids.

Quality and Cost

Furniture costs vary according to the level of quality of the items. A three seat sofa with the customer's own material selection in "A" quality may cost from $1800 to $2000. A desk chair may cost from $500 to $800, depending on quality. If a customer requests "A plus" quality, any price is possible. A three seat sofa with a $100 per yard COM (Customer's Own Material) might cost $1500 for the fabric alone before shipping cost or taxes. An "A plus" desk chair might cost $1500 or more.

When deciding on the quality of furniture for a project, the designer must be sure that the client is being realistic about today's costs. He may be asking for "A plus" quality with a "B" pocketbook. The designer must reassure him that the space will still look good with "B" quality furniture if he cannot afford the "A" or "A plus" variety. On the other hand, if the client cannot afford all new "B" quality furniture and wants to go to "C" grade, the designer may have to be quite inventive. "C" grade furniture will not last long and, in the long run, may not prove to be economical. It usually looks and is cheap. Most designers avoid recommending the use of "C" grade furniture. Perhaps, in such a case, a compromise could be reached where half of the existing furniture is retained for future replacement and any new furniture purchased is "A" or "B" quality.

Built-in Features

Sometimes it is necessary to include isometric drawings describing a grouping of files or a counter configuration in order to clarify the budget. Figure 6.3 is an example of a combination of a budget with isometric drawings. An isometric drawing descriptively shows three sides of an object with far less effort than a perspective drawing. It is used for illustrative purposes. The designer may have many similar groupings and can have one total cost for numerous separate items.

For custom furniture and built-ins, the designer should consult a cabinet-maker. The designer should develop some design sketches and concepts on the types of wood and joinery for the project. The cabinet maker can then estimate the costs involved based on this information. Cabinetmaking is very expensive and should not be "guesstimated" by the designer alone.

Flooring

In order to estimate flooring, the designer first determines the area of space to be covered. For carpet, this is measured in square yards; for most other types of flooring, square footage is most commonly used. These include sheet vinyl, vinyl composition tile (VCT), quarry tile, marble, terrazzo, raised floor, wood planking, or wood parquet. The simplest way to obtain an accurate budget for flooring is to consult with a flooring dealer/installer. The dealer will calculate the yardage of carpet and the footage of hard surface flooring required. One

Budget Work Sheet

Client				Date	
Location				Project No.	

Code	Total Quantity	Description & Breakdown	Unit Net Cost	Total Net Cost
			Total	

Figure 6.2

XYZ COMPANY
CHICAGO, ILLINOIS

CABINETS

Code	Total Estimated Quantity	Description	Unit Cost	Estimated Total Cost
K-01	1	Special design 6-section wall hung credenza in English brown oak, clear lacquer finish. Size: 9'-0" x 1'-6". Leather top: American Leather #E0564 Terracolors, Copper. Bronze hardware and trim. Components: three double door storage cabinets. Refer to Drawing F-14.	$3,000.00	$ 3,000.00
K-02	1	General Fireproofing #706HC 5-section credenza in American oak, clear lacquer finish. Size: 81" W. x 20-1/2" D. x 23" H. Mirror chrome hardware and trim. Pedestals left to right as facing: 1 #HC-6, storage cabinet, door hinged left. 3 #HC-1, tray drawer, box drawer, file drawer. 1 #HC-7 storage cabinet, door hinged right. All pedestals to lock.	1,800.00	1,800.00
K-03	1	General Fireproofing counter with files and storage. Refer to Drawing F-27.	2,600.00	2,600.00
K-04	1	General Fireproofing counter with files and storage. Refer to Drawing F-28 (attached).	1,000.00	1,000.00
K-05	1	Special design Kardex cabinet in American oak with clear lacquer finish. Size: 34-1/2" W. x 26" D. x 33'1/2" H. Sliding reference shelf. Mirror chrome hardware and casters.	1,200.00	1,200.00
K-06	1	General Fireproofing storage	300.00	300.00

Figure 6.3

		cabinet. Refer to Drawing F-29.		
K-07	1	General Fireproofing counter with storage. Refer to Drawing F-30.	1,800.00	1,800.00
K-08	1	General Fireproofing counter with storage. Refer to Drawing F-31.	1,600.00	1,600.00
K-09	2	General Fireproofing counter with storage. Refer to Drawing F-32.	1,800.00	3,600.00
K-10	1	General Fireproofing counter with storage. Refer to Drawing F-33.	1,300.00	1,300.00
K-11	1	General Fireproofing counter with storage. Refer to Drawing F-34.	1,300.00	1,300.00
K-12	3	General Fireproofing storage cabinet. Refer to Drawing F-35.	350.00	1,050.00
K-13	2	General Fireproofing storage units. Refer to Drawing F-36.	600.00	1,200.00
K-14	1	General Fireproofing counter with storage. Refer to Drawing F-37.	1,700.00	1,700.00
K-15	2	General Fireproofing counter with files. Refer to Drawing F-38 (attached).	3,000.00	6,000.00

Total Estimated Cost Cabinets $29,450.00

Figure 6.3 (continued)

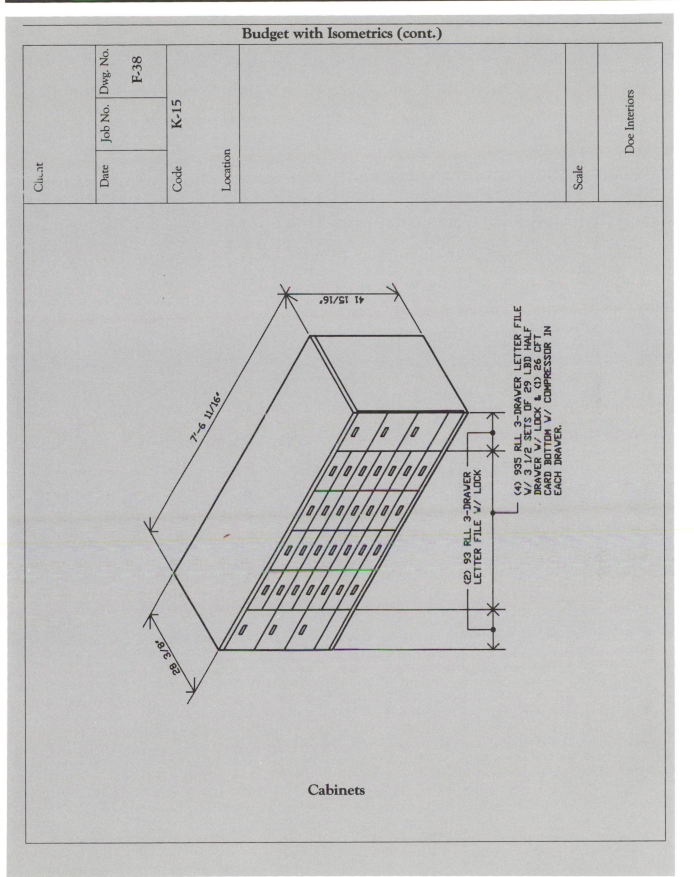

Cabinets

Figure 6.3 *(continued)*

87

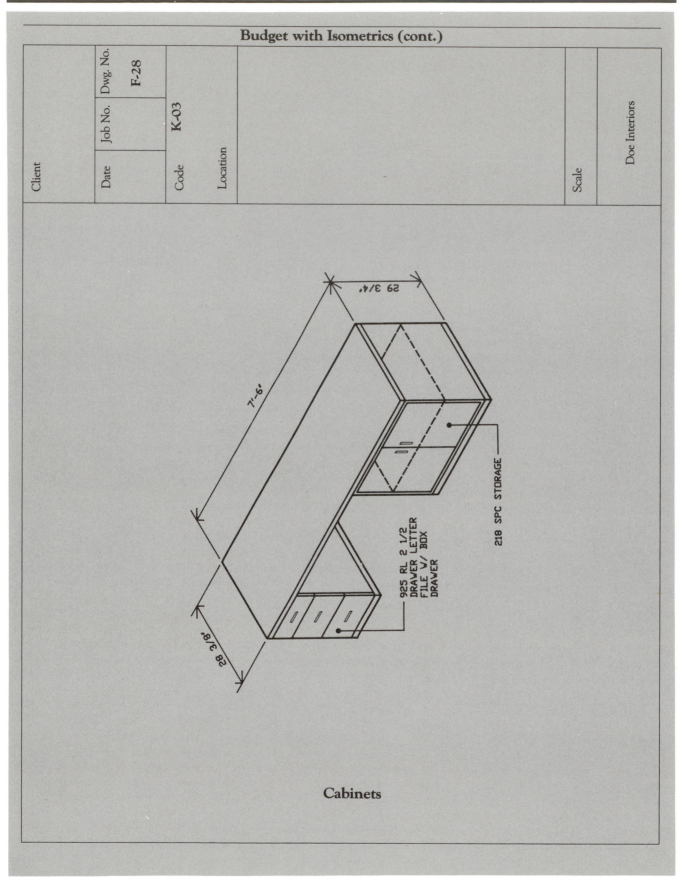

Cabinets

Client			
Date	Job No.	Dwg. No. F-28	
	Code	K-03	
	Location		
			Scale
			Doe Interiors

925 RL 2 1/2 DRAWER LETTER FILE W/ BDX DRAWER

218 SPC STORAGE

29 3/4"

7'-6"

28 3/8"

Figure 6.3 (continued)

common mistake often made when figuring the square yardage of carpet is to divide the usable square footage of the area by nine. This does not yield the carpet yardage required. A waste factor to account for the seaming direction and the size of fill pieces must be calculated and included in all carpet and vinyl flooring estimates. The most accurate way to accomplish this is to consult a contractor specializing in each type of flooring specified.

The same flooring dealer/installer can calculate an estimated budget cost for carpet or hard surface flooring if the particular material has not yet been selected. An allowance for material can be included. If the actual material is known, the dealer's price will be an accurate estimate of the costs for flooring. The designer should inquire about any discounts available if a large volume of one material is purchased.

The designer should ensure that everything is included in the flooring budget. Such items include padding, tack strip, reducer strips, adhesive, delivery, installation, clean up, restretching of carpet for one year, and initial polishing of tile or wood floor. Sometimes the flooring budget (or an allowance) is included in the construction budget; the designer should check with the project architect to be sure that the item is not estimated twice. The designer should verify that the construction plans are compatible with the project's design.

Window Treatment

There are many window treatment possibilities; draperies, curtains, slim line blinds, vertical blinds, roll-up shades, decorative draped shades, black-out shades with shadow-boxes, and solar treatment are some alternatives. Before estimating for windows, the designer must ascertain which type of treatment is appropriate for the client. Specialists in the chosen window treatment can then be asked to provide cost estimates for items which match the design concept. All items such as material, fabrication, hardware, delivery, installation, and repair of ceilings, window pockets, or sills after installation should be included in the window treatment cost estimate. Such items are dependent upon the chosen type of treatment.

Wall Finishes

There are many types of wall finishes available, including wood paneling, vinyl wallcovering, silk paper or grasscloth, stretched fabric panels, paint, acoustical, or hard surface for durability. All of the various wall finishes are estimated differently. For this reason, manufacturers or dealers should be consulted to obtain proper material and installation costs for these items.

Paint or Wallcoverings

Paint or wallpaper can be estimated by the square foot of wall area or by the lineal foot of partition. Estimating wallcovering, however, is difficult and confusing at best. A paperhanger or painter should be consulted for a proper wallcovering estimate. The paperhanger takes into account the width of the paper or vinyl and the number of "rolls" that are packaged together. Silk paper and handprints are usually 27 inches wide, packaged in single, double, and triple rolls. Commercial vinyl wallcovering is usually 54 inches wide, packaged by the linear yard.

Wallcovering is another area that is often included in the construction budget. The architect should be consulted to ensure that the proper items are specified for construction. For example, unaware of the designer's concept, the architect may have budgeted paint throughout. The difference between the cost of paint and the cost of wallcovering is significant. The cost of vinyl wallcovering can be three or more times that of painting.

Paneling

For wood paneling, the designer should consult a cabinetmaker. The cost will greatly depend on the wood selected. For example, elm burl is far more expensive than white oak. There may be a variation in cost depending on the detailing. The following questions must be answered:

- Will there be reveals around the panels?
- Will they be book matched or slip matched?
- How will they be installed?

For other wall treatments such as scuff resistant Kydex, the designer should consult a carpenter to obtain a proper estimate. This material is cut to fit and then glued to the wall. It has to be braced until the glue is set.

Fabric

Stretched fabric walls are frequently installed by drapery contractors. Thus, the drapery contractor can be consulted about wall and window treatment at the same time. Sometimes the designer creates a decorative three dimensional pattern for a wall out of stretched fabric panels. The mechanics of wrapping the forms and mounting them on the wall is quite complex, therefore, an expert should be consulted.

Acoustical Treatment

For acoustical treatments, the designer may have to consult with an acoustical engineer. If the designer wishes to provide some sound absorption for noisy machinery, he may specify carpet for the wall. A carpet dealer, should be consulted for an estimate. Other acoustical treatment might require a fabric type wallpaper. In this case, a paperhanger is consulted. For a better quality sound barrier, a separate wall with acoustical material in the pocket between the two walls must be constructed. Fabric is often stretched on the superstructure of the new wall. Prices for this work usually can be obtained from carpenters.

Accessories

Accessories are often overlooked. However, these seemingly insignificant items can add up, as large quantities are usually necessary. This category includes:

- Desk Accessories
  - desk pad
  - calendar
  - memo box
  - pencil cup
  - ashtray
  - letter tray—single or double
  - waste basket
  - pen and pencil set (for executives only)
  - clock (for executives only)
  - letter opener (executives only)
  - scissors (executives only)

- Cafeteria/Dining Room
  - table linens—tablecloths and napkins
  - flatware
  - china
  - glassware
  - ashtrays
  - clock
  - vases
  - trays
- Reception Areas
  - desk accessories as stated above
  - vases
  - umbrella stand
  - ash urn
- Conference Rooms
  - wastebasket
  - memo box
  - pencil cup
  - ashtrays
  - vases
- Corridors and Entrances
  - umbrella stands
  - ash urns

Most furniture dealers carry desk accessories and can assist the designer with pricing these items. Executive dining, cafeteria, and combination conference/lunch room table accessories are quite specialized and the designer should consult a wholesale distributor for pricing. It may be helpful to call a local hotel for assistance in locating a wholesale dealer for these items.

Plants

The designer should find a reliable commerical interior plant specialist to assist with estimating the planting costs. The cost of plants varies tremendously with species and size. Therefore, the plant specialist should first select plants which are practical for the environment, taking into account the light, temperature, and humidity in the area as well as the budget. The specialist also selects appropriate size containers for the plants. Once the size, type, and container have been determined, the designer can obtain an accurate estimate for plants.

Clients who are over budget at the end of a project often cut out the plant budget. However, planting is one of the important finishing touches of a project and can influence the way in which a space is perceived. For this reason, the designer must plan an accurate budget from the start and must stick to it. This will assure that there is enough money in the budget for the important finishing touches such as plants.

Artwork

Artwork in any building is one category that is subject to tremendous variation. Cost and quality depend greatly on the client's intent. A client may simply be interested in finishing up the space with some complementary artwork. It is relatively easy to develop a budget for complementary artwork. If the design firm employs a corporate art consultant, this person can develop an appropriate package for the project. This might consist of posters, prints, lithographs, and wall hangings.

On the other hand, many corporations are becoming more interested in investing in fine art as it has a proven track record of escalating in value. If the client is an art collector, he must first specify the amount that he is willing to spend on art. After this has been determined, the designer must help the client find what he likes. The designer charges an hourly fee for this service, usually stipulated in the contract.

Signage

As with accessories, signs tend to get overlooked as inconsequential. However this category can add up in the long run. For a comprehensive system, large numbers of signs may be necessary. The cost of signs, like the cost of artwork, depends on what the client has in mind. Some firms decide to use only room numbers if employees change offices frequently. If the client requires only room number signs and floor signs, the budget for signs will not be large. On the other hand, if the space is an open design, name signs, directional signs, and floor directories may be necessary to help visitors find their way. The cost of signs, in this case, will be significant.

A sign specialist can usually recommend the latest types of signage available and can provide an overall estimate. Changeable signs may be an option, so that when a person leaves the company an insert car be ordered instead of reordering the entire sign. This may cost more initially, but the cost of changeable signs is a lot less than the cost of permanent signs if there is a high turnover rate in the company.

Contingency

Even the most thorough estimator should include a contingency, in case either the designer or the client suddenly thinks of any small item to be added to the scope of the work. A contingency can be 5–15% of the subtotal of the budget. If the estimate is accurate a 5% contingency may be used. Any unused portion is not included in the final tabulation of costs. This allows for underbudgeting, minor errors, and omissions as well as a few changes and new additions by the client, without having to ask the client to increase the overall budget. A client is never happy about raising the budget after an agreement has been reached unless he makes a major change. The designer's goal should still be to complete the project within the budget and to use little or none of the contingency amount.

Types of Budgets

The method used to develop a budget depends on a number of factors: the job size, the amount of detail required, the amount of time given to develop the budget, and its purpose. A small company may want costs defined by room, by individual person, or by type of office. A large company may prefer that the budget be formulated by department or by division. An even larger scale project may require a floor by floor budget. No matter how large or small the project is, the same categories are included in the budget and the same principles are used.

If a budget is relatively long, it should be prefaced with a frontispiece and a table of contents so that the various categories can be readily found. The pages should also be numbered.

Square Foot Estimate

At the conceptual stage, the client will want a rough idea of how much it will cost to complete the interiors portion of the job. Without a lot of predetermined details, the best approach is to estimate by the square foot. This can be done using the latest figures from trade journals, annual pricing manuals such as Means *Interior Cost Data*, and other similar sources. For example, if the client is going to buy all new furniture and furnishings in a medium to good price range, the current national average price may be $45.00 per foot depending on what items are included. If rental footage (as opposed to usable footage) is used for the multiplier, the budget should cover the contingency and all the furnishings items: accessories, plants, poster art. Using the rental square footage just adds a little padding to the budget which is an extra safety precaution. If the project is in a city where usable and rental square footage are the same, the designer should add more to the estimated cost to cover plants, art, and contingency. If 50% of the existing furniture is to be reused, the budget might be $25.00 per square foot instead of $45.00. An example of this type of budget is shown in Figure 6.4.

By Person or by Room

This type of budget is usually done for a small firm or for the top executives of a large firm. This method becomes too lengthy and cumbersome if used for a large project.

Basically, each item in a particular space is listed, counted, and priced. Items such as carpet, draperies, and wallcovering may be included in the individual office budget. The total "package" of the complete office may be very important to a client, especially lawyers, hence the inclusion of these items. Many firms give a new employee an allowance and he then decorates his office in his own taste and style. Other companies view new office furnishings as a "perk" and may allow an employee to redecorate his office, but they do not want a manager to spend more than a vice president. This method is most appropriate for simple refurbishing projects involving single executive offices or suites of rooms.

The furniture to be purchased is itemized by office. Draperies, wallcovering, and flooring are frequently divided into categories by department, division, or floor. For a repeated area, such as reception areas on different floors that are furnished similarly but in different colors or patterns, the same process is used. Figure 6.5 is a budget for such a repeated area.

If the specifications are complete at this point the designer may elect to list all the detailed information in the budget. Figure 6.6 is an example of a detailed estimate. On the other hand, the designer may only have a layout and may be waiting for budget approval before actually selecting any materials. In this case the budget is quite simplified. Figure 6.7 is an example of a simplified budget.

XYZ COMPANY
CHICAGO, ILLINOIS

RENOVATION BUDGET LICENSING DIVISION

Rental square footage:

20th Floor	11,146
19th Floor	3,387
Total Square Footage	14,533

Budget Estimate:

Construction (Carried over from Architect's Budget):

20th Floor	11,146 sq. ft. @ $38.50	$ 429,121.00
19th Floor	3,387 sq. ft. @ $35.50	120,239.00
Total Construction		$ 549,360.00

Interiors (25% of Furniture will be existing):

Total 14,533 sq. ft. @ $30.00	$ 435,990.00
Artwork	50,000.00
Total Interiors	$ 485,990.00

Total Construction and Interiors	$1,035,350.00
10% Contingency	103,535.00
Grand Total	$1,138,885.00

Items not included:

        Telephones and cable
        Equipment (i.e., computers, typewriters, copiers)
        Taxes, freight, and delivery
        Relocation costs

Figure 6.4

XYZ COMPANY
CHICAGO, ILLINOIS

BUDGET FOR RECEPTION AREA FURNISHINGS
Floors: 3, 4, 5, 6, 7, and 8

Item	Quantity (each floor)	Description	Estimated Unit Net Cost	Estimated Total Net Cost
		FURNITURE		
Desk	1	Walnut Secretarial Desk, lacquer finish, wrapped vinyl top, modesty panel to the floor, size: 72" W x 32" D with right hand return 32" W x 20" D.	$ 1,300.00	$ 1,300.00
Secretarial Chair	1	Secretarial Chair upholstered in black grosgrain carpet casters.	170.00	170.00
Visitor's Chairs	2	Armchairs with swivel base, polished chrome covered in wool C. O. M.	500.00	1,000.00
Sofa	1	5 seat 'L' shaped Sofa Consisting of: 3 corner chairs 3 armless chairs 2 special plastic laminate end tables Covered in wool C. O. M.	3,100.00	3,100.00
Drum Table	1	Molded fiberglass drum table, 20" Diam.	100.00	100.00
Drum Table	1	Molded fiberglass drum table, 24" Diam.	130.00	130.00

Figure 6.5

Item	Quantity	Description	Estimated Unit Net Cost	Estimated Total Net Cost
		ACCESSORIES		
Ashtray	4	Ashtrays, colored porcelain inside, polished aluminum outside.	12.00	48.00
Calendar Pad	1	Calendar Pad with black Scheaffer White Dot ball point pen, arches in mirror fin-ish anodized aluminum base.	50.00	50.00
In & Out Basket	1	Double Letter Tray, black plastic	25.00	25.00
Vase	1	Frosted glass Vase 4 1/2" diam. x 4 7/8" H.	40.00	40.00
Wastebasket	1	Black poly vinyl Wastebasket	12.00	12.00
Print	2	Framed Lithographs	500.00	1,000.00
		Total Cost Furniture & Accessories		$ 6,975.00
		10% Contingency		698.00
		Total		$ 7,673.00
		Grand Total: 6 Floors @ $7,673.00		$ 46,038.00

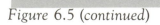

Figure 6.5 (continued)

XYZ COMPANY
CHICAGO, ILLINOIS

OFFICE OF MR. W.V. FRANK

Item	Quantity	Description	Estimated Unit Net Cost	Estimated Total Net Cost
Desk	1	Special design Table with St. Laurent marble top and stainless steel frame. Size: 29 1/2" H x 36" D x 66" W.	$ 3,500.00	$ 3,500.00
Telephone Cabinet	1	Special design Telephone Cabinet in black lacquer.	2,400.00	2,400.00
Desk Chair	1	Lehigh #1150 high back Swivel Chair, covered in American Leather, Connoisseur quality	1,500.00	1,500.00
Visitor's Chairs	4 existing	Ward Bennett #1070 Chair with lacquer finish. Reupholstered in American Leather, Connoisseur quality Dark green.	400.00	1,600.00
Lounge Chairs	3 existing	Ward Bennett #1075 Lounge Chair with lacquer finish. Reupholstered in Thorp #T-32012 Nile Mohair.	500.00	1,500.00
Coffee Table	3	Special Design Burl Drum Table, 16" H x 36" Diam.	1,000.00	3,000.00
Sofa	1	Ward Bennett #2094 Sofa, plain upholstery Size: 84" W x 33" D Upholstery in Thorp #T-32012 Nile Mohair	2,300.00	2,300.00

Figure 6.6

Item	Quantity	Description	Estimated Unit Net Cost	Estimated Total Net Cost
End Table	1	Antique Chinese Drum	$ 3,500.00	$ 3,500.00
Carpet	1	20th Century Oriental blue/green Area rug Approximate size: 15'-9" x 24'-6".	10,000.00	10,000.00
Draperies	2 pair	Stationary lined over Drapery Panels. Fabric: Thaibok #221A; Green silk.	800.00	1,680.00
Casement Curtains		Wall to wall accordian-fold Casement Curtains Fabric Lazarus, Ithaca, white/beige 43'-6" linear feet required.	45.00	1,957.00
Accessories		Allowance for accessories and planting.		1,200.00
		Total Office		$ 32,557.00
		Plus 10% Contingency		3,256.00
		Grand Total		$ 35,813.00

Figure 6.6 (*continued*)

XYZ COMPANY
CHICAGO, ILLINOIS

OFFICE OF MR. S.J. ROSE

Item	Quantity	Description	Estimated Unit Net Cost	Estimated Total Net Cost
Desk	1	Special design semi-circular burl table desk with stainless steel frame.	$ 4,500.00	$ 4,500.00
Telephone Cabinet	1	Special design burl telephone cabinet.	3,000.00	3,000.00
Desk Chair	1	High back paneled swivel chair. Covered in black leather.	1,500.00	1,500.00
Visitor's Chairs	6	Sled base chairs covered in red velvet.	650.00	3,900.00
Sofa	2	Tufted sofa 96" Wide. Covered in Brown American leather.	3,000.00	6,000.00
Coffee Table	1	Special design large burl coffee table. Size: 36" x 72".	1,500.00	1,500.00
Carpet	1	Oriental area rug. ALLOW.	10,000.00	10,000.00
Draperies	2 pair	Stationary lined over-drapery panels; silk taffeta fabric.	1,000.00	2,000.00
Casement Curtains		Wall to wall accordian-fold casement curtains. 43'-6" linear feet required.	45.00	1,958.00
Accessories		Allowance for accessories and planting.		1,200.00
		Total		$ 35,558.00
		10% Contingency		3,556.00
		Grand Total		$ 39,114.00

Figure 6.7

The designer should summarize the information detailed in the budget on a recapitulation sheet. List each person or each room. Add the total costs for each, add the contingency, and arrive at a grand total. This is the most important page of the budget and one that the client will look at first. For this reason, the recapitulation or "recap" sheet may be placed at the beginning of the estimate. Figure 6.8 is a sample recap sheet.

By Department or Division

Clients often request budgets written by department or division because these are separate cost centers within the firm. Each financial unit might be charged all, or a portion, of the cost of the work being done. These units might take up part of a floor or more than one floor, depending on their size. The designer may be able to work with simplified lump-sum amounts, such as total costs of furniture, carpet, or draperies per floor. Charts of furniture per room are kept separately as back-ups and are not part of the published departmental budget unless the client wishes to review these details. Figure 6.9 is an example of this type of budget. If the client requests more detailed information, this entails developing an in-depth formal budget. Like items are combined for lump sum costs. Examples are all desks, all chairs, all tables, all files, etc. Figure 6.10 shows an in-depth formal budget. The designer also needs a recapitulation for this type of budget. Once again it should be placed on top of the report since it is the most important sheet to the client. Figure 6.11 is an example of a recap sheet by department or by division.

Floor by Floor

This is another logical way to divide up a project into units that can be dealt with more easily than the project as a whole. There are no special advantages or disadvantages to budgeting by floor. The method is usually determined by client preference or cost center. Figure 6.12 is an example of a floor by floor budget and Figure 6.13 is a recapitulation of the same.

Taxes

Sales taxes are frequently paid on the actual item, but do not apply to freight, delivery, and installation. Cost should be "built-in" to the budget. To break out these items at this point in the project would be too time consuming and too costly to the client to make it a worthwhile exercise.

Telephone

Telephone systems are complex, requiring coordination of intercoms, signals, bells, special features, and private lines. Telephone estimates should be left to the telecommunication experts, and are usually handled directly by the client. If installing a new system, coordination is required with the manufacturer selected. Most designers do not possess the technical knowledge required to plan or budget a telephone system.

Equipment

As with telephone systems, budgets for typewriters, calculators, computers, word processors, and copiers should be obtained from specialty suppliers or manufacturers. Consultants may be called in to make recommendations and present budgets. The special equipment involved in any project depends on the client. In some cases, the client may simply order a copy machine, in others, maybe a test

XYZ   COMPANY
CHICAGO, ILLINOIS

Location	Unit Cost Including Contingency	Total Cost Including Contingency

23rd Floor

Office of Mr. W. V. Frank	$ 35,813.00	
Conference Room of Mr. W. V. Frank	24,275.00	
Office of Mr. S. J. Rose	35,558.00	
Conference Room of Mr. S. J. Rose	24,172.00	
Office of Mr. A. Cook	24,800.00	
Office of Mr. C. Jones	30,500.00	
Office of Mr. A. Smith	25,650.00	
Office of Mr. R. Cohen	35,400.00	
Office of Mr. W. Black	15,900.00	
Office of Mr. J. Palmer	8,500.00	
Conference Room	25,631.00	
Main Reception Area	20,593.00	
South Secretarial/Reception Area	20,752.00	
2 Secretarial Areas	25,000.00	

Total Cost 23rd Floor Executive Offices	352,544.00
Allowance for Art Work	150,000.00
Total	$502,544.00
10% Contingency	50,254.00
Grand Total	$552,798.00

Figure 6.8

XYZ COMPANY
CHICAGO, ILLINOIS

Division	Cost Per Floor	Total Cost

Saffert Records

2nd Floor

Furniture	$200,000.00	
Carpet	50,000.00	
Drapery	7,000.00	
Special Paint & Wallcovering	25,000.00	
Reception Furnishings	10,000.00	
Total Cost 2nd Floor		$292,000.00

3rd Floor

Furniture	$100,000.00	
Carpet	25,000.00	
Drapery	1,300.00	
Special Paint & Wallcovering	10,000.00	
Reception Furnishings	2,558.00	
Total Cost 3rd Floor		$138,858.00
Total Cost Saffert Records		$430,858.00

Dela Production

3rd Floor

Furniture	$ 50,000.00	
Carpet	12,500.00	
Drapery	2,000.00	
Special Paint & Wallcovering	6,000.00	
Reception Furnishings	2,558.00	
Total Cost Dela Production		$ 73,058.00

Corporate Advertising

3rd Floor

Furniture	$ 50,000.00	
Carpet	12,500.00	
Drapery	1,500.00	
Special Paint & Wallcovering	8,000.00	
Reception Furnishings	2,558.00	
Total Cost Corporate Advertising		$ 74,558.00

Figure 6.9

102

RECAPITULATION OF
COMBINED FURNITURE AND FURNISHINGS BUDGET

XYZ COMPANY
CHICAGO, ILLINOIS

Item	Estimated Unit Cost	Estimated Total Cost
Total Cost Desks	$ 200,000.00	
Total Cost Credenzas, Counters & Storage	60,000.00	
Total Cost Chairs & Benches	150,000.00	
Total Cost Sofas	20,000.00	
Total Cost Tables	45,000.00	
Total Cost Files & File Units	60,000.00	
Total Cost Shelving	20,000.00	
Total Cost Known Freight Charges	10,000.00	
Total Cost Furniture & Equipment		$ 565,000.00
Total Cost Planting (Seasonal Planting Not Included)	20,000.00	
Total Cost Accessories	42,000.00	
Total Cost Carpet	200,000.00	
Toal Cost Drapery	10,000.00	
Toal Cost Art Work	150,000.00	
Total		$ 987,000.00
10% Contingency		98,700.00
Grand Total		$1,085,700.00

Figure 6.10

103

RECAPITULATION OF BUDGET ESTIMATE
BY DIVISION

XYZ COMPANY
CHICAGO, ILLINOIS

	Total Cost
Saffert Records	$ 430,858.00
C & Y Publications	80,000.00
Corporate P. R.	125,000.00
R & D	40,000.00
Licensing	25,000.00
National Fitness	130,000.00
G. P. Publications	150,000.00
Dela Production	73,058.00
Corporate Advertising	74,558.00
J. M. Music	35,000.00
Total	$1,163,474.00
10% Contingency	116,347.00
Grand Total	$1,279,821.00

Figure 6.11

FURNITURE AND FURNISHINGS BUDGET
BY FLOOR

ABC BANK
ANYWHERE, USA

Second Floor

Location	Code	Estimated Unit Cost	Estimated Total Cost
Main Banking Room - Room 2-08			
14 Officers Desk	D-01	$ 3,000.00	$ 42,000.00
3 Secretarial Desks, Rt. hand return	D-02R	3,300.00	9,900.00
2 Secretarial Desks, Left hand return	D-02L	3,300.00	6,600.00
1 Reception/Information Desk	D-03	6,000.00	6,000.00
14 Officers Swivel Arm Chairs	C-04	600.00	8,400.00
6 Secretarial Posture Chairs	C-11	230.00	1,380.00
28 Side Arm Chairs	C-05	450.00	12,600.00
6 Lounge Chiars covered in leather	C-01	1,700.00	10,200.00
8 Lounge Chairs covered in fabric	C-01	1,600.00	12,800.00
1 Sofa	S-01	3,000.00	3,000.00
3 Lounge Tables with glass top	T-06	1,000.00	3,000.00
4 Lounge Tables with granite top	T-07	1,300.00	5,200.00
1 Vitrine	A-01	1,700.00	1,700.00
2 Check Desks	D-11	15,000.00	30,000.00
1 Plant and Planter - Allow	P-01	1,800.00	1,800.00
1 Plant and Planter - Allow	P-02	900.00	900.00
7 Plants and Planters - Allow	P-03	400.00	2,800.00
Accessories - Allow			12,000.00
Total			$ 170,280.00
Conference Room - Room 2-09			
1 Conference Table	T-01	$ 2,300.00	$ 2,300.00
1 Credenza	K-01	2,600.00	2,600.00
8 Conference Chairs	C-05	500.00	4,000.00
Accesories - Allow			600.00
Total			$ 9,500.00
Collections, Loans, and Discount - Room 2-13			
8 Secretarial Desks, Right hand return	D-10R	$ 650.00	$ 5,200.00
4 Secretarial Desks, Left hand return	D-10L	650.00	2,600.00
18 Secretarial Chairs	C-10A	200.00	3,600.00
4 Clerical Swivel Chairs	C-08A	225.00	900.00
1 Counter with Storage	K-07	1,800.00	1,800.00

Figure 6.12

Location	Code	Estimated Unit Cost	Estimated Total Cost
1 Counter with Storage	K-08	1,600.00	1,600.00
2 Counters with Storage	K-09	1,800.00	3,600.00
1 Counter with Storage	K-10	1,300.00	1,300.00
1 Counter with Storage	K-11	1,300.00	1,300.00
1 Counter with Storage	K-12	350.00	350.00
1 File Unit	F-05	1,700.00	1,700.00
1 File Unit for Computer Print Outs	F-06	1,900.00	1,900.00
Accessories - Allow			3,950.00
		Total	$29,800.00

Lobby - Room 2-19

Location	Code	Estimated Unit Cost	Estimated Total Cost
2 Plants and Planters - Allow	P-02	$ 900.00	$1,800.00

Bridge Room 2-19

Location	Code	Estimated Unit Cost	Estimated Total Cost
2 Benches	C-14	1,800.00	3,600.00
2 Plants and Planters - Allow	P-02	900.00	1,800.00
2 Plants and Planters - Allow	P-03	400.00	1,600.00
Accessories - Allow			800.00
		Total	$7,800.00

Carpet

Location	Code	Estimated Unit Cost	Estimated Total Cost
116 Yards Gray/Copper Carpet	R-01	28.00	3,248.00
336 Yards Morocccan Area Rugs	R-02	123.00	41,328.00
32 Yards Moroccan Carpet	R-03	135.00	4,320.00
		Total	$48,896.00
Total Cost Second Floor			$268,076.00

Figure 6.12 (*continued*)

RECAPITULATION OF FLOOR BY FLOOR
FURNITURE AND FURNISHINGS BUDGE

ABC BANK
ANYWHERE, USA

Total Cost Basement	$102,000.00
Total Cost Mezzanine	13,500.00
Total Cost Second Floor	264,126.00
Total Cost Third Floor	10,900.00
Total Cost Fourth Floor	160,326.00
Total Cost Fifth Floor	115,923.00
Total Cost Sixth Floor	65,861.00
Total Cost Seventh Floor	99,642.00
Total Cost Eighth Floor	25,095.00

Total	$857,373.00
10% Contingency	85,737.00
Grand Total	$943,110.00

Figure 6.13

kitchen, darkroom, sound studio, video conference room, or projection booth is part of the plan. The major costs for the latter, more complex equipment areas usually are included in a separate budget.

Approvals

It is most important that the client approve the budget in writing. This may be a simple signature, date, and statement that it is accepted, but the approval *must* be in writing. If there is ever a dispute over how much has been spent, the approved budget states what was included and for what amount. If there are any changes in the project the designer must also get the estimated cost of the revisions approved by the client *in writing*. This protects the designer in case the contingency (if included) does not cover the extra costs. In addition, the actual approval initiates the job. It means that the designer can begin spending money and ordering the materials (if the specifications are finalized).

Always remember that the client is the one who approves the budget, and all changes pertaining thereto. The client does not appreciate costs over budget, regardless of how wonderful the end result. If the designer has estimated carefully and has included an accurate contingency, he should have no trouble staying within or below the budget.

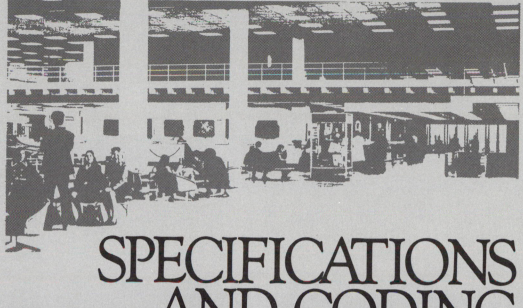

SPECIFICATIONS AND CODING FOR FURNITURE

CHAPTER SEVEN

SPECIFICATIONS AND CODING FOR FURNITURE

The main purposes of writing specifications are to enable the designer or the client to receive comparable bids and to assure required quality. Without detailed specifications, there can be a great deal of confusion and misinformation, and possible contractual conflicts. Furniture codes help identify each item of furniture and furnishings and allow the designer or any other professional involved to refer readily from one document to another.

Specifications are prepared when the preliminary square foot budget has been finalized. The designer must now sit down with manufacturer's price lists and representatives to work out all the details.

In writing the specifications, the following questions are considered for each item:

- Who is the manufacturer?
- What is the catalog number?
- What is this item? (i.e., two seat sofa, swivel chair, carpet, drapery)
- What size is this item?
- What color or finish is this item?
- Out of what material is this item fabricated?
- What upholstery is on this item?
- Any special hardware? (i.e., carpet casters, hard surface caster, locks to be keyed alike, gang locks)
- Any other characteristics that are special about the item? (i.e., is it used in conjunction with another item?)
- Special properties? (e.g., preservative treatment for fibers)
- Are there any modifications to the "standard" product (e.g., special seat or arm height on a chair)

Figure 7.1 contains examples of furniture specifications, in this case for desks.

Code	Description
D-1R	Manufacturer, #25301-L, 30" x 60" single pedestal desk, steel, standard leg, with 1 box and 1 file drawer in left side pedestal, center drawer with lock. Color: #087 Antique White, with #02 Light oak laminate top, with right hand return #25603-R 20" x 42", steel, standard leg, with 1 box and 1 file drawer, with stationary inserts, in color #087 Antique White, with #02 Light Oak laminate top.
D-1L	Manufacturer, #25201-R 30" x 60" single pedestal desk, steel standard leg, with 1 box and 1 file drawer in right side pedestal, center drawer with lock. Color: #087 Antique White with #02 Light Oak laminate top, with left hand return #25703-L, 20" x 42" steel, standard leg, with 1 box and 1 file drawer with stationary inserts. Color: #087 Antique White, with #02 Light Oak laminate top.
D-2	Manufacturer, #25100, 30" x 60" double pedestal steel desk, standard leg, 3 box drawers in pedestal on right side, center drawer with lock. Color: #087 Antique White, with #02 Light Oak laminate top.
D-3	Manufacturer, #1131, 36" x 72", double pedestal desk, with 1 box and 1 file drawer in left pedestal, center drawer with lock. Color: light oak with chrome base.
D-4R	Manufacturer, #14432, 60 x 30, single pedestal desk with 1 box and 1 file drawer in Left side pedestal, center drawer with lock with #15433, 39" x 19-3/4" Right Hand return with stationary pedestal, both in light oak with chrome base.

Figure 7.1

A furniture coding system should be simple and easy to understand. Prefixes used should be logical and should describe the type of item. If the same system is uniformly employed, everyone in the design firm will understand it. The coding system should be explained to the client. Examples of prefixes and the items they might represent are listed below:

A	shelving
C	chair
CPT	carpet
CT	ceramic tile
D	desk
DR	drapery
F	file
K	cabinet, credenza, bookcase
L	lamp
MS	miscellaneous (i.e., planter, step stool, bulletin board)
P	panel
QT	quarry tile
S	sofa
T	table
VT	vinyl composition tile
X	desk accessories

The designer must next actually write the item specifications. First, numbers are assigned to each item. The items most often used on the project are assigned low numbers. For example, a secretarial desk may be a "D-1L", which means it is desk number 1 with a typing return on the left. The same right hand desk is a "D-1R". The secretary chair could be numbered "C-1". Similarly, a "D-2" clerical desk might have a "C-2" clerical chair. If the chair codes for the most frequently used chairs match the desk codes, it is easier to spot a mistake on the plans. (As good as the draftsmen are, they may not always be able to read everyone's handwriting!). A variation on a particular item is often noted with an alphabetic designation, for example, "C-4" may be a chair with an oak frame and "C-4A" may be the same chair with a walnut frame.

Upholstery fabrics may also be coded. As long as a chart is kept with the color swatches attached and the codes in order, the system is easy to use. A side chair (Code C-5) may be available in five colors. These may be noted as: "C-5-A, C-5-B, C-5-C, C-5-D, C-5-E."

The panels in systems furniture may be specified in different colors, therefore, separate color codes are used for each one. The designer should continue use of an alphabetical code for panel colors. It is best not to skip code numbers; keep going in sequence as items are added to the specs. Figure 7.2 is an example of a code development sheet. This type of sheet also serves as a quick reference to look up a code number.

Working Documents

These documents become the mainstay of the project from which everything can be double checked. This makes for a more orderly installation. The following sections contain descriptions and examples of the working documents.

Code	Description
C-1	Secretarial chair
C-2	Desk chair
C-3-A	Side chair - Burnt Orange
C-3-B	Side chair - Kelly
C-3-C	Side chair - Blue
C-3-D	Side chair - Chocolate
C-3-E	Side chair - Tan Velvet
C-3-F	Side chair - Java Velvet
C-3-G	Side chair - Dark Brown Velvet
C-3-H	Side chair - Terra Cotta Velvet
C-3-I	Side chair - Tangerine
C-3-J	Side chair - Stone Blue Velvet
C-3-K	Side chair - Black
C-3-L	Side chair - Beige
C-3-M	Side chair - Char. Brown
C-3-N	Side chair - Grey/Beige
C-3-O	Side chair - Red
C-4-A	Exec. desk chair - Oak Frame Brown Fabric
C-4A-A	Exec. desk chair - Walnut frame, Brown fabric
C-5-A	Stack chair - Orange
C-5-B	Stack chair - Black
C-5-A	Dolly for stack chairs
C-5-C	Stack chair - Deep Orange
C-6	Conference chair
C-7	Drafting stool

Figure 7.2

Furniture Plans

The designer now codes and adds to the furniture plans anything that has not yet been specified. Equipment is usually labeled (e.g., VDT, printer, copier), even though it may not be the designer's responsibility. The use of a well documented coding system makes the specifications clear and usable to anyone who wishes to look up a particular item shown on the drawings. This alone saves time otherwise spent answering questions. Figure 7.3 is an example of a coded plan.

Location Charts

These charts list by code the room number and each item that goes into a particular room or space. Such charts are especially valuable if the furniture is not properly tagged for installation. Figures 7.4 and 7.5 are examples of location charts.

It is generally good practice to mark or color in the items on the drawings as they are noted in the location charts as a double check. At the completion of this process, everything on the furniture plan should be colored. In this way, anything that has not been specified or that the draftsmen missed will be easily detected. The designer should be aware of *every item* that is represented on the plans. Any discrepancies should be cleared up with the appropriate parties as early as possible so that there are no surprises at the time of installation.

Technical Specifications

This is the document that, in conjunction with the drawings, goes out to bid, becomes a part of a contract between the client and the furniture dealer/installer, directs the process for all parties and, frequently, prevents ambiguities and disputes. The intent for each article will be given in the body of this chapter. More specific information is shown in the sample specification documents at the end of this chapter. These specifications have been written for a fairly large project to demonstrate the level of detail necessary to fully protect the designer and the client. All specifications, when used as part of a contract, written or implied, have legal implications and consequences for both the designer and the client. An attorney should be consulted whenever there are any concerns regarding such legal matters. These specifications may be used for any project with modifications tailored to the specific needs of each client. This task is greatly simplified when a word processor is used. Certain documents are normally included with the specifications. These are described below.

Instructions to the Bidders

The designer must inform the selected bidders of such things as:

- The parties involved in the project
- What constitutes the "bidding documents"
- How to prepare the bids
- How and when to submit the bids
- How to modify the bids
- Bidder's qualifications
- How laws and regulations affect the contract
- How the contract will be awarded
- Schedule of occupancy

Figure 7.6 is a sample *Instructions to Bidders* (shown at the end of this chapter).

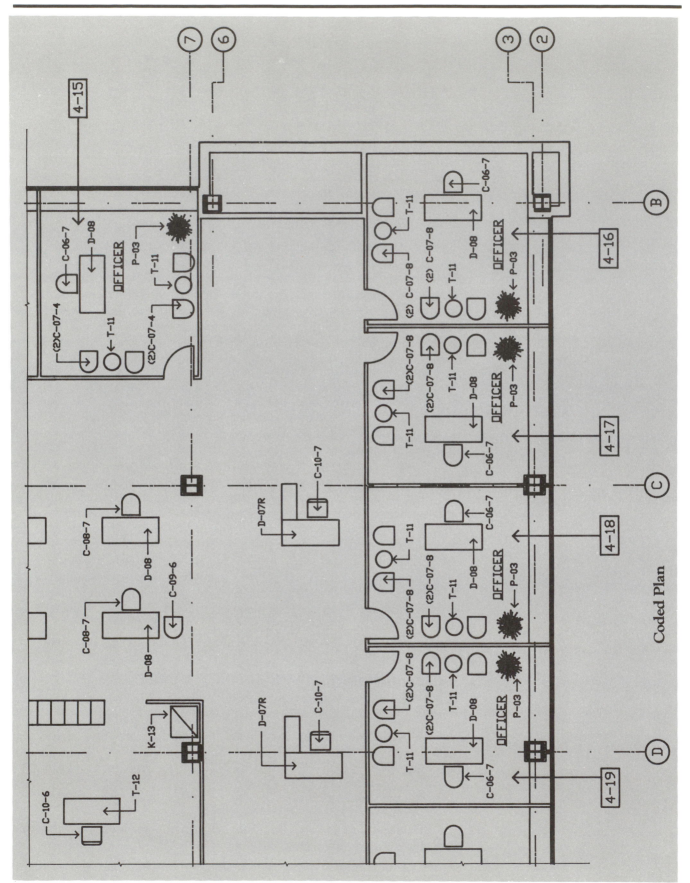

Figure 7.3

Coded Plan

116

Location Chart Type I

Doe Interiors

Client

Date

Page _____ of _____

Floor

Furniture Type

Room Number

Revisions

Total Remarks

Code | Mfg. | Fabric Code

Figure 7.4

Location Chart Type 2

Doe Interiors

Client

Page ———— of ————

Furniture Type

Date

Floor

Code | Mfg. | Fabric Code

Room Number

Revisions

Total | Remarks

Floor

Floor

Figure 7.5

General Conditions

This section of the specifications spells out the general scope of the project and the roles and responsibilities of the contractor, designer, and client, and how each party is to carry out its respective responsibilities. The General Conditions may include requirements regarding drawings, samples, ordering, expediting, scheduling, delivery, installation, cleanup, inspection, and acceptance. This document often covers guarantees, taxes, royalties, and patents, trade regulations, permits, insurance, termination of contract, payment to contractor and liens. Other requirements, such as warehousing, necessary if the site is not ready on time, may be included. An example of a format for the General Conditions section is shown in Figure 7.7.

Installation, Materials, and Workmanship

In this section, general information about the installation is given for the contractor. For example, "all files must be bolted together side by side for stability". This section should define, for example, the required quality of materials and workmanship. Other information may be given regarding finishes, joinery, dimensions, keying, fabrication, and welding. Figure 7.8 is an example of this document (shown at the end of this chapter).

Particular Conditions

These are conditions that may be unique to a particular project. For example, the client may want to have a future stocking and/or warehousing plan. Any sections here are prepared as needed. An example of stocking program requirements is shown in Figure 7.9 (shown at the end of this chapter).

Furniture Specifications

Furniture specifications, while not complicated and often seemingly repetitive, are extremely important and must be written carefully. The designer must be sure to include all pertinent information about each item. The designer must specify all the necessary component parts and finishes of each item. Some furniture can be quite complex. For example, a particular bucket chair requires selection of the following:

- Upholstery
- Fabric treatment
- Shell material
- Shell color
- Shell edging color
- Base and frame finish
- Base type
- Caster type

If all of these individual specifications are not addressed, the manufacturer's computer may reject the order. This inevitably causes shipping delays. It is much better to do extensive research up front with the manufacturer's representative rather than to play "catch up" later.

Systems furniture is very complex and the designer should spend a great deal of time with the sales representative to get everything specified accurately. This is important because there are numerous separate pieces and if any of these are missing at the time of installation, workstations will be incomplete. Figures 7.10, 7.11, and 7.12 are examples of furniture specifications, for chairs, files, and tables, respectively.

FURNITURE AND FURNISHINGS SPECIFICATIONS
FOR
(CLIENT)

SECTION 1
INSTRUCTIONS TO BIDDERS

You are invited to submit a firm proposal on the following requirements:

GENERAL FURNITURE CONTRACT – Category 1 Furniture

     FOR: (Client and location where the work
                                               will be performed)

1-01   DEFINITIONS

     A.   The following terms, as used in this Contract, are
          respectively defined as follows:

          1.   "Agreement": The written contract between the Owner and
               the Contractor in the form attached hereto.

          2.   "Contract Documents": The Instructions to Bidders;
               General Conditions, Installation Materials and
               Workmanship, Contractor's Proposal and unit prices,
               Agreement between Contractor and Owner, and the Drawings
               and Specifications, including all modifications thereof
               included in the documents before execution and any other
               documents included in the Agreement as part of the
               Contract. The term "contract" shall be considered as
               synonymous with the term "Contract Documents".

          3.   "Owner": (CLIENT)

          4.   "Designer": (DESIGNER)

          5.   "Contractor": The successful person, firm or
               manufacturer for the work included in these
               specifications and designated as such in the Agreement
               with the Owner.

          6.   "Subcontractor": The person, firm or manufacturer to
               whom the Contractor lets work required for the
               performance of his own contract agreement with the
               Owner.

          7.   "General Contractor": (GENERAL CONSTRUCTION CONTRACTOR)

          8.   "Contract Administrator": (PERSON DESIGNATED AS SUCH BY
               DESIGNER)

Figure 7.6

9. "Specifications": The Instructions to Bidders, General Conditions, Installation, Materials and Workmanship and the item specifications.

   a. The General Conditions shall apply to each and every section of the specifications.

   b. Where "as directed", "as required", "as permitted", "as authorized", "as approved", "as accepted", "as selected" or words of similar import are used, unless otherwise stated, the direction, requirement, permission, authorization, approval, acceptance or selection shall be by the Designer or Owner.

   c. "Provide", as used in the specifications, means furnished and installed complete and ready for use by the Owner.

10. "Drawings": Those drawings enumerated in the Schedule of Drawings.

   a. Where "as shown", "as indicated", "as detailed" or words of similar import are used, unless otherwise stated, reference is made to the drawings accompanying the specifications.

11. "Work": All obligations undertaken by the Contractor pursuant to the Contract Documents. Work includes, but is not limited to, the furnishing of all material, labor, equipment, supplies, plant, tools, transporation, supervision, insurance, taxes and all other services, facilities and expenses necessary for the full performance and completion of the requirements of the Contract Documents. Work also means that which is produced, constructed, or built pursuant to the Contract Documents.

12. "Building": The building in which the work is to be performed.

   a. "Site" or "Premises": The location(s) in which work under this Contract is being performed, and such adjacent areas as may be designated for Contractor's use for a specified limited period of time by the Designer or Owner.

13. "Proposal": A bid submitted in accordance with the terms and conditions of Article 1-05 hereof, including the Unit Pricing Forms, Statement of Contractor's Business Organization and Guarantee.

Figure 7.6 (continued)

1-02   BIDDING DOCUMENTS

    A.   Bidding Documents consist of:

        1.   Instructions to the Bidders
        2.   General Conditions
        3.   Installation, Materials and Workmanship
        4.   Specification proposal forms for category <u>Furniture</u>
        5.   Drawings
        6.   Location Charts
        7.   Furniture plans dated _____; Drawings, Numbers: _____.

    B.   Each Contractor will be issued two (2) complete sets of Bidding Documents for bidding purposes. These sets should be returned to the Contract Administrator within thirty (30) days of bid opening date.

        1.   Additional sets of drawings and specifications may be obtained from the Designer for $25.00 per set.

        2.   Drawings and specifications will be available for reference at the offices of the Designer.

        3.   The successful Contractor will be allowed to retain his copies of the drawings and specifications.

        4.   All drawings, specifications, and copies thereof, furnished by the Designer or Contract Administrator are the property of the Owner. They are not to be used in any other work, and are to be returned to the Designer by the successful Contractor at the completion of the work or on the earlier termination of the Contract.

    C.   All inquiries relating to the Bidding Documents shall be directed by bidders in writing to the office of the Designer. Replies from the Designer will be forwarded to all bidders in writing.

        1.   No inquiry received within 120 hours of the time fixed for receipt of bids will be given consideration. No oral interpretation will be made to any bidder as to the meaning of any of the Contract Documents.

1-03   ADDENDA

    A.   Any revisions or Addenda to the Specifications, issued during the bidding period, will be issued to all bidders, shall be included in the Proposal, and will be considered a part of the Contract at the time of the award.

Figure 7.6 (*continued*)

1-04   PREPARATION OF BIDS

    A.   After all bidders have received the Bidding Documents, one coordination meeting will be held in _____(City)_____ with all required representation by the Owner and the Designer. This meeting will be scheduled and bidders should submit all questions in advance. All decisions made will be distributed to all bidders in writing.

        1.   The successful Contractor shall be subject to and operate under the direction of the Designer to the end that complete coordination of each project will be affected.

    B.   The following items will be excluded from the General Furniture and Furnishings Contract:

        1.   Items contracted by the Owner to the General Construction Contractor.

        2.   Special items designed specifically for the Owner by the Designer.

        3.   Drapery and casements.

        4.   Carpet.

        5.   Certain decorative objects and one-of-a-kind accessories to be provided by the Designer.

        6.   Planting.

        7.   Tapestries.

        8.   Signage and Directories.

        9.   Art work.

    C.   Bidder's quotation to include all necessary services to provide, deliver and install Furniture and Furnishings complete and ready for use based on Bidder's net cost from his suppliers plus a surcharge on a percentage basis.

    D.   Before submitting quotations, Bidders shall examine the applicable Drawings and Specifications to insure the completeness of the Work, and shall notify the Designer in writing of any discrepancies. Supplementary parts necessary to complete the Work, though such parts are not shown or specified, shall be included.

    E.   Owner will provide free access to elevators.

    F.   Delivery and installation will be done during normal working hours.

Figure 7.6 (*continued*)

1-05   SUBMISSION OF BIDS

A.   Proposals to be entitled to consideration shall be submitted in triplicate on proposal forms prepared by the Designer. All spaces in the forms shall be filled in with subtotals at the bottom of each page. Taxes shall not be included as part of the bid. Freight, delivery and installation shall be an estimated percentage of the total materials cost. This percentage shall be stated in the proposal.

1.   Proposal must be signed in the firm or corporate name and must bear the signature of a principal duly authorized to execute contracts for the bidding party. The bidder's name must be fully stated. Where Proposals are signed by an agent of the bidder, evidence of his authority to act as the bidder's agent shall accompany the Proposal. The name of each person signing the Proposal shall be typed or printed below his or her signature.

2.   Proposal form shall be signed by the Bidder.

3.   Any erasures or corrections in the Proposal forms must be initialed by the Bidder.

4.   Specifications are attached as a part of the Contract Documents. These specifications describe in detail each item to be included by the Bidder in the Proposal. The Sheets list the code number by which the item is located on the drawings.

B.   Before submitting proposals, Bidders shall study all conditions and limitations to be encountered during delivery and installation and fully understand the Specifications and scope of Work. Such examination will be presumed and no allowances will be made to Contractor for extra labor or materials required or on account of any difficulty encountered which might have been foreseen had such examination been made.

C.   Bidders shall submit, with their Proposal, the names addresses and qualificaions of proposed Subcontractors, workrooms and installers for the Owner's and Designer's approval.

D.   Any proposed variations, deviations or qualifications of any nature in the requirements herein specified shall be fully noted in the Proposals or in an accompanying letter. Failure to provide such a statement will be interpreted to mean that the bidder agrees to meet all requirements of the Contract Documents.

E.   Proposals will be placed in sealed envelopes with the name of the bidder and the contents clearly identified and labeled "Do not open prior to 12:00 noon, ___(day, date)___".

Figure 7.6 (continued)

    F.   Proposals, in triplicate, will be received in the office of <u>(the Owner and Owner's present address)</u> not later that 12:00 noon, <u> (day, date) </u>. Proposals received after this time will <u>not</u> be considered. The bid opening will be held at 12:00 noon on <u> (day, date) </u>.

    G.   Any bidder may withdraw his/her bid by letter or with proper identification by personally securing his/her bid proposal at any time prior to the time stated for the opening of bids. No telephone requests for withdrawal of bids will be honored. No bidder may withdraw his/her bid after the time stated for the opening of bids unless such bid has not been accepted by the Owner within 60 days after such time.

1-06   BID MODIFICATION

    A.   Modification of Proposals will be considered only if received by letter prior to the time stated for the opening of bids. The indication "Bid Modification" must be on the envelope and the envelope labeled "Do not open prior to 12:00 noon, <u> (day, date) </u>" in order to prevent opening of stated letter prior to opening of bids.

    B.   No verbal modification will be considered.

1-07   QUALIFICATIONS OF BIDDER

    A.   The Owner may make such investigation as he deems necessary to determine the ability of the bidder to perform the work, and the bidder shall furnish to the Owner all such information and data for this purpose as the Owner may request. The Owner reserves the right to reject any bid if the evidence submitted by, or investigation of, such bidder fails to satisfy the Owner that such bidder is properly qualified to carry out the obligation of the Contract and to complete the work contemplated therein.

1-08   LAWS AND REGULATIONS

    A.   The bidder's attention is directed to the fact that all applicable Federal and State laws, municipal ordinances, and the rules and regulations of all authorities having jurisdiction over the project shall apply to the Contract throughout, and they will be deemed to be included in the Contract the same as though herein written out in full.

1-09   CONTRACT AWARD

    A.   The competency and responsibility of the bidders and proposed subcontractors will be considered in making the award. Conditional bids will not be accepted.

    B.   The Owner reserves the right to reject any or all bids and

Figure 7.6 (continued)

to waive any formalities; whichever in the Owner's opinion appears most advantageous to the Owner.

C. Following the award of any Contract, cost reduction refinements may be incorporated in each item of work through a cooperative development and refinement of each item by the Contractor, Designer and Owner. Any resulting reductions in unit prices will accrue to the Owner.

D. If written notice of the acceptance of a Proposal is mailed, telegraphed or delivered to a bidder within 60 days after the date of the opening of the bids, or at any time thereafter before a bid is withdrawn, the bidder agrees to execute and deliver a contract in the form prescribed by the Owner in accord with the bid as accepted and the selected bidder agrees to furnish a Performance, Labor and Material Payment Bond or sureties as the Owner may approve, within 10 days from the date of execution of the Contract.

E. The successful bidder will be required to execute a contract in the form attached. See pages _____. The Contract Documents including the Agreement and accompanying schedule of agreed upon items and unit prices will be used as a basis of ordering from the Contractor by the Owner from _____ __(date)__ through ___(date)___.

F. The successful Contractor shall be committed to support the unit prices for 6 months through September 1, 19__ with increases granted thereafter only upon 30 days written notice of the increase in the manufacturer's list price and proof of same. The same discount shall be maintained to the Owner during the full term of the Contract.

  1. Should the Contractor be able to negotiate better quantity discounts from the various manufacturers the Contractor shall pass these addditional discounts along to the Owner.

G. The Contract Documents shall constitute the agreement between the Owner and the Contractor and cover insurance, regulations and use of Owner's facilities, the method of payment, cases for cancellation or termination of the Contract and all other terms and conditions required by the Owner.

H. It is understood that each bidder has carefully examined the Bidding Documents and thoroughly understands the conditions under which the work will be done.

I. No pleas of ignorance of conditions that exist or that may exist hereafter or of conditions or difficulties encountered

Figure 7.6 (continued)

in the execution of the work under the Contract will be
accepted as an excuse for any failure or omission on the
part of the Contractor to fulfill in every detail all the
requirements of the Contract.

J. No pleas whatsoever will be accepted as a basis for claims
for extra compensation, or for an extension of time.

K. Any contract awarded will be construed according to all
governing laws and is non-assignable by the Contractor
without the written consent of the Owner.

L. Bidder agrees that his/her Proposal may be held by the Owner
as an irrevocable offer for a period of 60 days from the
date of bid opening and for such further period as such
Proposal shall not have been withdrawn as provided herein.

1-10 SCHEDULE OF OCCUPANCY

It is anticipated that the Owner will occupy his new quarters on
or about _____.

Figure 7.6 *(continued)*

FURNITURE & FURNISHINGS SPECIFICATIONS
FOR
(CLIENT)

SECTION 2
GENERAL CONDITIONS

2-01   EXECUTION, CORRELATION AND INTENT OF DOCUMENTS

A.   All instruments constituting the Contract Documents are
complementary and what is called for by any one shall be as
binding as if called for by all. The intention of the
Contract Documents is to include all labor, materials,
equipment and transportation to the place where the subject
matter of the Contract is to be used or enjoyed by the Owner
and shall include the installation thereof as called for by
the terms of the Contract Documents.

B.   These specifications are separated into titled sections for
convenience only and not to dictate or determine the trade
or craft involved. Such separations shall not operate to
make the Contract Administrator or Designer an arbiter for
the division of responsibility between Contractor and
subcontractor, and between subcontractors, nor shall such
separation relieve the Contractor of the responsibility for
the satisfactory completion of the entire work regardless of
the trade divisions. No work shall be left in an unfinished
condition owing to disagreement between the various
subcontractors or between the subcontractors and the
Contractor as to where the work of one begins and ends in
relation to the work of the other.

1.   Nothing in the Contract Documents shall be deemed or
construed to impose upon the Owner any obligation,
liability, or duty to a subcontractor, or to create any
contractual relation between the Owner and any
subcontractor.

2-02   INSPECTION OF THE PREMISES

A.   The Contractor shall be held to have examined the job site
before commencing delivery and installation, and to be
cognizant of the conditions under which he/she will be
obliged to operate in performing the work, including any
obstructions, unloading facilities, location and size of
elevators, amount of work, character and nature of the work,
the equipment and facilities needed preliminary to and
during the execution of the work, and any other
consideration which may affect the work in any manner.

1.   The Contractor shall report to the Designer any
condition which, in the Contractor's opinion, may in any

Figure 7.7

way prevent completion of the installation in a first
class manner.

2. The commencement of work without such notification shall
    be construed as an acceptance by the Contractor of all
    existing conditions and as a waiver of all claims or
    questions relating thereto. No allowances will
    subsequently be made in behalf of the Contractor for
    reason of any error or assumption on his/her part,
    including extra labor, compensation or materials,
    extension of time, or on account of any difficulty
    encountered which might have been foreseen had such
    examination been made.

2-03   DRAWINGS AND SPECIFICATIONS

A. The Designer shall furnish instructions by means of bill of
    materials, drawings, specifications, and necessary location
    charts for the proper execution of the work. All such
    instructions shall be consistent with the Contract
    Documents, or approved modifications, or true developments
    thereof, and reasonably inferable therefrom. The work shall
    be executed in conformity therewith and the Contractor shall
    do no major work without proper drawings and instructions.
    In giving such instructions, the Designer shall have
    authority to make minor changes in the work, not involving
    extra cost nor inconsistent with the intent of the Contract
    Documents.

B. Contractor shall examine all applicable Drawings, bill of
    materials, Specifications, and location charts to insure the
    completeness of the work, and shall notify the Designer in
    writing of any discrepancies. Supplementary parts necessary
    to complete the work, though such parts are not expressly
    shown or specified, shall be included. If any such
    differences or conflicts between Drawings, bill of
    materials, Specifications and location charts not called to
    the Designer's attention prior to delivery and installation,
    the Designer shall decide which of the conflicting
    requirements will govern, and the Contractor shall rectify
    the situation immediately in accordance with the Designer's
    decision.

C. Wherever typical parts or sections of the work are
    completely detailed on the drawings, and other parts or
    sections which are essentially of the same construction are
    shown in outline only, the complete details shall apply to
    the work which is shown in outline.

D. Dimensions of work shall not be determined by scale or
    rule. Figured dimensions shall be followed at all times.
    If figured dimensions are lacking on drawings, the Designer
    shall supply them on request of the Contractor.

Figure 7.7 (continued)

E.   The Contractor shall maintain one complete set of drawings, specifications and shop drawings at each job site in good order, available to the Designer and the Owner's representative. The drawings, specifications and shop drawings shall be kept up to date by replacing obsolete sheets with revised sheets as they are issued.

F.   All copies of drawings and specifications furnished by the Designer shall remain the property of the Owner. Said copies are not to be used in any other work or project whatsoever and are to be returned to the Designer upon completion of the work.

2-04   CONTRACTOR'S DRAWINGS

A.   The Contractor shall prepare installation floor plans, color coded, and coordinated with the approved tagging system, to properly locate, lay out and install the entire work. Drawings are to be submitted for the approval of the Designer prior to the start of any installation. The Contractor is responsible for delivering each item to the floor shown on the Designer's layout drawings and placing it in its proper location.

B.   The term "shop drawings" as used herein includes fabrication, erection, layout and setting drawings; manufacturers' standard drawings; schedules, descriptive literature, catalogs and brochures, and all other descriptive data pertaining to materials, furnishings, equipment, accessories, and methods of construction as may be required to show that the materials, furnishings, equipment, etc., conform to the requirements of the Contract Documents. As used herein, the term "manufactured" applies to standard units usually mass produced, and "fabricated" means items specifically assembled or made out of selected materials to meet individual design requirements. Shop drawings shall establish the actual detail of all manufactured or fabricated items; indicate proper relation to adjoining work; incorporate minor changes of design or construction to suit actual conditions.

C.   When required, shop drawings shall be submitted to the Designer for approval and shall show in scale the design, dimensions, reinforcement and all other pertinent data and information. Construction, methods of assembly, engineering and manufacturing shall be the responsibility of the Contractor. Disapproved shop drawings shall be corrected and resubmitted until approved. Delay in submitting or revising shop drawings shall not constitute a reason for not complying with the delivery schedule.

1. All shop drawings must be complete in every detail,

Figure 7.7 (continued)

130

properly identified with the name of the project and
dated. Each lot submitted must be accompanied by a
letter of transmittal referring to the name of the
project and location for identification of each item,
and stating qualifications, departures or deviations
from the Contract Documents if any. Shop drawings for
each project shall be numbered consecutively and the
numbering system shall be retained throughout all
revisions. Each drawing shall have a clear space for
the approval of the Contractor and the Designer.

2. Submit one (1) reproducible sepia transparency and one
(1) blueprint of each drawing, including fabrication,
erection, layout and setting drawings and such other
drawings as required under the various sections of the
specifications until final approval is obtained.

3. Each subcontractor shall submit all shop drawings and/or
manufacturer's descriptive data through the Contractor
for the Designers's approval. All shop drawings shall
be thoroughly checked by the Contractor for completeness
and for compliance with the Contract Documents before
submitting them to the Designer and shall bear the
Contractor's stamp of approval, certifying that they
have so been checked. Any shop drawings submitted
without this stamp of approval and certification, and
shop drawings which, in the Designer's opinion are
incomplete, contain numerous errors or have not been
checked or only checked superficially, will be returned
by the Designer for resubmission by the Contractor.

4. In checking shop drawings the Contractor shall verify
all dimensions and field conditions and shall check and
coordinate the shop drawings of any section or trade
with the requirements of all other sections or trades
whose work is related thereto, as required for proper
and complete installation of the work. The Designer
will review and approve shop drawings for design,
general methods of construction and detailing; however,
approval of such drawings shall not relieve the
Contractor, subcontractor, manufacturer, fabricator or
supplier from responsibility for any deficiency that may
exist or from any departure or deviations from the
requirements of the Contract Documents unless he/she
has, in writing, called the Designer's attention to such
deviations at the time of submission, nor shall it
relieve the Contractor from responsibility for errors of
any sort in shop drawings or schedules, nor from
responsibility for proper fitting of the work, nor from
the necessity of furnishing any work required by the
Contract Documents which may not be indicated on shop
drawings when approved. The Contractor shall be solely
responsible for any quantities which may be shown on the
shop drawings.

Figure 7.7 (*continued*)

5. The Designer will check the shop drawings, manufacturer's descriptive literature, catalog cuts and brochures with reasonable promptness and will return them to the Contractor with the Designer's stamp and signature applied thereto, indicating the appropriate action to be taken.

6. As the work progresses each subcontractor shall, under the direction of the Contractor, keep a complete and accurate record of all approved changes or deviations from the Contract Documents, including the Drawings, Specification and shop drawings, indicating the work as actually installed. All such changes shall be neatly and correctly shown on a print of the Drawing affected, or in the Specifications with appropriate supplementary notes. This record set of prints of the Drawings, shop drawings and Specifications shall be kept at the job site for inspection by the Designer and Owner.

7. At the completion of the work, each subcontractor shall certify, by endorsement thereof, that each of the revised prints of the Drawings and Specifications for his/her part of the work is complete and accurate. Prior to the Contractor's application for final payment, and as a condition to its approval by the Designer and Owner, each subcontractor shall deliver the record Drawings and Specifications, arranged in proper order, indexed and endorsed as previously specified, to the Contractor, and the Contractor shall assemble these records for all parts of the work, review them for completeness and submit them to the Designer.

2-05   SAMPLES

A. The Contractor shall submit such samples of natural materials, fabricated items, equipment, accessories, fabrics, hardware, devices, appliances or parts thereof as called for in the specifications, and any other samples as may be required by the Designer for approval prior to fabrication.

B. All work, shall be in accordance with the approved samples.

1. All samples shall be submitted in triplicate properly identified with the name of the Contractor, the name of the project, the code, the description and the date, and shall be accompanied by a letter of transmittal containing similar information. Each tag or sticker shall have clear space for the approval stamps of the Contractor and the Designer.

Figure 7.7 (continued)

2.   All samples shall be checked by the Contractor for
      compliance with the Contract Documents before
      submitting them to the Designer and shall bear the
      Contractor's stamp of approval certifying they have
      so been checked. Any samples submitted without this
      stamp of approval, and samples which, in the
      Designer's opinion are incomplete or which have not
      been checked or only checked superficially, will be
      returned unchecked by the Designer for resubmission
      by the Contractor.

3.   The Designer will review and approve samples for
      aesthetics, general design and technical compliance;
      however, approval of such samples shall not relieve
      the Contractor, subcontractor, manufacturer,
      fabricator or supplier from responsiblility for any
      departures or deviations from the requirements of
      the Contract Documents unless he/she has, in
      writing, called the Designer's attention to such
      departures or deviations at the time of submission.
      Samples shall be furnished in time so as to allow
      the Designer a reasonable time for consideration.
      Delay in submitting samples shall not constitute a
      reason for not complying with the delivery
      schedule. The Designer will check the samples with
      reasonable promptness and will return them to the
      Contractor with the Designer's stamp and signature
      applied thereto, indicating the appropriate action
      to be taken. One approved sample of each item will
      be returned to the Contractor. The remaining
      samples will be retained by the Designer for the
      Owner's use.

2-06   SUPERVISION: SCHEDULES

A.   The Contractor shall give efficient supervision to the
      work exercising his/her best skill and attention. The
      Contractor shall carefully study and compare all
      drawings, specifications, location charts and other
      instructions to insure the completeness and accuracy of
      the work before proceeding with the order and shall
      forthwith report to the Designer any error, inconsistency
      or omission. The Contractor shall subsequently proceed
      with the work in accordance with instructions from the
      Designer concerning any such error or omission.

B.   Supplementary parts for furniture or furnishings
      necessary to complete the work, though such parts are not
      shown or specified, shall be included.

C.   Within 10 days after finalizing the contract, the
      Contractor shall submit to the Designer, for approval, a
      preliminary work schedule for submission of: Shop
      Drawings, Samples, the beginning of manufacture, and the
      completion of the various parts of the work; each such

Figure 7.7 (continued)

schedule to be subject to change from time to time if there are changes in the construction schedule.

D.   The Contractor shall be solely responsible for properly laying out the work, and for all lines and measurements for all of the work executed under the Contract Documents. The Contractor shall verify the figures shown on the drawings before laying out the work and will be held responsible for any errors or inaccuracies resulting from failure to do so. The Designer or duly assigned representatives will in no case assume the responsibility for laying out the work.

2-07   ORDERING AND EXPEDITING

A.   Acceptance of a contract for furniture and furnishings covered by these specifications shall indicate the Contractor's intent to comply with the indicated delivery dates in accordance with the Owner's schedule of occupancy. Furniture will not be accepted for installation or storage prior to the indicated delivery date. If delivery cannot be made within the time specified, the Contractor must notify the Designer in writing immediately and submit estimated costs for interim rental furniture for the Owner's approval.

1.   Contractor shall make all necessary arrangements for rental furniture upon the Owner's approval. The incurred rental fee and pick-up and delivery charges shall be invoiced separately at the completion of the project.

B.   Specifications prepared by the Designer are to be strictly followed in all particulars by the Contractor. No substitutions at variance with specifications issued by the Designer will be made.

1.   The Owner reserves the right to reject any or all materials that do not conform to the specifications.

C.   Contractor agrees to assign a competent and experienced individual within his/her organization as General Project Manager to work with Owner and Designer and that the individual will have the assistance of the required staff, experienced in order writing, expediting, installing and inspecting of merchandise in order to insure complete and timely performance.

D.   Contractor shall survey the Owner's requirements for keying arrangements of desks, files and cabinets such as keying alike of banks of files, master keying, etc.

E.   Contractor will promptly place orders with the various

Figure 7.7 (continued)

manufacturers in accordance with the specifications of the Designer and obtain timely acknowledgement of all orders.

F. Copies of all purchase orders and acknowledgments of orders placed with outside sources are to be submitted to the Designer so that the Designer is kept fully informed on a continuing basis as to the Contractor's performance. Each order must be marked with Designer's code, quantity, and room number.

G. The Contractor agrees to keep in close touch with each manufacturer after placing orders for the purpose of forestalling delays in shipment. The Contractor shall have the responsibility of expediting the manufacture and delivery of all items covered herein on a continuous basis until final completion of installation. A semi-monthly progress report indicating the status of each order is to be transmitted to the Owner and Designer on the first and 15th of each month.

H. Contractor shall notify the Designer in writing with copies to Owner of any unusual scheduling problems; unavailability of fabrics or any other conditions which may affect delivery promptly upon learning of such conditions so that the Designer may consider specification changes to avoid such prospective delay.

    1. If the Contractor (or subcontractor) is delayed at any time in the progress of the work by any act or neglect of the Owner or by any separate Contractor employed by the Owner, or by changes in or suspension in the work ordered by Owner, or by strikes, lockouts, fire, or any other causes beyond the Contractor's reasonable control or power to avoid and due to no fault of the Contractor, the Contractor shall promptly give the Designer written notice thereof, stating all particulars. If the Designer finds such delay to be attributable to no fault of the Contractor and beyond the Contractor's reasonable control or power to avoid, and that such delay will, in the judgment of the Designer necessarily delay the completion of the work, the Owner shall determine whether and to what date the completion of the work shall, in fairness to both parties, be extended because of such delay.

I. Duplicate copies of all invoices shall be submitted to the Designer for approval prior to their submission to the Owner for payment.

J. The acceptance of the final payment for each project by the Contractor shall be held to be a waiver of any and all claims against the Owner arising out of or in

Figure 7.7 (continued)

135

connection with the Contract.

K.   Contractor shall upon request by the Owner furnish Owner
      and Designer with copies of paid invoices from
      Contractor's suppliers for materials furnished under this
      Contract.

2-08   TAGGING SYSTEM

A.   The Contractor shall be responsible for using a
      comprehensive tagging system specified by the Designer
      and in accordance with the Designer's drawings, codes
      specifications and location charts for furniture and
      furnishings to be shipped to the job from each and every
      manufacturer. Contractor to submit this tagging system
      to the Owner and Designer for approval. Tags must remain
      on all items after their placement until inspection is
      made by the Designer or Owner. If any piece of furniture
      arrives on the job without identification, it shall be
      the responsibility of the Contractor to identify it or it
      will be returned to the Contractor at the Contractor's
      expense. Contractor shall remove all tags after
      inspection and approval.

2-09   INSPECTION

A.   Contractor will inspect the progress of manufacturing at
      the various production factories whenever, in the opinion
      of the Contractor or Designer, such inspection is
      necessary or desirable to insure faithful adherence to
      specifications, samples, quality standards, and
      completion of manufacturing and shipment within the
      specified time. Inspection report must be submitted to
      Designer and Owner promptly. Any items found not to be
      in accordance with the specifications will be rejected.

B.   The earliest possible delivery of all small furniture
      orders shall be made to the Contractor's local warehouse
      in order that inspections be made, any shortages remedied
      and any necessary corrections accomplished without delay
      in Owner's schedule for installation. In all cases the
      Contractor will inspect merchandise as received in
      Contractor's warehouse and in the event there is evidence
      of possible damage in any instance such merchandise shall
      be completely unpacked for thorough inspection. Unpacked
      inspections will also be made at the time of receiving of
      specific items as directed by Designer

C.   Designer and Owner shall have the right to inspect
      materials during production or while stored in
      Contractor's warehouse at any time.   Any items found not
      to be in strict accordance with specifications will be

Figure 7.7 (continued)

rejected at Contractor's expense.

2-10   WAREHOUSING

A.   Local warehousing will be performed by the Contractor as
      required without additional cost to the Owner unless the
      Contractor is required to store any items of furniture
      and furnishings after the agreed upon installation date
      due to delays in construction of Owner's building or
      other delays required by Owner. The Owner shall be
      obligated to Contractor for storage charges subsequent to
      agreed date on the basis of Contractor's actual costs for
      the warehousing space utilized for such purpose. Costs
      shall in no event exceed public warehousing rates or
      charges.

2-11   DELIVERY AND INSTALLATION

A.   Contractor shall submit for each project, the names,
      addresses, and qualifications of proposed subcontractors,
      workrooms, and installers for the Owner's and Designer's
      approval.

B.   The Contractor shall furnish a competent superintendent
      at the site of the work as may be necessary for the
      proper coordination and supervision of the work and to
      ensure completion of the work in accordance with all
      requirements of the Contract Documents and to the entire
      satisfaction of the Designer. The superintendent shall
      receive all deliveries, check for transit damage and
      supervise the installation.

C.   The Contractor shall work with the Designer to develop a
      delivery schedule compatible with the construction
      schedule and shall be responsible for all such delivery
      and installation dates. The Contractor shall furnish
      sufficient forces to ensure completion of work in time.

D.   Work shall be performed during regular working hours
      except that in the event of emergency, and when required
      to complete the work within the time stated in the
      Contract, work may be performed on night shifts,
      overtime, Sundays and holidays when written permission to
      do so has been obtained from the Owner.

E.   The Contractor shall be responsible for securing a
      schedule for the availability of spaces forming the scope
      of Contract obligation from the General Contractor so as
      to assure the completion of work within the required
      time. No material shall be shipped to the job site
      except in accordance with written delivery schedules

Figure 7.7 (*continued*)

approved by the Owner and Designer.

F.   Deliveries shall be made according to the Owner's
     requirements. Contractor shall cooperate with the
     General Contractor in arranging schedules for deliveries,
     available unloading space and the use of building
     elevators and facilities. Owner will provide free access
     to elevators.

     1.   In the event the Contractor needs space for the
          storage of materials and/or equipment required in
          connection with the work, the Contractor shall store
          such materials and equipment in such space as is
          specifically authorized and provided by the General
          Contractor on behalf of the Owner for such purpose,
          and in no other space or location in, on, or about
          the building.

     2.   The Contractor shall not enter or have access to any
          space in the building in order to perform the work
          without first having given timely notice to the
          Owner so that the necessary arrangements may be made
          and the Owner's permission obtained.

G.   In the event of unforeseen delays of any nature that
     would prevent delivery according to schedule, the
     Designer shall be notified by telephone in order to
     attempt to make adjustments in the elevator schedule. It
     is understood that the Contractor's schedule will not be
     permitted to upset the day's established delivery
     schedule in order to accommodate irregular deliveries.
     Deliveries that cannot be completed within the time
     reserved shall be made at the end of the scheduled day at
     Contractor's expense even though it becomes overtime.

H.   If any item arrives on the job without proper
     identification, it shall be the responsibility of the
     Contractor's representative to identify it or it will be
     returned to the Contractor at the Contractor's expense.

I.   Contractor shall furnish to the Owner and Designer,
     immediately after receipt of any interior furnishings
     receiving reports listing each item of interior
     furnishings received at the job site, and any damaged or
     rejected items.

J.   Tags or labels must remain on the furniture until the
     placement is checked, and inspection is made by the
     Designer.

K.   The Contractor shall remove daily all packaging and
     crating materials from the work area.

L.   All delivered units shall match the approved shop
     drawings. Units which are marred, chipped or otherwise

Figure 7.7 *(continued)*

damaged shall be repaired and/or replaced to the complete satisfaction of the Designer and Owner.

M. After installation of units in their proper location, all protection shall be removed and all surfaces thoroughly cleaned to the complete satisfaction of the Designer and Owner.

N. The Contractor shall be responsible for all cutting and patching necessary for the installation of the work. All cutting shall be done promptly and all repairs shall be made as necessary to leave the entire work in good condition, including all cutting, fitting, and drilling of metal, wood, and other materials as specified or required for proper assembly, fabrication, installation and completion of all work under the Contract, and including any patching as may be necessary.

    1. Permission to patch any areas or items of work shall not constitute a waiver of the Designer's right to require complete removal and replacement of said items of work if, in the Designer's opinion, said patching does not satisfactorily restore quality and appearance of same.

O. All items shall be delivered and installed in accordance with the Designer's floor plans.

    1. All large accessory items shall be unboxed and placed according to the location charts.

    2. All desk accessories for occupied desks shall be unboxed and placed on the desks. All such accessories for people to be hired in the future shall be left boxed and shall be placed in the supply store room.

P. Security measures as required to protect stored or installed interior furnishings shall be provided by the General Contractor or the Owner. Completed areas shall be closed to traffic until the Designer and Owner have inspected and accepted all interior furnishings in such areas.

Q. Owner will designate a representative authorized to accept or reject on behalf of Owner items delivered, placed, and installed by Contractor. All items shall be considered finally accepted only after inspection by and written approval is obtained from the Owner or duly assigned representative.

2-12   CLEANING UP AND MAINTENANCE

A. The premises and the areas in which the work is performed

Figure 7.7 (continued)

shall be maintained in a reasonably neat and orderly
condition by the Contractor and kept free from
accumulations of waste materials and rubbish during the
progress of the work and until completion thereof. The
Contractor is responsible for the removal of all crates,
cartons, wrappings and other flammable waste materials or
trash from the building at the end of each working day.
If the premises are not maintained properly, the Owner
may have any accumulations of waste materials or trash
removed and charge the cost to the Contractor, as the
Designer shall determine to be just.

B. Floors shall be "broom-cleaned", or its equivalent during
the course of the work. Additional cleaning of carpeting
and of all other items which are provided as a part of
the Contract, including removal of dust, stains and
finger marks from all finished wood, metal, marble, glass
or other surfaces shall be performed by the Contractor as
required before Final Acceptance of the work by the
Owner.

C. Upon completion of the work, the Contractor shall remove
from the premises all installation equipment and all
surplus materials and rubbish resulting from the work.
Contractor shall submit to the Designer three copies of
manufacturer's maintenance instructions for all items of
furniture and furnishings.

2-13   PROTECTION OF WORK AND PROPERTY/SAFETY

A. Contractor shall be responsible for the care and
protection of each item of furniture and furnishings
herein specified including specifically (but without
limitation) adequate protection from soil and dirt and
damage to finish and joinery due to temperature and
humidity variations during transport and warehousing,
until it has been placed in the specified location by the
Contractor, adjusted and inspected by Contractor and
Designer and accepted by Designer/Owner; provided,
however, that Contractor shall not be required to place
any item until work of others in locations specified for
such items has been completed suitably for making and
securing such placement.

B. Contractor shall be responsible for risk of damage or
loss, and Owner will not be responsible until acceptance,
for any damage or loss of any item herein specified
caused by fire, wind, theft, vandalism, malicious
mischief, negligence, act of providence, or any other
cause.

Figure 7.7 (*continued*)

1.   If any loss or damage occurs prior to acceptance by the Owner, the Contractor shall promptly repair or replace the part or parts lost, damaged, or destroyed, as directed, at no cost to the Owner.

C.   In entering, passing through, or working in any such space in the building in the performance of the work, the Contractor shall at all times furnish and maintain proper protection for the floors, walls, ceilings, fixtures, equipment, furniture and/or other property of the Owner. Contractor shall repair or replace any damaged adjoining work as directed without additional cost to the Owner.

D.   The Contractor shall be governed by applicable government, insurance and building regulations in the receiving, handling, and storage of all materials, installation equipment, removal of debris, etc., as required for all work herein specified.

E.   The Contractor shall consult the Owner concerning building and safety regulations, arrangements for use of existing building facilities, if any, etc.

F.   The Contractor shall exercise special care in keeping all areas clean, and strictly adhere to all safety, fire and other regulations concerning the use of the building.

1.   Adequate precautions shall be taken against fire throughout all the Contractor's and subcontractor's operations, Flammable material(s) shall be kept to an absolute minimum and, if any, shall be handled and stored in accordance with goverment and insurance requirements.

G.   The Contractor shall take all necessary precautions to ensure the safety of the public and of workmen on the job, and to prevent accidents or injury to any persons on, about, or adjacent to the premises where the work is being performed. The Contractor shall comply with all laws, ordinances, codes, rules and regulations relative to safety and the prevention of accidents.

2-14   DESIGNER'S STATUS AND DECISIONS

A.   The Designer shall be the Owner's representative during the construction and installation period and shall observe the work in process on behalf of the Owner, but shall not be responsible for the Contractor's failure to carry out the work in accordance with the Contract Documents. The Designer shall have authority to act on behalf of the Owner only to the extent expressly provided in the Contract Documents or otherwise in writing, which

Figure 7.7 (continued)

141

shall be shown to the Contractor.

    1.   Contractor's moving and installing personnel shall cooperate with, and be responsible to the Designer and Owner.

B.   The Designer shall determine the amount, quality, acceptability, and fitness of the several kinds of work and materials which are included under this Contract and shall decide all questions which may arise in relation to said work and the construction thereof. All such decisions shall be binding and final.

C.   The Designer shall decide the meaning and intent of any portion of the specifications and of any drawings where the same may be found obscure or be in dispute.

2-15   USE AND OCCUPANCY PRIOR TO ACCEPTANCE BY OWNER

A.   After preliminary acceptance of any part of the work, the Owner shall have the privilege of occupying and using or permitting others to occupy and use such part of the work in advance of completion and final acceptance of the entire work.

B.   In the event that the Owner desires to exercise the privilege of partial occupancy prior to completion and final acceptance of the entire work as provided above, the Contractor shall cooperate with the Owner in making furnishings available for said use for part of the work to be occupied, and if the furnishings required to furnish such services are not entirely completed at the time the Owner desires to occupy the aforesaid part of the work, the Contractor shall make every reasonable effort to complete same as soon as possible to the extent that the necessary furnishings can be put into operation and use.

2-16   CHANGES IN THE WORK OR QUANTITIES DURING AND SUBSEQUENT TO THE CONTRACT

A.   The Owner reserves the right at any time to make changes through the Designer in specifications as to any additions or omissions of material. Such additions, or omissions shall be based on the established unit prices for each item.

B.   If such changes shall be considered to work a hardship on the Contractor or to incur an extra charge or extra time, it shall be the Contractor's responsibility to immediately submit an estimate of the cost and time to

Figure 7.7 (continued)

142

the Owner and Designer. Such changes shall be equitably adjusted and the Contract and/or schedule shall be modified in writing accordingly. No charge will be accepted that is not agreed upon and supported by a Change Order.

C.   The Owner may order additional furniture and furnishings, and other items within the categories set forth in these General Conditions of the same specifications and unit price as items theretofore actually furnished by the Contractor which may be required for installation or use in Owner's building at any time during the contract period. Items will be supplied by the Contractor to the Owner upon the same terms and conditions as provided by the Contractor for the original installation.

2-17   CORRECTION OF WORK BEFORE FINAL PAYMENT

A.   The Contractor shall promptly remove from the premises all materials and equipment and all work condemned by the Designer as failing to conform to the Contract Documents. The Contractor shall promptly replace and re-execute all work under Contract in accordance with the Contract Documents and without expense to the Owner and shall bear the expense of making good all work of other Contractors destroyed or damaged by such removal or replacement.

1.   The Owner reserves the right to withhold a portion of the total payment until any defective work is remedied and any missing items are delivered.

B.   If the Designer and Owner deem it inexpedient to correct work damaged or work not performed in accordance with the Contract Documents, an equitable deduction through negotiation shall be made from the amounts due or to become due the Contractor.

C.   If the Contractor does not remove condemned work and materials within a reasonable time, fixed by written notice, the Owner may, at the expense of the Contractor, remove them and store the material. If the Contractor does not pay the expenses of such removal within ten days' time thereafter, the Owner may, upon ten days' written notice, sell such materials at auction or at private sale and shall account for the net proceeds thereof only after deducting all the costs and expenses that should have been borne by the Contractor.

2-18   CORRECTION OF WORK AFTER FINAL PAYMENT

A.   Neither the final payment nor any provisions in the

Figure 7.7 (continued)

Contract Documents shall relieve the Contractor of
responsibility for faulty materials, equipment or
workmanship and, unless otherwise specified, the
Contractor shall remedy any defects due thereto and pay
for any damage to other work resulting therefrom which
shall appear within the guarantee period. The Owner
shall give written notice of such observed defects with
reasonable promptness. All questions arising under this
Article shall be directed to the Designer and the
Contract Administrator.

2-19   OWNER'S RIGHT TO DO WORK

A.   If the Contractor should neglect to prosecute the work
      properly or fail to perform in accordance with the
      Contract Documents, the Owner, after three days' written
      notice to the Contractor, may without prejudice to any
      other remedy, make good such deficiencies and may deduct
      the cost thereof from amounts due or to become due the
      Contractor, provided however, that the Designer shall
      approve both such action and the amount charged to the
      Contractor.

2-20   ACCEPTANCE OF THE WORK

A.   Preliminary acceptance of the work will be made after
      preliminary inspection by the Designer when, in the
      opinion of the Designer, the work has been substantially
      completed in accordance with the requirements of the
      Contract Documents, except for minor adjustments, repairs
      or deficiencies, so that the Owner can occupy the
      building or portions thereof for the use for which it was
      intended.

B.   Final acceptance will be made after final inspection by
      the Designer when all requirements of the Contract
      Documents appear to have been completed. Upon final
      acceptance of the work, the Owner may take over the
      premises for occupancy and use thereafter.

2-21   GUARANTEE

A.   Neither the final nor partial payment, nor any provision
      in the Contract Documents, nor partial or entire
      occupancy of the premises by the Owner shall constitute
      an acceptance of work not done in accordance with the
      Contract Documents or relieve the Contractor of any
      liability under the Contract Documents in respect of any
      express or implied warranties, responsibility for faulty
      materials or workmanship or otherwise. All merchandise

Figure 7.7 (*continued*)

furnished by Contractor hereunder is unconditionally guaranteed for one (1) year against defects in materials or workmanship from the date of final acceptance of the work by the Owner. The Contractor shall remedy any defects in the installation, materials, and workmanship and pay for any damage to other work resulting therefrom, which shall appear within a period of (1) one year. The Owner will give notice of observed defects with reasonable promptness.

B.   If defects appear due to faulty installation, workmanship or material within the guarantee period, Contractor shall repair or replace same without charge to Owner after receiving notice thereof. All other service which may be required by Owner in connection with the merchandise furnished by the Contractor after installation will be provided by the Contractor at the regular hourly rates prevailing for the trades required. Contractor will provide such service at the Owner's convenience through its own mechanics or subcontractors employed by it and Contractor shall charge only the effective hourly rate with no profit added. Replacement merchandise and parts required other than those to be furnished by the Contractor under guarantee will be provided at the same rates as the basic products sold under these General Conditions.

C.   Contractor represents and warrants that the material included in his/her proposal is not manufactured nor sold by the Contractor in violation or infringement of any USA or foreign patent or copyrights and the Contractor agrees to indemnify the Owner against any liability by reason of the use of such material.

D.   Contractor guarantees that no materials or supplies for the work shall be purchased by the Contractor or by any subcontractor subject to any chattel mortgage or under a conditional sale contract or other agreement by which an interest is retained by the seller. The Contractor warrants full title to all materials and supplies used in the work, and that they are free from all liens, charges, claims or encumbrances.

E.   Contractor shall provide Owner with a written guarantee stipulating the conditions of A,B,C, and D above.

F.   Within 10 days after the signing of the Contract the Contractor shall submit to the Designer three copies of written guarantee signed by each furniture manufacturer guaranteeing the furniture for a period of at least two years against defects in materials and workmanship.

Figure 7.7 (*continued*)

2-22   CONTRACT SECURITY

        A.   Within ten days of receipt of the written Notification of
              Selection, the successful Contractor shall enter into a
              formal Contract with the Owner and within ten days of the
              execution of the Contract, the Contractor shall provide a
              Performance, Labor, Material and Payment Bond in the
              amount of $_____.

        B.   The Bond shall be signed and sealed by an authorized
              representative of the Bonding Company and an authorized
              officer or representative of the Contractor; a notarized
              certificate of the authority of those signing the Bond,
              if not officers, shall be attached thereto.

        C.   The Performance and Payment Bond shall guarantee the
              performance of the duties placed on the Contractor by the
              Prevailing Wage Act, as well as all other duties required
              by the Contract Documents, and shall indemnify the Owner
              from any liability or loss resulting to the Owner from
              any failure of the Contractor to fully perform each or
              all of said duties.

2-23   TAXES

        A.   The Contractor shall pay for all Federal, State and Local
              taxes on all materials, labor or services furnished, and
              all taxes arising out of the operations under the
              Contract Documents. Such taxes shall include, but not be
              limited to, Occupational, Sales, Use, Excise, Old Age
              Benefit and Unemployment Taxes, customs duties, and all
              income taxes and other taxes now in force or hereafter
              enacted prior to final acceptance of the work. The
              Contractor shall assume all liability for the payment of
              unemployment benefits payable under applicable Federal or
              State laws to individuals who were employed by the
              Contractor during the term of this Contract.

2-24   ROYALTIES AND PATENTS

        A.   The Contractor shall pay all royalties and license fees
              and shall defend, indemnify and hold the Owner and the
              Designer harmless from any and all suits, demands or
              claims for infringement on any patent rights.

        B.   The approval of any method of construction, invention,
              appliance, process, article, device or material of any
              kind by the Designer or Owner shall only be an approval
              of its adequacy for the work, and shall not be an
              approval of the use thereof by the Contractor in

Figure 7.7 (continued)

146

violation of any patent or other rights of any third party.

2-25   TRADE REGULATIONS

A.   Where applicable, the Contractor shall comply with all union regulations governing inter- and intra-state trucking and delivery and installation and local regulations, particularly in regard to mechanics doing installation work on the premises. It shall be the Contractor's responsibility to make sure that no situation is allowed to develop, i.e.: jurisdictional disputes or job shut down, that would either interfere with the work being done by the Construction Company or delay the scheduled furniture requirements of the Owner.

B.   Wherever any provision of any section of the specifications conflicts with any agreements or regulations of any kind at any time in force among members of any Trade Associations, Unions or Councils, which regulate or distinguish what work shall or shall not be included in the work of any particular trade, the Contractor shall make all necessary arrangements to reconcile any such conflict without delay, damage or cost to the Owner and without recourse to the Designer or the Owner.

1.   In case the progress of the work is affected by any undue delay in furnishing or installing any items of material or equipment required under the Contract because of a conflict involving any such agreement or regulation, the Designer may require that other material or equipment of equal kind and quality be provided at no additional cost to the Owner.

C.   The Contractor or subcontractors, installers, etc., in order to avoid labor disputes, shall employ only such labor as will, to the satisfaction of the Owner, work in harmony with the other individuals employed by the Owner and shall not use materials or means which might cause strikes or other labor troubles by any person employed in or about the Owner's building.

1.   Any Contractor or subcontractor not normally employing union labor shall make all provisions necessary to avoid any resulting disputes with labor unions and shall be responsible for any delays, damages or extra costs caused by employment of such non-union labor.

Figure 7.7 (*continued*)

147

2-26   PERMITS, LAWS AND REGULATIONS

   A.   The Contractor shall obtain and pay for all permits,
          licenses and certificates of inspection necessary for the
          execution of the work; shall give all notices and comply
          with all laws, ordinances, codes, rules and regulations
          bearing on the conduct of the work; and shall pay all
          fees required by law. If the Contractor observes that
          the drawings and specifications are at variance
          therewith, the Designer shall be promptly notified in
          writing, and any necessary changes shall be made. If the
          Contractor performs any work which is contrary to such
          laws, ordinances, codes, rules and regulations, the
          Contractor shall be responsible to make all changes as
          required to comply therewith and shall bear all costs
          arising therefrom.

2-27   INDEMNIFICATION OF OWNER AND DESIGNER

   A.   The Contractor shall indemnify, protect and hold harmless
          the Owner and Designer from loss or damage and shall
          reimburse the Owner and Designer for any expense,
          including legal fees and disbursements, because of any
          misrepresentation or the breach of any warranty or
          covenant made in the Contract Documents, including
          without limitation, litigation and on account of
          infringement or alleged infringement of any letters
          patent or patent rights by reason of the work or
          materials sold by the Contractor or any subcontractors
          engaged for the work.

   B.   The Contractor shall defend any and all suits brought
          against the Owner and/or the Designer by any employee or
          other persons for damage to property and/or injury
          (including death) alleged or claimed to have been caused
          by or through the performance of the work under the
          Contract. Contractor shall indemnify and hold harmless
          the Owner and/or Designer from and against any and all
          claim or claims arising out of the work performed by the
          Contractor or subcontractors or sub-subcontractors. The
          Contractor shall pay, liquidate and discharge any and all
          claims or demands for bodily injury (including death),
          and/or loss of or damage to any and all property caused
          by, growing out of or incidental to the performance of
          the work performed by the Contractor, including damage to
          the building and other property of the Owner and
          including all damages for the obstruction of private
          driveways, streets, and alleys, and all costs and
          expenses of suits and reasonable attorneys' fees. In the
          event of any such injury (including death), loss or
          damage (or claim or claims therefor), Contractor shall
          give immediate notice thereof to the Contract

Figure 7.7 (continued)

Administrator and Designer.

2-28   INSURANCE

A.   The Contractor shall secure, pay for and maintain until
      all work is completed, such insurance as will protect
      himself from claims under Worker's Compensation Acts,
      Worker's Occupational Diseases Act, and from any other
      claims for damages to property or for bodily injury
      (including death), which may arise from operations under
      this Contract.

      1.   It shall be the Contractor's responsibility to
            guarantee that any subcontractors employed by him
            carry the necessary Worker's Compensation insurance.

B.   Prior to commencement of any work, the Contractor shall
      furnish to the Contract Administrator Certificates of
      Insurance in an approved form executed in triplicate by
      insurance companies approved by the Owner to evidence
      coverage by the Contractor as set forth below.
      Certificates which deviate from this form or which, in
      the Contract Administrator's opinion, are incomplete will
      be returned for resubmission by the Contractor. The
      Contractor shall keep said insurance in full force until
      all work is completed and accepted by the Owner,
      including work required by Article 2-21 GUARANTEES. Said
      insurance shall not be materially changed, or cancelled
      without 30 days advance notice to Owner and Contract
      Administrator. Notification of material change or
      cancellation shall be by registered mail to the Owner and
      Contract Administrator at their regular place of
      business.

C.   The Contractor shall carry insurance(s) as may be
      required by Federal, State and Local ordinances.
      Contractor shall verify that all subcontractor and sub-
      subcontractors also carry the required insurance(s) as
      outlined below and require evidence of coverage prior to
      commencing work.

      1.   The Contractor shall name the Owner and Designer as
            an "additional insured" under the Comprehensive
            General Liability coverages provided and shall
            submit certificates of insurance evidencing same, at
            the limits specified, prior to commencement of work.

D.   Contractor's Insurance

      Coverage Minimum Limits Of Liability

Figure 7.7 (continued)

1. Worker's Compensation
    and Occupational
    Disease: Statutory Limits

2. Employers Liability: $500,000 (Coverage B)

3. Comprehensive General
    Liability Insurance:

    a. General Coverage

        Bodily Injury $1,000,000 per occurrence

        Property Damage $1,000,000 per occurrence

    b. Coverage to include
        the following:

        1) Contractual Liability
            Including the Indemnification
            of Owner and Designer

        2) Contractor's
            Protective Liability

        3) Product Liability and completed operations
            up to one year after final acceptance of the
            completed work by the Owner.

4. Comprehensive Automobile
    Liability Insurance:

    Bodily Injury $1,000,000 each person
                            $1,000,000 each occurrence

    Property Damage $1,000,000 each occurrence

    This insurance must include non-owned,
    hired or rented vehicles as well as
    owned vehicles.

5. Property Insurance: The Contractor shall secure,
    pay for and maintain whatever Fire or Extended
    Coverage Insurance he may deem necessary to protect
    himself against loss of any materials or equipment
    which are a part of this Contract and loss of owned
    or rented capital equipment and tools, including any
    tools owned by mechanics, and any tools, equipment,
    scaffolding and stagings owned or rented by the
    Contractor.

Figure 7.7 *(continued)*

      a. It shall be the responsibility of the Contractor to indemnify the Owner for all unaccepted work and/or furnishings.

    6. <u>Fire Insurance:</u> The Contractor shall name the Owner and Designer, as their interests may appear as "joint loss payee" for all goods, furniture and materials covered under this contract and for which the Owner and Designer has a right or interest.

    7. In the event of a loss, the Contractor shall waive all rights of subrogation against Owner or Designer should a dispute arise as to origin of the loss or responsibility.

E. <u>Property Insurance on Structure(s):</u> Fire Insurance and Extended Coverage on the building(s) in which the work of the Contractor is to be performed will be maintained by the Owner.

2-29   SEPARATE CONTRACTS

A. The Owner reserves the right to let other contracts in connection with this work. The Contractor shall afford other contractors reasonable opportunity for the introduction and storage of their materials and the execution of their work, and shall properly connect and coordinate his/her work with theirs.

B. If any part of the Contractor's work depends for proper execution or result upon the work of any other contractor, the Contractor shall inspect and promptly report to the Designer any defects in such work that render it unsuitable for such proper execution and results. The Contractor's failure to do so shall constitute an acceptance of the other contractor's work as fit and proper for the reception of his work, except as to defects which may develop in the other contractor's work after the execution of his work.

    1. To ensure the proper execution of subsequent work, the Contractor shall measure work already in place and shall at once report to the Designer any discrepancy between executed work and the drawings or other specifications.

C. The Contractor, where separate contractors or their subcontractors are employed on the work, will not hold the Owner responsible for loss or damage or injury caused by any fault or negligence of such other contractors or subcontractors for recovery from them for any such damage or injury.

Figure 7.7 (continued)

151

D.   Wherever work being done by any such contractors or
     subcontractors is contiguous to work covered by the
     Contract Documents, the respective rights of the parties
     shall be established by the Designer to secure the
     completion of the various portions of the work in general
     harmony.

E.   If any separate contractor or his subcontractor shall
     suffer loss or damage through any acts or omissions on
     the part of the Contractor, or any of his subcontractors,
     the Contractor shall reimburse such other contractor or
     his subcontractor by agreement, if they will so settle.
     If such separate contractor or his subcontractor shall
     assert any claim against the Owner on account of any
     damage or loss alleged to have been so sustained, the
     Owner shall notify the Contractor, and the Contractor
     shall save the Owner harmless against such claims to the
     extent provided in Article 2-27 "INDEMIFICATION OF OWNER
     AND DESIGNER".

2-30   SUBCONTRACTS

A.   The Contractor shall, prior to delivering any furniture,
     notify the Designer in writing of the names of
     subcontractors proposed for the principal parts of the
     work and for such others as the Designer may direct and
     shall not employ any that the Designer may find
     objectionable.

B.   The Contractor shall assume full responsibility to the
     Owner and Designer for the acts and omissions of his
     subcontractors and of persons either directly or
     indirectly employed by them, and for the acts and
     omissions of persons directly or indirectly employed by
     him.

C.   The Contractor shall assume to bind every subcontractor
     and every subcontractor agrees to be bound by the terms
     and conditions of these Contract Documents, as far as
     applicable to this work unless specifically noted to the
     contrary in a subcontract approved in writing as adequate
     by the Contract Administrator and Designer.

D.   Nothing in the Contract Documents shall be deemed or
     construed to impose upon the Owner an obligation,
     liability, or duty to any subcontractor, or to create any
     contractual relation between the Owner and any
     subcontractor.

2-31   OWNER'S RIGHT TO TERMINATE CONTRACT

A.   If the Contractor: shall be adjudged a bankrupt, or shall

Figure 7.7 (continued)

make a general assignment for the benefit of creditors, or if a receiver shall be appointed on account of insolvency or shall refuse or shall fail, except in cases for which extension of time is provided, to supply enough properly skilled workmen or proper materials, or shall fail to make prompt payment to subcontractors or for material or labor, or disregard the instructions of the Designer, or is unable to complete the work properly or by the time scheduled for completion, or otherwise be guilty of a violation of any provision of the Contract Documents, then the Contract Administrator, upon the recommendation of the Designer may, without prejudice to any other right or remedy and after giving the Contractor seven days' written notice, terminate the Contract. Upon said termination, the Owner shall take possession of the premises and of all materials, tools and appliances thereon and have assigned, if so desired, the Contractor's subcontracts and material orders, and finish the work by whatever method the Owner may deem expedient.

B.   In such case, the Contractor shall not be entitled to receive any further payment. Without limiting any other remedy which Owner or Designer may have in equity or at law, if the expense of finishing the work, including compensation for additional managerial and administrative services, paid the Contractor, the Contractor (or the surety or sureties on the performance bond) shall be liable for the payment of the amount of such excess to the Owner. The expense incurred by the Owner as herein provided and the damage incurred through the Contractor's default, shall be certified to the Contract Administrator by the Designer.

2-32   ASSIGNMENT

A.   Neither party to the Contract shall assign the Contract or sublet it as a whole without written consent of the other, nor shall the Contractor assign any monies due or to become due hereunder without the previous written consent of the Owner.

B.   Any assignment of monies due under the Contract made without the written consent of the Owner shall be held invalid, and the assignee in such case shall acquire no rights against the Owner.

2-33   PAYMENT

A.   Payment shall be made after acceptance to the Contractor in accordance with the terms of the Contract Documents. Invoices in the required form shall be submitted in duplicate to the Designer for approval.

Figure 7.7 (continued)

B.   Payments may be withheld as may be necessary to protect the Owner from loss on account of defective work not remedied; claims filed or reasonable evidence indicating probable filing thereof; failure of Contractor to make payments to subcontractors or for material or labor; damage to another contractor or to the property of the Owner or others; unauthorized deviations by the Contractor from the Contract Documents and other good and sufficient reasons as determined by the Designer.

    1.   When the above grounds are removed, further payments shall be made for amounts withheld because of them.

2-34   LIENS

A.   Neither the final payment nor any part of the retained percentage for each project shall become due until the Contractor shall deliver to the Owner in form acceptable to the Owner:

    1.   A signed release of all liens, charges, incumbrances or claims from himself, subcontractors, suppliers of material or others in connection with the work, or arising out of the work;

    2.   An affidavit that so far as the Contractor has knowledge or information, the releases include all the labor and material for which a lien could be filed; and

B.   If any lien remains unsatisfied, after all payments are made, the Contractor shall refund to the Owner all monies that the latter may be compelled to pay in discharging such a lien, including all costs and a reasonable attorney's fee.

2-35   ACCEPTANCE OF FINAL PAYMENT CONSTITUTES RELEASE

A.   The acceptance by the Contractor of final payment for a project shall be and shall operate as a release of the Owner from all claims and all liability to the Contractor for all things done or furnished in connection with the work and for every act and neglect of the Owner and others relating to or arising out of this work. No payment, however, final or otherwise, shall operate to release the Contractor or his sureties from any obligations under this Contract or the Performance and Payment Bond.

Figure 7.7 *(continued)*

154

INSTALLATION, MATERIALS, AND WORKMANSHIP

FURNITURE & FURNISHINGS SPECIFICATIONS
FOR
(CLIENT)

SECTION 3
INSTALLATION, MATERIALS & WORKMANSHIP

3-01   GOVERNMENTAL REGULATIONS

A.   Materials and their installation shall comply with all requirements and restrictions in reference standards of all governmental agencies, Federal, State and Local, and any other agencies that have jurisdiction.

3-02   INSTALLATION - GENERAL

A.   Installers must be arranged for and provided for by the Contractor as the Contractor's subcontractor. Installer must have a minimum of five (5) years experience in the installation of furniture and furnishings similar to those specified herein. The Contractor shall assume responsibility for all of the work referred to in this Contract, including final installation and cleaning of all items at the job site. The Contractor and subcontractor(s) are responsible for supplying the manufacturer's materials and products specified by the Designer as necessary to complete the work.

1.   The Contractor's or subcontractors' employees whose work or conduct is unsatisfactory to the Owner or Designer, or who are considered by the Designer to be deficient in the skills required by the work or otherwise objectionable, shall be dismissed from the work immediately upon notice from the Designer.

2.   Materials shall be installed only under the supervision of the Contractor's qualified technical representative.

3.   All work shall be erected by skilled workpersons, especially trained in this type of work by the manufacturer or his authorized representatives.

4.   The method of leveling all floor supported units must be of a concealed, adjustable type acceptable to the Designer. Shims shall be avoided wherever possible, and used only where approved by the Designer. Exposed shims will not be allowed. Shims will only be allowed if the manufacturer guarantees that shims used will be totally concealed and attached with adhesive or two-sided tape so that shims cannot become dislodged.

5.   All files and storage cabinets shall be bolted together side to side. All overfile storage

Figure 7.8

155

cabinets and all counter tops shall be securely fastened to the equipment below. All equipment shall be leveled plumb and true prior to bolting.

B.   Special care shall be taken in the handling of the furniture to avoid its being either scratched or otherwise defaced during the course of installation. Any materials showing evidence of such mishandling shall be replaced at the expense of the Contractor.

C.   Units which have members that are warped, bowed, deformed or otherwise damaged or defaced shall not be installed. Contractor shall remove and replace such members as directed.

D.   The Contractor must meet with the Designer and the Owner's representative, and manufacturer(s) necessary at the project site to review the furniture installation, procedure and coordination with other trades prior to the delivery and installation of all furniture and furnishing covered under this Contract.

3-03   MATERIALS AND WORKMANSHIP

A.   All materials shall be new and both workmanship and materials shall be the very best of its respective kind of each of the several trades employed. All work shall be executed in strict accordance with dimensional design requirements of the drawings and specifications and under direct supervision of competent representatives of the Contractor. Tolerances on over-all assembly dimensions shall be within plus or minus 1/32 inch.

B.   Methods of fabrication, assembly, and erection, unless otherwise specifically stated, shall be at the discretion of the manufacturer whose responsibility it shall be to guarantee to the Contractor satisfactory performance as herein specified.

C.   Metal and wood furniture shall be fabricated and rigidly assembled by skilled workpersons of the highest grade known to the trade and to the complete satisfaction of the Designer. Reinforcing as required to ensure a rigid and secure assembly shall be provided where necessary, even if not detailed on the drawings. Exposed surfaces shall be free from dents, tool marks, warpage, buckle, glue and open joints. All joints, corners, and miters shall be accurately fitted and rigidly secured with hairline contacts. Fastenings shall be concealed. Threaded connections shall be made up tightly so that threads are entirely concealed.

1.   Metal work shall be fabricated and fastened so that work will not be distorted nor the fasteners overstressed from the expansion and contraction of the metal.

Figure 7.8 (continued)

156

2. All welding shall be in accordance with appropriate recommendations of the American Welding Society and shall be done with electrodes and/or by methods recommended by the manufacturer of the alloys being welded. All welds behind finished surfaces shall be so done as to minimize distortion and to assure no discoloration on the finished side. All weld spatter and welding oxides on finished surfaces shall be removed by descaling and/or grinding. All weld beads on exposed finish surfaces shall be ground and/or polished to match and blend with finish on adjacent parent metal. All welding shall be of adequate strength and durability with joints tight, flush, smooth and clean.

3. All soldering shall be in accordance with the recommendations of the manufacturers of the parent metals involved. Soldering shall be employed only for filling or sealing of joints, and shall not be relied upon for mechanical strength. Immediately after soldering, all fluxes shall be removed by washing with a strong neutralizing solution, followed by clean water rinse and drying.

4. Sheet metal work shall be formed, fabricated and erected accurately, to shapes and dimensions shown, with all lines, angles and surfaces in true alignment, plumb, level and in proper plane.

5. The proper thickness of metal, adequate stiffeners, supports and proven details of assembly shall be used so that the finished product will conform to the highest standards of the industry.

6. Members and joints shall be reinforced with steel plates, bars, rods or angles for rigidity and strength as needed to fulfill performance requirements.

7. Metal surfaces, after being ground and/or polished, or where subject to severe forming operations, shall be cleaned of all extraneous material, thoroughly rinsed with clear water and dried.

8. All lubricants used in the fabrication shall be removed before painting or plating finish work begins.

9. All work shall be fitted and assembled in the shop insofar as practicable. Units which are too large for shipment to project site shall be marked and disassembled, retaining units in sizes as large as possible for shipment and erection.

10. All dimensions for recessed file unit(s) and landscape panel runs shall be verified in the field.

Figure 7.8 (*continued*)

11. All exposed work shall be carefully matched to produce continuity of line and design.

12. All finishes shall match samples as approved by Designer in all respects.

13. Glueing of plastic laminate surfacing materials and of face veneers shall, where possible, be by the hotplate method and glued surfaces shall be in close contact throughout. Glue stains will not be permitted.

D. Manufactured materials shall be delivered in the original packages, containers or bundles bearing the name of the manufacturer and the brand.

    1. Temporary coverings, provided at the Contractor's option to protect the work during shipment, storage and installation, shall be carefully selected to avoid development of deleterious effects in the work.

E. All manufactured articles, materials and equipment shall be applied, installed, connected, erected, stored, used, cleaned and conditioned in accordance with the manufacturer's written specifications or instructions unless hereinafter specified to the contrary. The Contractor shall furnish to the Designer two copies of these specifications or instructions before proceeding with the work. Manufacturer's manuals shall include certification or laboratory test reports as may be required to show compliance with these specifications. Indicate by transmittal form that a copy of each set of instructions has been transmitted to the Installer.

F. Desks and credenzas appearing in the same room shall, unless otherwise noted, be keyed alike so that one key shall open both desk and cabinets.

G. No stamped, printed or other manufacturer identifying markings shall appear on any exposed surfaces of any item furnished under these specifications. This does not apply to Underwriters' labels where required, nor to the manufacturer's name and rating plates on mechanical and electrical equipment.

H. Any work, materials, furniture or equipment which does not conform to these requirements or the standards set forth in the Contract documents may be disapproved and condemned by the Designer, in which case it shall be removed and replaced by the Contractor as provided in Article 2-17, CORRECTION OF WORK BEFORE FINAL PAYMENT.

Figure 7.8 (*continued*)

PARTICULAR CONDITIONS

FURNITURE & FURNISHINGS SPECIFICATIONS
FOR
(CLIENT)

SECTION 4
STOCKING PROGRAM

4-01   INTENTION OF OWNER

A.   It is the intention of the Owner to have the successful
Contractor maintain a stocking program of the basic items
most often used in new facilities as a rapid ship
program.

1.   This enables the Owner to quickly set up facilities
in various cities and avoids the high cost of
renting furniture.

2.   Offices to be set up through the stocking program
are intended to be "start up" operations and are
relatively small. Major projects will be ordered
through the usual methods when longer lead times
prevail.

4-02   REQUIREMENTS OF THE STOCKING PROGRAM

A.   All furniture and furnishings in the stocking program
must be able to ship within two weeks of the receipt of
the order by the Contractor.

B.   All items removed from stock must be replaced within two
weeks so that the stock is not depleted for a lengthy
period of time.

C.   There shall be no charge to the Owner by the Contractor
for maintaining this stocking program.

4-03   LISTING OF ITEMS TO BE STOCKED

A.   Items are listed by code and an abbreviated description.
For detailed specifications see STANDARD SPECIFICATIONS,
Section 5. (Attach list and quantity of each item to be
stocked.)

Figure 7.9

FURNITURE AND FURNISHINGS SPECIFICATIONS
FOR (client)
SECTION 5

<u>Chairs</u>

Code	Description
C-1	Metalstand #OSP Secretarial chair, swivel, fabric back and seat in 100% nylon, Titeweve. Color: #6625 - chocolate, polished chrome finish. Kevi Dual Wheel Casters.
C-2	Metalstand #ORA, swivel/tilt desk chair, fabric back and seat, 100% nylon Titeweve. Color: #X6625 chocolate, polished chrome finish. Kevi Dual Wheel Cpt. casters.
C-3A	Metalstand #OSA Side chair with arms, sled base. Polished chrome finish. Fabric back and seat 100% nylon Titeweve. Color: #X1525 burnt orange.
C-3B	As per C3A except. Fabric: Red #X555.
C-3C	As per C3A except. Fabric: Kelly #X8525.
C-3D	As per C3A except. Fabric: Blue #X0625.
C4	AGI #826-4, swivel/tilt, high back desk chair, oak arms and base. Fabric back and seat. Uph: Grade 8, 100% nylon. Color: #18 brown, carpet casters.
C5	"Amseco" action stacker chair #8700, Plastic chair seat and back, polished chrome tubular frame. Color: Flame Red.
C5A	As per C5. Except. Black.
C5B	Amesco Dolly for 25 Action Stacker chairs #8690.
C6	Metalstand #OHSA. High back side chair with arms, sled base. Polished chrome finish. Fabric back and seat. 100% nylon velvet color: #9798 Terra Cotta.
C7	"Kinetics" #100/143 drafting stool Polished chrome base. Fabric back and seat 100% nylon. Color: KN-09 chocolate.
C8A	"Vecta-Colville #500781 Lounge/club chair. Upholstered in Nylo-Giant. 100% nylon. Grade: 6000. Size: 36"w x 34"d x 29"h. Fabric: Putty #243.
C8B	As per C8 except. Fabric: Camel #244.
C8C	As per C8 except. Fabric: Burnt Orange #233.
C8D	As per C8 except. Fabric: Terra Cotta #232.

Figure 7.10

FURNITURE AND FURNISHINGS SPECIFICATIONS
FOR (client)
SECTION 5

<u>Files</u>

Code   Description

F1   Office Specialty #86-362 FFL 2 drawer Lateral
                File Cabinet. Legal size. Fixed Front Doors
                with lock. Hanging File Folder Frames. Size:
                36"W X 18"D X 27.5"H. Color: #087 Antique
                White. Top: light oak laminate #PL- 36 color
                02.

F2   Office Specialty #86-365 FFl 5 drawer Lateral
                File Cabinet. Legal Size. Top Drawer to have
                retractable door, 4 fixed front file drawers
                with lock below. Hanging File Folder Frames.
                Size: 36"W X 18"D X 65"H. Color: #087 Antique
                White.

F3   Office Specialty #85600L, 5 drawer vertical file
                cabinet legal size with lock, hanging file
                folder frame. Size: 18"W X 28"D X 59"H. Color:
                #087 Antique White.

F4   Cole Steel #4030 5 drawer blueprint cabinet.
                Size: 40 7/8"W X 15 3/4"H X 28"D. Color: #44
                Desert Sand. Base to be specified as per
                requirements.

F5   Office Specialty #86-36-3FF 3 drawer lateral
                file, legal size, fixed front drawers with
                lock. Hanging File Folder Frames. Size: 36"W X
                18"D X 39 1/2"H. Color: #087 Antique White.
                Top: Light Oak Laminate #PL- 36 color 02.

F6   Office Specialty 86-36-60 Lateral Computer Print
                Out File with 4 L-36 EDP Drawer Fronts. Size:
                36" X 18" X 65"H. Color: #087 Antique White
                4-EDP-36 Inserts.

F7   Ulrich Fireproof Map File #3624. Size: 43"W X
                31"D X 35 1/2"H. Color: Beige.

F8   Stacor #TF-24 Mobile Tub Map File with reference
                table #R24. Size: 24" X 36" with a #24 cover
                for file tub.

F9   Murphy Fire King #2-21-C 2 drawer legal fire
                file. Size: 27 11/16"H X 23 3/4"W X 31 1/2"D.
                Color: White.

Figure 7.11

FURNITURE AND FURNISHINGS SPECIFICATIONS
FOR (client)
SECTION 5

Tables

Code	Description
T-1	Intrex Cube Table series Hexahedron #92010. Size: 24" X 24" X 21"H. Finish: 37 oak Lo Glare
T-2	Intrex Coffee Table series Deacon #91201. Size: 30" X 30" X 16"H. Finish: #37 Oak Lo Glare
T-3	Vecta Ginko #620-902 Cafeteria Table. Size: 36" square, 2" thick top. Black Vinyl Plastic Edge. Heat fused thermostat finished base, #18 Adobe, #27 Natural Oak Laminate top.
T4	Vecta-Ginko #665-906/907 conference table. Boatshaped 12'L X 4'W, 2" thick top, self edged, (2) 24" heatfused thermostat "T" Base legs in bronze +/12 with Oak Laminate Top. Color: #27 Natural.
T5	Office Specialty #25000 work table. Size: 60"W X 30"D X 29"H with #02 White Oak Laminate Top and Polished Chrome Legs.
T6	Intrex Drum Table seres #11050. Size: 15"D X 22"H. Finish: #37 Oak Lo Glare.
T7	Stacor thriftmaster #TH 3862 4 post steel drafting table. Tool and Shallow drawers. Finish: Hard baked light sand beige enamel. Size: 37 1/2" X 60" X 37".
T9	Intrex Series 92010 Hexahedron. Size: 30" X 30" X 21"H. Finish: #37 Oak, Lo Glare.
T10	Vecto-Ginko #607-903 Conterence Table. Size: 54" Diameter, 2" thick top self edged 2/42 heatfused thermostat base in bronze +/12, oak laminate top #27 Natural.
T11	Stacor #ST-50 Vertizontal V series drafting table. Size: 37 1/2" X 50" includes rear bookshelf, microplane board and pencil trough. Color: shell and stone grey with vinyl cover.

Figure 7.12

SPECIFICATIONS AND CODING FOR FINISHES AND FURNISHINGS

SPECIFICATIONS AND CODING FOR FINISHES AND FURNISHINGS

The finishes and furnishings portion of an interior design project includes all interior finishes, flooring, wallcoverings, and accessories. This chapter contains suggested methods for specifying and coding each one, with examples. For easy reference, all figures are located at the end of the chapter.

Carpet   The Instructions to the Bidders and General Conditions sections of the specifications for furniture, as discussed in Chapter 7, would also be basically applicable for carpet. Only minor changes in terminology are made with the General Conditions, except in the following categories:

- Inspection and Warehousing
- Delivery and Installation
- Guarantee
- Maintenance
- Testing

Typical changes/additions which can be made in the General Conditions for carpet are shown in Figure 8.1. The Materials and Workmanship section of the specifications might be rewritten as demonstrated in Figure 8.2. The actual material specifications (see Figure 8.3) should include, at a minimum, the information listed below:

- Content
- Width
- Pile Height
- Yarn ply
- Rows per inch
- Pitch
- Construction
- Face weight
- Total weight
- Backing
- Flammability

- Smoke density
- Fungicide
- Static control
- Wear guarantee

Window Treatment

There are so many variations of window treatment available that it might be helpful to utilize standard Instructions to the Bidders and General Conditions (see Chapter 7) with slight terminology modifications. Fabrication and installation methods and specifications for different types of window treatment can usually be obtained from manufacturers and suppliers. Each type may have unique requirements:

- Full height drapery, lined or unlined
- Full height sheers
- Sheers in the window or to the sill
- Curtains, lined or unlined, in the window or to the sill
- Black out shades with a shadow box
- Roll up shades
- Roman shades
- Austrian shades
- Bamboo shades
- Vertical blinds
- Slim line blinds
- Tinted glass (applied to window)
- Solar treatments
- Beaded curtains
- Swags and valances

Each type may require different hardware. For instance, pinch pleated draperies are hung on a track usually surface mounted to the wall; accordion or ripple pleated draperies have snap on hangers and can hang from a recessed or surface mounted ceiling track. The track snaps into a channel which is recessed into the ceiling and hung from the black iron. Sometimes a decorative rod is installed above the window and the drapery is simply slipped onto the rod and gathered. The draw-direction of the drapery is also important in determining the location of the pull cord. Draperies may open in the center or may be one way draw in either direction. The draw direction, opening, stack location, cord location, and type of drapery should be indicated on the window treatment plans.

Within each of the above window treatment categories are numerous variations. For example, vertical blinds are usually available with three inch, four inch, and five inch vanes. They are made of many possible types including fabric, plastic, metal, and solar materials. Vertical blinds are available with a top track only or top and bottom track. Each has its advantages and disadvantages and the selection often depends on the site conditions. The draw direction is also important for specifying vertical blinds. Figure 8.4 shows sample drapery specifications.

Wallcoverings

Wall treatment is usually selected by the designer. This information is specified on the finish plans whenever possible—this assures a more coordinated project. If applicable, the designer gives the information to the project architect or construction manager who has it incorporated into the working drawings. The interior wall finishes may warrant a separate drawing, possibly to be priced independently. Figure 8.5 is an example of a partial finish plan.

Materials and workmanship requirements may be included in the specifications or on the finish plans (see Figure 8.5). If the designer is responsible for obtaining bids, the standard specifications sections should be used.

Various types of finishes are listed below:
- Wallpaper: vinyl, paper, silk, grasscloth, fabric—installed by a paperhanger
- Paint: installed by painter
- Wood paneling: installed by a carpenter or cabinetmaker
- Stretched fabric wall: installed by a drapery contractor or upholsterer
- Hard surface for protection: installed by carpenters
- Acoustical: carpet by carpet installers; stretched fabric with insulation behind installed by carpenters or upholsterers; and acoustical tile installed by carpenters
- Mirror: installed by a glazier
- Rough plaster, stucco, or sand paint: installed by painter

Accessories

Accessories are usually included under general furniture and furnishings, therefore, the previously described specifications can still be utilized. Specifying desk accessories is difficult because there are so many small items to include. It is helpful to make packages of accessories. For example, accessory package code "X-01" for secretarial desks might contain the following:

Accessory Package X-01 (secretarial)

1 Wastebasket	(Mf.), (Catalog #), (Material), (Color)
1 Double letter tray	(Mf.), (Catalog #), (Material), (Color)
1 Memo box	(Mf.), (Catalog #), (Material), (Color)
1 Pencil cup	(Mf.), (Catalog #), (Material), (Color)
1 Ashtray	(Mf.), (Catalog #), (Material), (Color)

The number of packages ordered is the same as the quantity of secretarial desks on the project. Making packages of accessories simplifies the ordering process dramatically as well as the location charts. Figure 8.6 is a sample accessories specification if items are specified individually.

Accessories for hallways and lobbies should not be overlooked. Umbrella stands are necessary for carpeted entrances and coat closets. Ash urns for lobbies and corridors and at elevators are also included in this category. A special category includes tableware and linens, necessary for dining facilities. A wholesale representative may be consulted for specific requirements. The following items may be specified for dining areas:
- Flatware: stainless, silver plate, or sterling (including serving pieces)
- China: stoneware, bone china (including serving pieces)

- Glassware: glass, crystal
- Linens: table cloths or place mats and napkins
- Vases
- Ashtrays
- Candle holders
- Trays

Refurbishing

It is always amazing how good furniture can look after being refurbished. Refurbishing is also a major cost saver when compared with buying new furniture. A client might consider refurbishing if he has some good quality existing furniture.

Refurbishing work should be done with minimum inconvenience to the client. Sending out all of the conference chairs to be reupholstered at the same time may constitute a hardship (unless substitute furniture is obtained for the interim), but sending out half of them at a time would probably work. The designer and the client should determine an appropriate schedule for reupholstering. It may be necessary to wait until the client is in the new space for some of this work to be done. Refinishing and respraying are usually accomplished after the move-in. Both of these can be done at night. This eliminates the possibility of refurbishing furniture and then having it damaged in the move. The designer has to work closely with the client to determine the best procedure.

Scheduling

If there are 20 offices each containing two chairs to be reupholstered, the designer can send out 20 chairs at a time (one from each office). Most employees can do without a second guest chair for a few weeks. If the first 20 chairs are scheduled to be picked up two weeks before the move, these can be reupholstered and then delivered to the new location. This eliminates double handling of the chairs. The second batch of chairs can then be left behind by the mover for the reupholsterer to pick up, refurbish, and deliver to the new site. Figure 8.7 is a refurbishing schedule. The pick-up and delivery schedule would be established toward the end of the project.

Refinishing and Respraying

This work is often done after the physical move so the items will not be damaged in the move. Refinishing, if it is extensive, may be done off the premises in order to have a controlled environment in which to do the work. On the other hand, many refinishers work at night on the premises which saves money otherwise spent transporting the items.

Electrostatic respraying of steel files, desks, and cabinets is normally done at night. The metallic item to be painted is given an electrical charge so that the paint is attracted electrostatically.

Small Projects

For small jobs, detailed item specifications are still needed to get the right interior items ordered and delivered. The length of the general specifications, however, may be abbreviated. The Instructions to Bidders can be handled by letter or a verbal request for a quote. The General Conditions may be eliminated and the Materials and Workmanship sections generalized. For example, the following statement regarding carpet covers a lot of bases: "The contractor shall install the specified carpet utilizing the tackless method wall to wall over a 40-ounce pad complete and ready for use by the XYZ Company. All necessary adhesives, binder bars, and other incidentals shall be included so the installation will be a turn-key job."

The amount of protection the designer and client need on a particular project determines how detailed the specifications should be. The purpose of specifications is to protect all the parties involved in case of a legal dispute.

CHANGES TO GENERAL CONDITIONS FOR
CARPET SPECIFICATIONS

2-04   CONTRACTOR'S DRAWINGS

A. The Contractor shall prepare seaming plans, to properly locate, layout and install the entire work. Drawings are to be submitted for the approval of the Designer prior to the start of any installation. The Contractor is responsible for delivering and installing all carpet in its proper location.

1. All carpet will run in one direction.

B. Disapproved seaming plans shall be corrected and resubmitted until approved. Delay in submitting or revising seaming plans shall not constitute a reason for not complying with the delivery schedule.

1. All seaming plans must be complete in every detail, properly identified with the name of the project and dated. Each lot submitted must be accompanied by a letter of transmittal referring to the name of the project and location for identification of each item, and stating qualifications, departures or deviations from the Contract Documents if any. Each drawing shall have a clear space for the approval of the Contractor and the Designer.

2. Submit one (1) reproducible sepia transparency and one (1) blueprint of each drawing, until final approval is obtained.

3. In checking the seaming plans, the Contractor shall verify all dimensions and field conditions and shall check and coordinate with other trades whose work is related thereto, as required for proper and complete installation of the work. The Designer will review and approve seaming plans for design; however, approval of such drawings shall not relieve the Contractor, subcontractor, manufacturer, or supplier from responsibility for any deficiency that may exist or from any departure or deviations from the requirements of the Contract Documents unless he has, in writing, called the Designer's attention to such deviations at the time of submission, nor shall it relieve the Contractor from responsibility for errors of any sort in seaming plans or schedules, nor from responsibility for proper fitting of the work, nor from the necessity of furnishing any work required by the Contract Documents which may not be indicated on seaming plans when approved. The Contractor shall be solely responsible for the quantities of each carpet.

4. The Designer will check the seaming plans with reasonable promptness and will return them to the Contractor with the

Figure 8.1

Designer's stamp and signature applied thereto, indicating the appropriate action to be taken.

5.   As the work progresses the Contractor shall keep a complete and accurate record of all approved changes or deviations from the Contract Documents, including the work as actually installed. All such changes shall be neatly and correctly shown on a print of the Drawing affected. This record set of prints of the Drawings, seaming plans and Specifications shall be kept at the job site for inspecton by the Designer and Owner.

2-10   WAREHOUSING

A.   Local warehousing will be performed by the Contractor as required without additional cost to the Owner unless the Contractor is required to store any materials more than 30 days after the agreed upon installation date due to delays in construction of Owner's building or other delays required by Owner. The Owner shall be obligated to Contractor for storage charges subsequent to agreed date on the basis of Contractor's actual costs for the warehousing space utilized for such purpose. Costs shall in no event exceed public warehousing rates or charges.

B.   The Contractor shall provide an off-site storage facility for all overage and usable scraps of carpet, which shall be marked by carpet code and color for future use and repair.

C.   Overage shall be the property of the Contractor until required for installation or repair.

D.   The Contractor shall have complete responsibility for cartage of goods and for management and control of his off-site storage facility.

E.   Carpet that is stored must be turned at least once a month to prevent permanent "roll marks".

2-11   DELIVERY AND INSTALLATION

A.   Contractor shall submit for each project, the names, addresses, and qualifications of proposed subcontractors, workrooms, and installers for the Owner's and Designer's approval.

1.   All material shall be installed by mechanics experienced in this trade.

B.   The Contractor shall furnish a competent superintendent at the site of the work as may be

Figure 8.1 (continued)

171

necessary for the proper coordination and supervision of the work and to ensure completion of the work in accordance with all requirements of the Contract Documents and to the entire satisfacion of the Designer. The superintendent shall receive all deliveries, check for transit damage and supervise the installation.

C. The Contractor shall work with the Designer to develop a delivery schedule compatible with the construction schedule and shall be responsible for all such delivery and installation dates. The Contractor shall furnish sufficient forces to ensure completion of work in time.

1. The Contractor shall make arrangements with each manufacturer for preferential production and shipping schedules.

D. Work shall be performed during reqular working hours except that in the event of emergency, and when required to complete the work within the time stated in the Contract, work may be performed on night shifts, overtime, Sundays, and holidays when written permission to do so has been obtained from the Owner.

E. The Contractor shall be responsible for securing a schedule for the availability of spaces forming the scope of Contract obligation from the General Contractor so as to assure the completion of work within the required time. No material shall be shipped to the job site except in accordance with delivery schedules approved by the Owner and Designer.

F. Deliveries shall be made according to the Owner's requirements. Contractor shall cooperate with the General Contractor in arranging schedules for deliveries, available unloading space and the use of building elevators and facilities. Owner will provide free access to elevators.

1. In the event the Contractor needs space for the storage of materials and/or equipment required in connection with the work, the Contractor shall store such materials and equipment in such space as is specifically authorized and provided by the General Contractor on behalf of the Owner or by the Owner for such purpose, and in no other space or location, in, on, or about the building.

2. The Contractor shall not enter or have access to any space in the building in order to perform the work without first having given timely notice to

Figure 8.1 (*continued*)

172

the Owner so that the necessary arrangements may
be made and the Owner's permission obtained.

3.   The Contractor shall be responsible for verifying
     and confirming that all carpets proposed are of
     such a size (length and width of roll) that they
     can easily be brought into the building and to
     their specified locations by means other than
     special hoists.

G.   In the event of unforeseen delays of any nature that
     would prevent delivery according to schedule, the
     Designer shall be notified by telephone in order to
     attempt to make adjustments in the elevator schedule.
     It is understood that the Contractor's schedule will
     not be permitted to upset the day's established
     delivery schedule to accommodate irregular deliveries.
     Deliveries that cannot be completed within the time
     reserved shall be made at the end of the schedule day
     at Contractor's expense even though it becomes
     overtime.

H.   If any materials arrive on the job without proper
     identification, it shall be the responibility of the
     Contractor's representative to identify them or they
     will be returned to the Contractor at the Contractor's
     expense.

I.   The Contractor shall remove daily all packaging and
     scrap materials from the work area. Large scraps shall
     be removed and stored in the Contractor's warehouse
     for future repair work.

J.   Installed material shall match the approved Designer's
     flooring plans and the carpet seaming plans.

K.   After the carpet is installed all protection shall be
     removed and all surfaces thoroughly cleaned to the
     complete satisfaction of the Owner.

L.   The surface upon or against which carpet is to be
     installed will be provided by others and will be left
     ready for installation of carpet. The General
     Contractor, immediately prior to the installation of
     carpet, shall prepare all subflooring to be thoroughly
     dry, broom clean, free of droppings, grease, oil
     paint, varnish, sprinkled cement, plaster or any
     material that would interfere with the proper
     installation of carpet. (The Contractor shall not be
     responsible for the irregular contour of the floor to
     be covered.)

Figure 8.1 (*continued*)

M. The telephone and electrical pedestal floor outlets
    may be installed after the carpet is laid. (All
    telephone and electrical floor outlets shall be opened
    in advance of carpet installation.) The Contractor
    will cooperate with the General Contractor and related
    sub-contractors.

N. All cutting of carpet for floor outlets, pull boxes
    and trench duct covers shall be the responsibility of
    the Contractor. It shall be the Contractor's
    responsibility to develop a method of installing
    carpet over pull boxes and trench duct covers so as to
    allow carpet sections to be easily released for access
    to the under floor ducts, and replaced.

O. Security measures as required to protect stored or
    installed materials shall be provided by the General
    Contractor or the Owner. Completed areas shall be
    closed to traffic until the Designer and Owner have
    inspected and accepted all materials in such areas.

P. Owner will designate a representative authorized to
    accept or reject on behalf of Owner material delivered
    and installed by Contractor. All materials shall be
    considered finally accepted only after inspection by
    and written approval is obtained from the Owner or
    duly assigned representative.

Q. The manufacturer's recommended procedures for
    installing carpet shall be closely followed.

2-12   CLEANING UP AND MAINTENANCE

A. The premises and the areas in which the work is
    performed shall be maintained in a reasonably neat and
    orderly condition by the Contractor and kept free from
    accumulations of waste materials and rubbish during
    the progress of the work and until completion thereof.
    Remove all cartons, wrappings and other flammable
    waste.

2-36   TESTING

    At Owner's discretion, three (3) samples taken at
    random from carpet rolls will be sent to an
    independent testing lab for verification of
    specificatons.

Figure 8.1 (continued)

CARPET INSTALLATION, MATERIALS AND WORKMANSHIP

CARPET SPECIFICATIONS
FOR
(CLIENT)

SECTION 3
INSTALLATION, MATERIALS AND WORKMANSHIP

3-01   GOVERNMENTAL REGULATIONS

A.   Materials and their installation shall comply with all requirements and restrictions in reference standards of all governmental agencies, Federal, State and Local, and any other agencies that have jurisdiction.

3-02   INSTALLATION

A.   Installers must be arranged for and provided for by the Contractor as the Contractor's subcontractor. Installer must have a minimum of five (5) years experience in the installation of materials similar to those specified herein. The Contractor shall assume responsibility for all of the work referred to in this Contract, including final installation and cleaning of all carpet at the job site. The Contractor and subcontractor(s) are responsible for supplying the manufacturer's materials and products specified by the Designer as necessary to complete the work.

1.   The Contractor's or subcontractors' employees whose work or conduct is unsatisfactory to the Owner or Designer, or who are considered by the Designer to be deficient in the skills required by the work or otherwise objectionable, shall be dismissed from the work immediately upon notice from the Designer.

2.   Materials shall be installed only under the supervision of the Contractor's qualified technical representative.

3.   All work shall be installed by skilled workpersons, especially trained in this type of work by the manufacturer or his authorized representative.

Figure 8.2

175

B. The Contractor must meet with the Designer and the Owner's representative, and manufacturer(s) necessary, at the project site to review the installation, procedure and coordination with other trades prior to the delivery and installation of all carpet covered under this Contract.

C. The carpet installer shall cooperate with the electrical contractor and the telephone contractor and conform with the electrical and telephone requirements. All cutting of carpet for floor outlets and Trench Duct Covers shall be the responsibility of the carpet installer.

D. All carpet shall be installed over padding wall-to-wall with tackless stripping.

   1. Tackless stripping shall be securely fastened to the floor with best quality cement. Tackless stripping shall then be firmly nailed to concrete floor with steel nails at intervals of not more than eight inches. If the condition of the floor is such that steel nails will not hold securely in the concrete, the Contractor shall first drill and plug the floor before installing the tackless stripping.

   2. Tackless stripping shall be set at a correct distance from the base to permit the proper turning down and holding of the carpet.

E. All seams are to be taped in keeping with standard practice.

F. Where carpet terminates at door opening and resilient tile begins a half threshold shall be utilized.

G. All rubbish, wrapping paper, selvages shall be removed from the job site each day.

H. Manufacturer's recommendations for use of floor cement, adhesives, seam cement, pin tape and cross joining shall be adhered to at all times.

Figure 8.2 (continued)

I.   Spots and smears of floor cement and seam cement shall be removed immediately.

3-03   MATERIALS AND WORKMANSHIP

A.   All materials shall be new and both workmanship and materials shall be the very best of its respective kind of each of the serval trades employed. All work shall be executed in strict accordance with dimensional design requirements of the drawings and specifications and under direct supervision of competent representatives of the Contractor.

B.   The work shall include all labor, materials and services required including proper adhesives, seam cement, edge strips, carpet reducing strips etc., sufficient to produce a completed installation.

C.   Materials shall be delivered in the original packages, containers or bundles bearing the name of the manufacturer.

D.   All manufactured articles, materials and equipment shall be installed, stored, used and cleaned in accordance with the manufacturer's written specifications or instructions unless hereinafter specified to the contrary. The Contractor shall furnish to the Designer two copies of these specifications or instructions before proceeding with the work. Manufacturer's manuals shall include certification or laboratory test reports as may be required to show compliance with these specifications. Indicate by transmittal form that a copy of each instruction has been transmitted to the Installer.

E.   Any work, materials or carpet which does not conform to these requirements or the standards set forth in the Contract documents may be disapproved and condemned by the Designer, in which case it shall be removed and replaced by the Contractor as provided in Article 2-16, CORRECTION OF WORK BEFORE FINAL PAYMENT.

Figure 8.2 (continued)

     F.   Padding shall be as manufactured by General Felt Industries (GFI), Quality: Diplomat, 40 oz. rubberized hair and jute or approved equal.

     G.   Tackless strip shall be as manufactured by the Roberts Company or approved equal.

     H.   Half thresholds shall be as manufactured by Roppe Rubber Co. burnt umber #10 or approved equal.

     I.   Vinyl floor tile shall be as manufactured by Azrock Floor Products, quality: Custom Cortina, color: #V-824 Sesame, or approved equal.

3-04   MAINTENANCE

     A.   The Contractor shall furnish the Owner detailed printed instructions for janitoral maintenance procedure for maximum life and appearance of the carpet. Maintenance and patching methods, proper equipment, cleaning chemicals and materials, methods of application, spotting techniques and maintenance program, based on the amount of traffic for each area of the Owner's building.

     B.   All other services which may be required by Owner in connection with the carpet furnished by the Contractor after installation will be provided by the Contractor at the regular hourly rates prevailing for the trades required. Contractor will provide such service at the Owner's convenience through its own mechanics or subontractors employed by it. Replacement carpet and installation materials required other than those to be furnished by the Contractor under guarantee will be provided at the same rates as the basic products sold under these General Conditons.

          1.   Restretching as required for new carpet shall be provided under the one (1) year guarantee at no charge to the Owner.

3-05   OVERAGE

     A.   Maximum overage that will be considered by the Owner shall not exceed 3% of the total carpet requirements.

Figure 8.2 (continued)

CARPET SPECIFICATIONS
FOR
(CLIENT)

SECTION 5
CARPET SPECIFICATIONS

Carpet
5-01

Code   Description

CPT-1   Manufacturer: Stratton Industries Inc.
          Quality: -   Corporate Park II
          Color: -   CPX-1605 Java Beige
          Construction: -   Tufted, Bulky Cord Loop Pile
          Yarn: -   Woolex (55% Wool/45% Acrylic)
          Ply: -   3 Ply
          Gauge: -   1/4" (6.35 mm)
          Stitches/6 IN.   -   45
          Pile Height: -   13/32" (10.32 mm)
          Yarn Weight: -   50 oz. per sq. yd. (2034 g/m^2)
          Primary Back: -   Patchogue Plymouth's POLYBAC/AS)
          Secondary Back: -   Jute (Manufacturer reserves the
                                    right to use jute or ULTRA-LOC as
                                    equal secondary backing)
          Total Weight: -   98 oz. per sq. yd. (3323 g/m^2)
          Static Control: -   Permanent static control to reduce
                                    static build up
          Width: -   12 ft.
          Carpet Treatment: -   Treated with SCOTCHGUARD brand
                                    carpet protector.

          Flammability:
            ASTM E-85   -   Class B (Flame Spread rating of 75
            (Steiner Tunnel)   or less)
            ASTM E-648   -   Carpet only - meets National
            (Flooring   Bureau of Standards recommended
            Radiant   limits for commercial (Class II)
            Panel)   occupancies (critical radiant flux
                                    of .22-.45 watts/cm^2)
            ASTM E-662   -   Smoke density rating of 450 or
            (NBS Smoke   less in flaming mode
            Chamber)
            FF 1-70   -   Meets Methenamine Pill Test

Figure 8.3

DRAPERY SPECIFICATIONS

Section 4
Installation, Materials and Workmanship

3-01   GOVERNMENTAL REGULATIONS

    A. Materials and their installation shall comply with all requirements and restrictions in reference standards of all governmental agencies, Federal, State and Local and any other agencies that have jurisdiction.

3-02   INSTALLATION

See Figure 8.2 and use the information in 3-02-A-1-2-3 and B.

3-03   MATERIALS AND WORKMANSHIP

    A. See Figure 8.2 and use information in 3-03-A.

    B. All materials shall be used in accordance with manufacturer's directions unless the Designer issues written instructions to the contrary.

    C. All work to be executed under direct supervision of competent representatives of the Contractor.

    D. All items necessary to a complete drapery installation are to be included:

        1. All headings (flexible crinoline)

        2. All hooks and fastenings

        3. All carriers, pulleys, cords, floor pulleys

        4. Bottom weights

        5. All ceiling tracks (unless otherwise noted in specifications and drawings)

        6. All lining fabrics

        7. All casement and drapery fabrics

        8. Installation of all casement curtains, draperies and hardware

        9. Any additional materials necessary for fabrication and/or installaton

    E. All fabric shall be of the approved manufacture, type and quality specified and shall be free of any irregularities in weave or materials.

Figure 8.4

1. Contractor shall be responsible for inspection of fabric for defects and shall immediately bring to the attention of the Designer all faults and defects of material before fabrication is begun, so that a proper substitution can be made.

2. Three (3) cuttings of each fabric received are to be sent to the Designer for approval.

F. All approximate yardages and finish lengths are taken from Drapery Plan and are subject to final physical measurements by Contractor at job site. Contractor shall be responsible for all final yardage requirements. Contractor shall field check all dimensions before commencement of work and shall be fully responsible for same.

G. All casements and draperies shall be made so that they hang straight and true, and shall be tabled and squared a true 90 degrees to the warp thread at top and bottom of each width.

H. All seams shall fall within the folds.

I. All printed patterns shall be perfectly matched.

J. Complete work is to be clean and free of imperfections. All work is to be long folded after completion. Any completed work which is to be stored shall be stored in dust-proof cartons or bags.

K. All work is to be completely pressed before installation.

L. All draperies shall be fully hung out so as to eliminate the need for alteration after installation has been made.

M. All drapery shall clear the floor, convector or sill by no more that 1/2".

N. All draperies are to be steamed at the job site after they are hung to eliminate all fold and wrinkle marks.

O. Work failing in any manner to comform to the requirements of the Drawings and Specifications shall upon order of the Designer be promptly removed from the premises and replaced with the proper workmanship and material at the expense of the Contractor.

P. Refer to Designer's drawings for unlined casement locations (and direction of draw) and stationary lined

Figure 8.4 (continued)

drapery panel locations.

Q. Casement fabric shall be, code DR-1:
    Design Tex, Fabric #DT-2892
    Stable Loc Classic, Content: 67%
    verel 20.5% rayon,7.5% flax, 5% nylon
    Color: White/Flax. 48" wide,
    inherently flameproofed.

4-01 UNLINED CASEMENT CURTAINS

A. All casement curtains shall be unlined using a minimum
    of 150% additional fullness. Fullness shall be
    computed by adding 12" per opening for overlap and
    returns, and then multiplying by 250%.

B. No less than one half width of fabric may be used in
    any casement panel.

C. All hems shall be twice turned to contain three (3)
    thicknesses of fabric. Front hem shall be 2", back hem
    shall be 1". Bottom hem shall be 4", and bottom of cut
    edge shall be turned to bottom of drape so no shadow
    line appears. Side hems shall be made in same fashion.

D. Hems shall be blind stitched so that no stitches are
    visible on the face of the fabric. A mercerized
    preshrunk three cord cotton thread shall be used.

E. Heading shall be 4" wide with 4" wide washable
    stiffening, Pellon or equal doubled back to make four
    thicknesses of fabric including the stiffening.
    Heading shall be French pinch pleated.

F. All widths shall be hand cut on the thread, and all
    selvages shall be trimmed. Widths of fabric shall be
    joined by means of a serging process with an overlock
    stitch.

G. Casements shall be anchored to the wall or mullion at
    the back of each panel by means of an appropriate hook
    in the wall and ring in the drapery both top and
    bottom. Casements shall clear the sill or floor by no
    more than 1/2".

H. Bottom hems shall be properly weighted with covered
    corner weights provided at the front and back of each
    panel at each seam.

I. Hardware for unlined casements: (or approved equal)
    Track - Kirsch (heavy duty) #9035
    Nylon track glide - Kirsch #9400
    Overlap master track glides - Kirsch #9452
    Ball bearing track pulley - Kirsch #9327
    Cord tension pulley - Kirsch #9923.

Figure 8.4 (continued)

4-02   LINED DRAPERY STATIONARY PANELS

   A. All Lined Drapery Panels shall contain a minimum of
       300% additional fullness, based on the overall width
       shown on the Designer's Drapery Plan, and not on the
       width of the window. The draperies shall be pleated to
       standard 100% fullness (using a 4" space and a 4"
       pleat) and stacked back by hand to finished width at
       the time of installation.

   B. Draperies shall be lined with a good quality sateen,
       (minimum count of 104 x 64). Lining shall be hand
       tacked to face of fabric at each seam and at least
       once between the seams, the entire length of the
       drapery. Lining shall be attached at bottom by means
       of woven cotton swing tapes, 6" long, every 18".

   C. Front edge of drapery shall have a 3" turnback, which
       shall be interlined with flannel, hand tacked every 2"
       the length of the drapery. Lining shall be attached to
       this turnback.

   D. All hems shall be twice turned to contain three thick-
       nesses of fabric. Front edge shall be as outlined in
       Paragraph C above. Back edge shall be 1". Bottom hem
       shall be 4" and shall be weighted with #715 continuous
       lead tape weight. Bottom of cut edge, with tape weight
       attached shall be returned to bottom of drape so no
       shadow line appears. Front edge shall also contain a
       1-1/2" square cloth covered lead weight. Heading shall
       be 4" interlined with washable stiffening, Pellon or
       equal.

   E. Fabric shall be hand cut "on the thread". Selvages
       shall be trimmed and widths joined by means of a
       serging process with an overlock stitch. Hems shall be
       blind stitched and no stitches shall be visible on the
       face of the fabric.

   F. Hardware for Lined Drapery Panels:
               Track: Grant 2201
               End Stop: Grant 2205
               Carriers: Grant 2203

       Supply the above, plus any and all parts necessary and
       recommended by Manufacturer for efficient, trouble
       free operation.

   G. Lined Drapery Stationary Panels Codes:
               DR-2: Fabric to be selected
               DR-3: Fabric to be selected
               DR-4: Fabric to be selected
               DR-5: Fabric to be selected

Figure 8.4 (*continued*)

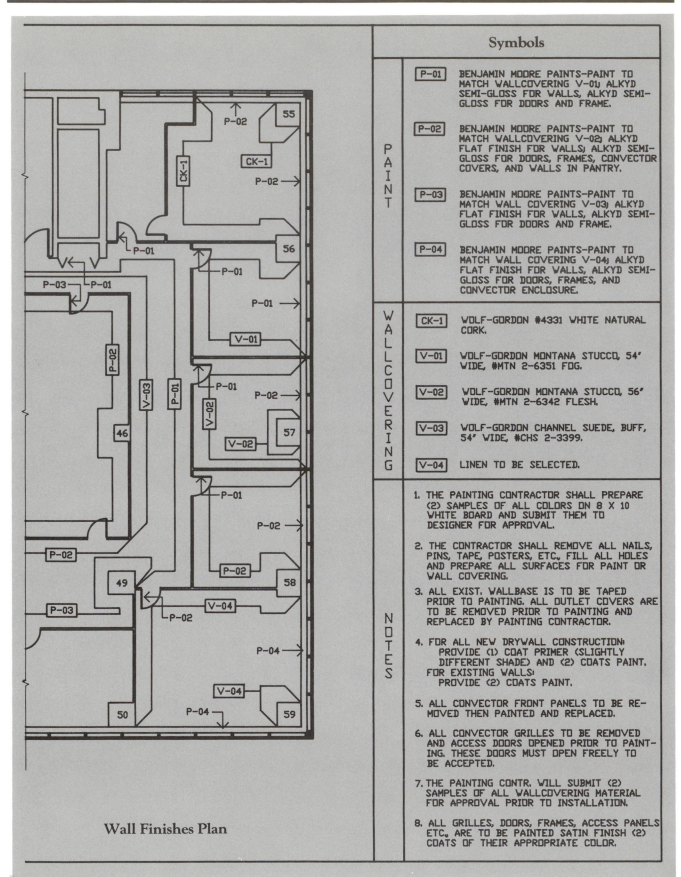

Wall Finishes Plan

Symbols

Figure 8.5

<u>Desk Accessories</u> (if individually specified)

Code	Description
X1	Desk Tray, Rubbermaid, #2510 Legal size. Color: dark brown, plastic
X2	Stacking posts for desk trays, Rubbermaid #2512 set of 2. Color: dark brown
X3	Memo box, Rubbermaid #2517, 4x6. Color: dark brown plastic
X4	Calendar Base, Rubbermaid, #2516 book-type. Color: dark brown plastic
X5	Calendar refill, Everready #B1-E717, Calendar re-fill pages for use with book style calendar base.
X6	Waste basket, Rubbermaid, #2956, rectangular 14.5" x 10.5" x 15"H. Color: dark brown plastic
X7	Ash tray, Rubbermaid #2509. Color: dark brown plastic
X8	Pencil cup, Rubbermaid #2520. Color: dark brown plastic
X9	Smokador legal letter tray #1801E(MC). Size: 10"x 15" x 15"h, mirror chrome finish, black interior
X-10	Smokador memo box #105(MC). Size 4" x 6" x 1.25"h, mirror chrome finish, includes paper.
X-11	Smokador book style calendar #1809(MC), Size: 9" x 5.625" x 2.375"h, mirror chrome finish, includes calendar.
X-12	Smokador ashtray #AT-118(MC). 5" diam mirror chrome finish with black interior.
X-13	Smokador pencil cup #1815(MC), 3" diam x 3.5"h mirror chrome finish, black interior.

Figure 8.6

REFINISHING SCHEDULE

Item	Quan.	Present Room No.	Reupholstery Fabric Code	Refinishing On Upholstered Pieces	Deliver to New Room No.
C-2	10	23-04 (conf.)	AB	Polish wood frames	26-15 (conf.)
C-4	4	23-05 (Mr. Bates)	AE	Refinish wood frames	26-16 (Mr. Bates)

Figure 8.7

BIDDING
AND PURCHASING

BIDDING AND PURCHASING

The main purpose of inviting bids for furniture, finishes, and furnishings for a project is to obtain the best possible price for the items to be acquired. The theory is that if a contractor knows he is competing with others, he may "sharpen his pencil", and take a few extra percentage points off his price in order to win the contract. If the project is large, there will almost always be many interested parties.

If the specifications have been properly written, the designer will be comparing prices for equal items and work. Then, the decision to be made is who can do the best job for the lowest price. If the specifications have not been written properly, incomparable bids will be received, and additional clarification from the vendors will be necessary. Or, a selected vendor may supply or install an incorrect item.

The designer should not simply accept the lowest bid. In most government work the low bidder must be chosen, however, the private sector does not have this requirement. The object is to choose the best combination of price, quality, and expertise.

Bid Package

The bid package, at this point, is almost complete. The Instructions to Bidders, the General Conditions, the Installation, Materials and Workmanship, and the Item Specifications have been written (see Chapters 7 and 8). To finalize the bid package, drawings must be complete. The bid pricing forms are added to the specifications along with a cover letter, or Invitation to Bid.

Proposal Forms
Sample proposal forms are shown in Figures 9.1 through 9.5. They consist of the proposal, unit pricing forms, statement of contractor's business organization, guarantee, and agreement. These forms must be filled in by each competitor and, when completed, constitute his bid. These forms are shown for illustrative purposes only. Such documents have legal implications. An attorney should be consulted concerning the preparation and use of such documents.

In the example proposal, the furniture is priced net FOB the factory. An estimated percentage should be added to cover the warehousing, delivery, and installation, which is billed at cost. The furniture can also be bid *delivered and installed* complete and ready for use. This is generally preferable unless the project is very large and shipments can be arranged directly from the plant to the job site. In this case, the client will save money by ordering FOB the factory, as double handling in and out of a local warehouse is eliminated.

The unit pricing forms may simply be copies of the item specification sheets with spaces for the prices to be filled in. Figures 7.10, 7.11, and 7.12 are examples of item specifications for furniture. The example shown in Figure 9.2 is for unit prices for carpet, but illustrates general bidding procedures for all categories.

Invitation to Bid

An example of a letter to the various bidders, or Invitation to Bid, is shown in Figure 9.6. The designer must now decide which vendors should be given the opportunity to bid.

Design firms, as well as clients, often have established bid lists of contractors considered acceptable. The designer may have to perform research necessary (i.e., Dun and Bradstreet reports, trade references, etc.) to ensure that all bidders are qualified to perform the work. This is especially important when the project is out of town and the designer is not familiar with the contractors bidding the work. If the project is very large, up to ten contractors may be invited to bid. Usually, however, three to five are sufficient. More than ten becomes unwieldy when performing a bid analysis.

Bid Receipt, Opening, and Analysis

The client may prefer that the designer receive, open, and analyze the bids. The designer would then present recommended choices. On the other hand, the client may want to be intimately involved with the selection process. He may want the bids received and opened in his office at a formal meeting. The bids might later be analyzed by the client's purchasing department.

No matter who receives the bids, it is important, when necessary, that the staff is alerted to expect sealed bids which are not to be opened. The envelopes should be time and date stamped as proof that they were received before the bid deadline. Late bids are usually rejected unless the contractor can prove extenuating circumstances beyond his control. If one bidder is given an exception, all bidders must be notified of the extension, and the client must delay the bid opening.

The bid opening is the point at which the designer discovers the accuracy of his budget. Once the bids are opened and the totals for each contractor noted, the client usually gives the bids to the designer to review and analyze. It is possible to do the analysis at the bid opening if the project is small, but this process is often too time consuming and tedious to accomplish at a large meeting. (Usually, a lot of people want to attend the bid opening out of curiosity.) The analysis is done later often by one person who has the time and resources to do so effectively and efficiently.

Analyzing bids means reading the proposals in detail to see if there are any deviations from the specifications. Sometimes, for example, a contractor substitutes one furniture manufacturer for another. The designer or the person analyzing the bids must determine if the substituted item is actually "equal" to the original item specified. In addition, a bidder might take exception to a clause or two in the bidding documents and exclude something from his proposal. In this case the reviewer must analyze the importance of what was eliminated, if it would have to be provided by someone else, and what it would cost.

Bid Negotiation and Award

Sometimes a client wishes to negotiate with the two or three lowest or most favorable bidders separately to see what, if any, additional concessions they will make.

Award Notification and Rejection

It is easy to write a letter saying "Congratulations, you are the winner of the bid for furniture and furnishings for the ABC Company". It is quite another to write a rejection letter. No one ever wants to do this, as it is seen as unpleasant. However, the designer should realize that this is a normal business procedure. An example of a rejection letter is shown in Figure 9.7. It is also considered a courtesy that the letter state the vendor who received the contract award. This prevents the other vendors from calling to ask who the successful bidder was.

Acceptance

The client must sign his acceptance on an Agreement form (an example is shown in Figure 9.5). If there are any agreed upon exclusions, variations, or changes, they should be so noted. Sometimes, a client wishes to have a covering purchase order in addition to the agreement. This is attached to the agreement and issued to the successful contractor as the formal document which starts the work.

Purchasing by Client or Designer

Sometimes a client does not wish to solicit bids. He may have a favored contractor(s) and may wish to simply negotiate the contract(s). This is his choice. If awarding each of the categories of the entire project to one or a few vendors, this is easily handled by the contracts previously described, with covering purchase orders and attached item specifications. On the other hand, sometimes a client purchases items directly from the manufacturers whenever possible. This usually generates a great deal more paperwork for the designer as the furniture/carpet dealer usually performs this work. Unfortunately, this extra paperwork is usually the responsibility of the designer, since he is frequently expected to purchase all items at a "designer's discount". Occasionally, the client can can get designer discounts extended to the corporation so that purchase orders can be written on the corporation's forms, but the designer may still be responsible for getting the orders issued.

Purchase Orders

A purchase order lists all the relevant information about the item or items being ordered. The designer should be able to copy the necessary information from the item specification sheets. If all items were thoroughly researched for the specifications, this should be a relatively easy task.

A sample purchase order form is shown in Figure 9.8. The terms and conditions, usually printed on the back of the purchase order, are shown in Figure 9.9. Purchase orders are often multiple copy forms of different colors. There is a copy for the vendor and one each for the originator, purchasing department, accounting department, and receiving.

The designer should be sure that every purchase order is signed by the client. This is extremely important. The order may have been written on the designer's letterhead, but the client is ultimately responsible for payment.

If the designer is ordering some items and paying the invoices, deposits are usually required by the manufacturers. The client therefore pays a 30% to 50% deposit up front on all orders either to the designer or the manufacturer. If a manufacturer requires a deposit, either the designer's or the client's check is usually acceptable. This method eliminates the problem of cash flow for the designer. Sometimes the vendors are willing to bill the client directly. In this case the designer is not involved in the payment of invoices at all, however, he should still verify all invoices and make payment recommendations.

Bill of Materials

A bill of materials can be considered a short order form. If, for example, the client has a national furniture standard that is bid out once a year, the specifications and prices are already established. Ordering, then, is simply accomplished using established codes and short descriptions of each item. A covering purchase order for a project can be issued with the bill of materials (BOM) attached. An example of a bill of materials is shown in Figure 9.10.

Verify Order Acknowledgments

It is imperative that confirmations from manufacturers are verified against the original orders. There may be a "typo" or a very different delivery date than that required. Such a mistake can mean that the wrong item was ordered or that the item will not be shipped on time. Moving day may be met with the unwelcome surprise of an incorrect or late item unless the acknowledgments are verified as early as possible.

If, upon checking the acknowledgments, an error is discovered, the vendor is notified immediately. If it is early enough in the project, the mistake can be corrected or an item substituted until delivery of the ordered item can be made. Acknowledgments are subtle. They do not call to attention any discrepancies from the order. They may have different shipping dates than were originally specified, which can be crucial to the project. If there is a furniture dealer working on the project, for example, he should check all acknowledgments and report any discrepancies to the designer and the client. If he does not check these documents in a timely fashion, a problem may be discovered too late.

Changes and Cancellations

Changes are, unfortunately, all too familiar to the project manager. Although he tries to keep these to a minimum, there are always some changes. Change order forms, such as that shown in Figure 9.11, should be used for all changes. These forms are used for whatever change is necessary: quantity, color, finish, fabric. It is up to the vendor to notify the designer of any charges for making the change. The designer must also make sure that the changes are actually made. Depending on the time frame, the item may not be cancelled without suffering a penalty. If an item is already in the production line, the manufacturer may not accept a cancellation or may accept it only with a restocking charge. The designer's leverage in this case may depend on the volume of work ordered. In any case, the client must be notified, in order to reconsider the decision based on this information. A typical purchase order cancellation is shown in Figure 9.12.

Expediting Deliveries

Tracking shipments and deliveries may be one of the most frustrating tasks that a contract administrator has to do. There are many things in this process that the project manager has no control over that can go wrong. For example, quality control rejects the item, the teamsters go on strike, or the truck driver takes two days off en route. The only thing the designer can attempt to do is to stay on top of the situation. The designer accomplishes this by periodically checking with the manufacturer and dealer to track the progress of the items. It is always better to alert the client to a potential problem early. This way, if items are going to be delivered late, it is possible to anticipate and prepare for delays.

Sometimes the problem is on the client's end; the space is not always built on schedule. If the furniture contractor has fulfilled his requirements and acquired all the necessary furniture on time, he is not liable for storage charges beyond the contract date. Usually, the contractor will make the warehousing arrangements for any items to be stored. The designer should negotiate, on behalf of the client, a monthly charge for storage if there is a long delay in construction.

Inspection of Delivered Items

The designer must inspect all furniture and furnishings when delivered to ensure that the items match the specifications. If there is any problem such as damage, incorrect finish, or incorrect fabric, the designer must immediately notify the furniture contractor. It is the contractor's responsibility to correct the problem.

Approving Invoices

Invoices are usually sent to the designer for approval prior to being sent to the client for payment. This is important because nothing should be paid for that is not one hundred percent correct. It is much easier to get something corrected when payment is withheld than it is when the invoice has been paid in full.

Sometimes 80% to 90% of a total contract is approved to be paid pending final checking and approval. Final checking and approval may take several months. For this reason, it is difficult to get interiors punch list items completed after the bulk of the work is done. No one ever wants to return to clean up the details. However, until these details are taken care of, some portion of the final payment should be withheld or these small items will *never* be finalized.

PROPOSAL FOR
GENERAL FURNITURE AND FURNISHINGS SPECIFICATIONS
FOR
(CLIENT)

Proposal submitted by _____ for all work required to complete the general furniture and furnishings requirement for _____(client)_____ dated _____, in accordance with the terms and conditions of the Contract Documents referred to therein. Terms used in this Proposal have the meanings assigned to them in the Contract Documents.

We the undersigned, having carefully examined the conditions affecting the work and being thoroughly familiar with the Bidding documents, do hereby offer to furnish all labor, materials, tools, equipment, plant, machinery, supplies, specified insurance, taxes and services necessary to complete the general furniture and furnishings requirement for _____ (client)_____. This Proposal is in accordance with the Specifications dated _____ including Addenda Numbers _____, _____, _____, and _____, issued prior to the date of opening of Proposals.

The individual material prices upon which this Proposal is based are attached.

Our estimate of the additional percentage of materials cost for freight, delivery, installation and warehousing is ____%. All such charges will be billed to the Owner at our cost. Supporting bills of lading and installation time sheets will be submitted as back up with our invoices.

UNIT PRICES:

The undersigned agrees that the unit prices submitted on the Proposal attachments entitled, "Unit Pricing Forms" submitted herewith, as outlined in the Instructions to the Bidders, will apply in the event that changes involving additions to or deductions from the work to be performed under the Contract are authorized by a written change order from the Designer to the Contractor, and that the unit prices are based on providing all furniture FOB factory in accordance with the requirements of the Contract Documents. The undersigned agrees to support the unit prices until _____(date)_____.

For any additional materials not included in the original Specifications, the undersigned agrees to submit a quotation upon request.

COMPLETION TIME:

The undersigned agrees that if awarded a Contract for the work bid for herein, work will commence under the Contract on the date the first

Figure 9.1

purchase order issued by the Owner is received, and the undersigned will efficiently, diligently and expeditiously conduct the work in a manner consistent with the Construction Schedule as established by the project architect and construction manager and as approved by the Designer.

The undersigned further agrees to cooperate with the General Contractor and with any other General Furnishings contractors to assure proper coordination in the installation of all items in a timely fashion.

REQUIRED INFORMATION:

The undersigned agrees to furnish for the Owner's approval the following information, complete and in the form prescribed, all within the stipulated times. The undersigned further agrees that failure to so furnish such information will be construed to be an unauthorized deviation by the undersigned from the Contract Documents, and as such will be cause to withhold any and all payment which may become due the undersigned.

    A. WITH SUBMISSION OF PROPOSAL:

        1.   Statement of Contractor's Business Organization, as attached to the Proposal.

        2.   Financial Statement, dated no earlier than January 1, (year).

        3.   Guarantee as attached to the Proposal.

    B. WITHIN TEN (10) DAYS AFTER THE NOTIFICATION OF CONTRACT AWARD

        1.   Performance Labor and Material Payment Bond, as outlined in the Instructions to the Bidders, Section 1-10.

        2.   Manufacturers' guarantees to the Contractor for materials and workmanship as outlined in the General Conditions Section 2-21.

        3.   Signed Agreement as outlined in the General Conditions.

In anticipation of compliance with the "GENERAL CONDITIONS" the undersigned hereby submits the names of the following surety companies

Figure 9.1 (continued)

who, subject to the approval of the Owner, would write the Performance and Payment Bond in the event he is awarded this Contract.

_____

_____

_____

Unless it is sooner rejected the Proposal made hereby shall be irrevocable until 12:00 noon, (day), (date) .

The undersigned hereby represents and warrants that the execution and delivery of this Proposal have been duly authorized by all requisite action, corporate or otherwise, of the undersigned and such execution and delivery will not result in the breach of any of the terms, conditions or provisions of any instrument to which the undersigned is a party or by which it may be bound, and the person signing this Proposal in behalf of the undersigned has full authority to do so.

If this Proposal is submitted by an individual or partnership, execute the following form:

Dated _____day of _____, 19___

_____
            Contractor

By:_____
Title

If this Proposal is submitted by a corporation, execute the following form:

Dated _____day of _____, 19___

_____
            Contractor

(SEAL)
Attest

_____   By:_____

_____   _____
                                        Title

Figure 9.1 (*continued*)

UNIT PRICING FORM
CARPET SPECIFICATIONS
FOR
(client)

Carpet Code	Quan. S.Y.	Description	Unit Prices	Total Cost
CPT-1	_____	Stratton, Corporate Park II, Java Beige	_____	
		Material Price Per Square Yard	_____	
		Padding Price Per Square Yard	_____	
		Labor and Sundries Per Square Yard	_____	
		Freight Per Square Yard	_____	
		Delivery Per Square Yard	_____	
		Warehousing Per Square Yard	_____	
		Per Square Yard Price Delivered and Installed	$_____	$_____
CPT-2	_____	Stratton, Devon Hall, White Sands	_____	
		Material Price Per Square Yard	_____	
		Padding Price Per Square Yard	_____	
		Labor and Sundries Per Square Yard	_____	
		Freight Per Square Yard	_____	
		Delivery Per Square Yard	_____	
		Warehousing Per Square Yard	_____	
		Per Square Yard Price Delivered and Installed	$_____	$_____
CPT-3	_____	Bigelow, Executive Privilege, Suede Tan	_____	
		Material Price Per Square Yard	_____	
		Padding Price Per Square Yard	_____	
		Labor and Sundries Per Square Yard	_____	
		Freight Per Square Yard	_____	
		Delivery Per Square Yard	_____	
		Warehousing Per Square Yard	_____	
		Per Square Yard Price Delivered and Installed	$_____	$_____

Figure 9.2

STATEMENT OF CONTRACTOR'S BUSINESS ORGANIZATION

This statement is attached to and is part of the Proposal for General Furniture and Furnishings Specification for _____(client)_____.

Submitted by:_____

_____

If the Proposal is submitted by an individual, execute the following form:

(a)   Firm Name _____
(b)   The Owner and Official Address _____
        _____
(c)   Number of Full-time employees _____
(d)   Name of non-owned installation co. _____

_____

If the Proposal is submitted by a partnership, execute the following form:

(a)   Firm Name _____
(b)   The Owner and Official Address _____
        _____
(c)   Names of all of the partners:
        _____   _____
        _____   _____
        _____   _____
(d)   Number of Full-time employees _____
(e)   Name of non-owned installation co. _____

_____

If the Proposal is submitted by a corporation, execute the following form:

(a)   Corporate Name _____
(b)   State in which incorporated _____
(c)   List the States in which you are authorized to do business
        _____
        _____
        _____
        _____

Names and titles of officers authorized to sign contracts.

_____   _____
                                            Title
_____   _____
                                            Title
_____   _____
                                            Title

(d)   Number of Full-time employees _____
(e)   Name of non-owned installation co. _____

Figure 9.3

GUARANTEE
TO
(client)
FOR
GENERAL FURNITURE AND FURNISHINGS

Contractor: _____

Client: _____

Period of Guarantee: <u>1 year from acceptance of the work</u>

In accordance with the provisions of Article 2-21 of the General
Conditions for the above mentioned project, the undersigned hereby
furnishes its guarantee in favor of Owner/Designer against defects in
materials and workmanship for the period of this guarantee and otherwise
with respect to all of the Contractor's obligations set forth in such
Article 2-21.

Dated this _____ day of _____, 19____

_____
Contractor

[S E A L]

ATTEST: By_____

By_____   Title_____

Figure 9.4

AGREEMENT
BETWEEN
<u>(successful contractor)</u>
AND
<u>(client)</u>
GENERAL FURNITURE AND FURNISHINGS

THIS AGREEMENT, made this ___ day of _____, Nineteen Hundred and ___,

by and between _____,

hereinafter called the "Contractor", and _____<u>(client)</u>_____,

hereinafter called the "Owner".

<u>WITNESSETH:</u>

      First: The Contractor and its successors for the
consideration hereinafter set forth, hereby agrees with the Owner, that
he/she will properly and sufficiently furnish and provide all materials
and equipment, and perform all labor and do all else required under the
terms and conditions of the Contract Documents referred to below in order
to complete the Furniture and furnishings requirement for _____
<u>(client)</u>_____.

      Second: If the Contractor shall properly and faithfully
fulfill this Contract, the Owner will pay the Contractor in a timely
manner in accordance with the terms and conditions of the Contract
Documents identified in the Third paragraph hereof, including, without
limitation, the Contractor's Proposal dated _____
itemizing the unit prices listed on the Unit Pricing Forms
dated _____,19__;

      Third: This Agreement for the General furniture and
furnishing base shall embrace and include all the Contract Documents
which are as follows:

    Contract Documents and
    Items Specifications, dated _____, 19

    Addendum No. 1,   dated _____, 19

    Addendum No. 2,   dated _____, 19

    Addendum No. 3,   dated _____, 19

Figure 9.5

      Proposal including Unit Pricing Forms, Statement of Contractor's
      Business Organization and Guarantee
                 dated _____, 19

      Notification of Award of Contract, dated _____, 19
      all of which are attached hereto, and made a part hereof.

All such Contract Documents are incorporated by reference as if fully set
forth herein.

The Contractor hereby represents and warrants that the execution and
delivery of this Agreement have been duly authorized by all requisite
action, corporate or otherwise, of the Contractor and such execution and
delivery will not result in a breach of any of the terms, conditions or
provisions of any instrument to which the Contractor is a party or by
which it may be bound, and the person signing this Agreement on behalf of
the Contractor has full authority to do so.

THIS AGREEMENT, shall be a ____(state)____ contract and shall be
interpreted and construed in accordance with the law of ____(state)____.

IN WITNESS WHEREOF, the parties have executed this Agreement in four
counterparts, the day and year first above written.

                        _____
                                  (client)

                        By_____

                        Title _____

ATTEST:

_____

                        _____
                               (Contractor)

                        by_____

                        Title _____

ATTEST:

_____
      (Secretary)

Figure 9.5 (continued)

INVITATION TO BID

_____(Date)_____

_____(Vendor)_____

____(Vendor Address)____

_____"_____"_____

RE: ____(Project)____

Dear _____:

        You are invited to submit a proposal for the general furniture
and furnishings requirement for _____(client)_____ at _____
(address of project)____. It is anticipated that a move-in on or
about _____(date)_____ will be possible based on the current
construction schedule.

        Enclosed for your use and reference, are two bid packages
consisting of:

                Instructions to the Bidders
                General Conditions
                Installation, Materials and Workmanship
                Particular Conditions
                Item Specifications
                Proposal forms
                Drawings dated _____

        There will be a general pre-bid meeting on ____(day)___,
____(date)____ at _____(location)_____ at __(time)__ to
review any questions you may have about the project.

        Your sealed bid should be submitted in triplicate to the
(client or designer) at _____(address)_____ no later
than 12:00 noon on __(day)__, _____(date)_____ .

Very truly yours,

(Contract Administrator)

cc: (client)
     (designer)

Figure 9.6

BID REJECTION LETTER

_____(Date)_____

_____(Vendor)_____

____(Vendor Address)____

_____"_____"_____

RE: _____(Project)_____

Dear _____:

   We wish to thank you for your recent quotation on the requirement for General Furniture and Furnishings for _____ (client)_____ at _____(location)_____.

   After careful consideration of all bids received, we regret to inform you that your bid was not accepted. The contract has been awarded to _____.

   Please be assured your company will be considered for any future requirement we may have for work of this type.

Very truly yours,

(Contract Administrator)

cc: (client)
     (designer)

Figure 9.7

Purchase Order

Req. No.	Originator	Approval	Remarks		Inv. No.	Account No.

Doe Interiors

Purchase Order No.

To

Job No.

Important: P.O. number must appear on all invoices, shipping notices, bills of lading, express receipts, packages and packing slips.

Four copies of invoice required.

Note: ☐
See standard shipping and billing instructions attached.

Ship To

Bill To

Date	Delivery Required	Terms	FOB/Delivered/Other	Routing

Quantity Ordered	Quantity Received	Description	Unit Price	Total Price

Mark For _____ By _____
Doe Interiors

Approved by _____

_____ Attach Cutting to Confirmation

This Purchase Order is placed with the seller on the understanding that shipment of the goods covered by this Purchase Order or acceptance of this Purchase Order in any other way shall constitute acceptance of all the provisions on the face and back hereof and that the entire contract between the buyer and the seller with respect to the said goods will be as stated herein.

Figure 9.8

Purchase Order Conditions

All shipments must be made as specified in this purchase order in standard commercial containers capable of safe delivery to the Buyer at the lowest lawful transportation and insurance rates. Commodity descriptions which produce the lowest lawful freight charges must be shown on bills of lading. Packing slips must be included in all packages. Original bill of lading must be mailed with invoice on date of shipment.

Goods rejected on account of inferior quality or workmanship will be returned to you and charges for transportation both ways plus labor, reloading, trucking, etc., shall be for your account. Goods rejected are not to be replaced except upon receipt of written instructions from us.

You are to assume all liability for all damage or injury caused by or to your workmen while engaged in the execution of this order.

Time is of essence of this purchase order. If the Seller fails to deliver the goods covered by this purchase order at the time or times called for delivery (whether for causes beyond its control or otherwise) the Buyer may, at its option, either cancel the delivery or require delivery as soon as the Seller is able to deliver. Failure of the Buyer to accept delivery if due to any cause beyond its reasonable control shall not constitute a default by the Buyer.

Acceptance of goods furnished pursuant to this purchase order, shall be subject to inspection and approval by the Buyer at the Buyer's premises to which the goods are to be delivered. At the Buyer's option, the goods may be rejected by the Buyer and returned for full credit or replacement at the Seller's expense if found to be non-conforming or not as warranted, not withstanding pre-payment.

The Buyer may sign for the receipt of shipments and may pay the Seller's invoices before arrival and/or inspection of the goods to avail itself of cash discounts without thereby waiving any of the provisions of this Purchase Order.

The Buyer will not pay charges other than those indicated on the face hereof. The Seller represents that the prices charged for the goods covered by this purchase order are not and will not be in excess of the maximum prices thereof established by law. All prices shown are net unless otherwise specified. Cash discounts will be calculated from the date an acceptable invoice is received by the Buyer or from the date the goods arrive at the Buyer's designated plant, whichever is sooner.

The Seller warrants that it has good title to the goods delivered pursuant to this purchase order, free and clear of any liens or encumbrances, that the goods will conform to the specifications and description appearing on the face of this purchase order and that they will be mercantable and free from defect in design, workmanship and material.

The Seller warrants that the goods delivered pursuant to this purchase order do not infringe any patents and in case the goods are used by the Buyer as recommended by the Seller or for a purpose for which they are regularly sold by the Seller, that such use will not infringe any patents. The Seller agrees to indemnify and save the Buyer and its customers harmless against any losses, claims, costs, damages or expenses resulting, directly or indirectly from a breach of the foregoing warranties.

The Seller warrants that the goods delivered pursuant to this purchase order will have been manufactured and produced and all work done will have been performed, in accordance with the requirements of applicable federal, state and municipal laws and regulations.

The contract resulting from acceptance of this purchase order is to be construed, and its performance governed by the laws of the state in which this order originates as shown by the address printed on the face hereof. Acceptance of this offer must be made on its exact terms and if additional or different terms are proposed by the Seller, Seller's response shall constitute a counter-offer. This purchase order and the contract resulting from its acceptance is not assignable voluntarily or by operation of law. You are to assume all liability for all damage or injury caused by or to your workmen while engaged in the execution of this order.

Figure 9.9

Bill of Materials

Date _____

Type _____   Page _____ of _____

Location _____   Requisition No. | | | | | |

Prepared By _____   Project No. | | | | | |

Quan.	Code	Description	Unit of Measure	Unit Price	Total
			Total	$	$

Figure 9.10

CHANGE ORDER

Client: _____   Change Order Number: _____
        _____   Date: _____
        _____   Project No.: _____
                                       Contract for: _____

To: (Contractor): _____   Purchase Order No.: _____
    _____
    _____

_____
You are directed to make the following changes in this contract:

_____

Contract to date is $_____.

The Contract Sum will be (increased)
    (decreased) (unchanged) by this
    amount $_____.

The new Contract Sum including this
    Change Order will be $_____.

The Contract Time will be (increased)
    (decreased) (unchanged) by   _____Days.

The Date of Substantial Completion as of the date of this Change Order
therefore is _____, 19____.

Authorized by:
_____   _____   _____
  (designer)   (contractor)   (owner)
by_____   by_____   by_____
   (date)   (date)   (date)

NOTE: Not Valid until signed by both the Owner and Designer.
Signature of the Contractor indicates his agreement herewith, including
any adjustment in the Contract Sum or Contract Time.

cc: Owner
       Designer
       Contractor

Figure 9.11

PURCHASE ORDER CANCELLATION

Cancellation No. _____   Date: _____

To: ____(Contractor)____   Re: Purchase Order No. _____

_____   Dated: _____

_____

Please cancel the items listed below:

Quantity	Description	Unit Price	Total Cost

Please acknowledge cancellation of these items by returning the attached copy signed with your acceptance.

DATE _____ BY _____Designer

DATE _____ BY _____Owner

DATE _____ BY _____Contractor

Figure 9.12

CHAPTER TEN

PLANTS

C H A P T E R   T E N

PLANTS

In selecting plants, the designer is looking for an effect that will complete the space and complement the design scheme. The foliage color, size, shape, height, spread, and outline are all important aesthetic considerations. But the environment in which these plants will live must also be considered or the client will end up with a lot of dead plants. If the designer is not practical at this stage, he can create a maintenance nightmare. Most designers and clients prefer plants such as Ficus Benjamina, Ming Aurelia, Schefflera, or other difficult to maintain plants to produce special visual effects, but they are simply not practical in many situations. Compromises may be necessary. If the designer does not have a working knowledge of plants he should consult with a local plant services contractor.

The designer should have a working knowledge of plants, in order to choose plants which will thrive in the office environment over time. The main features of some plants are flowers (i.e., Spathephylum); others have variegated leaves. A Warnecki has green and white spikey leaves while a Dracena Masangeana (commonly known as a corn plant) has green and yellow leaves. Pothos are available in green and white, green and yellow, and all green. There are also some red and green striped leaf plants. All of these variations can be used to create different, interesting effects in the space.

The amount of light a plant requires determines whether or not it will survive in an office environment. Some plants require a lot of light and/or water while others need very little of either. In selecting interior plants, the designer must know how much and what kinds of light the proposed space will have (daylight, fluorescent, incandescent).

The solar orientation of the space is also an important factor. A southern exposure provides much more direct sunlight than either an eastern or western exposure. All of these provide more sunlight than a northern exposure. Some plants require direct sunlight (i.e., a Ficus Benjamina) and will not live in northern diffused light. Daylight must also be considered because the lights in most offices are turned off over the weekends and holidays. If a plant is placed in an interior conference room that is not used often during the week, it will have to be a plant that can grow almost in the dark (i.e., Dracena Massangeana). The designer should check with a local nursery to see what types of plants are available and what is recommended for specific conditions.

Specifications

Regardless of whether the plant contract is to be bid or negotiated, a set of specifications is necessary. This enables all parties to work with the same information. Figure 10.1 is a sample specification for interior planting. As can be seen in this example, details about plant height and width, trunks, stems, branches or canes, foliage, root system, and growing medium are included in the specifications. Exact procedures for installation of the plants in decorative planters must be included. A schedule of individual plants selected, their location, height, and the planter or container to be used are also included in the specifications.

Lease or Buy

For accounting reasons, some clients wish to lease plants on a monthly basis instead of purchasing them. In the long run, however, buying the plants outright and paying monthly for a maintenance and replacement guarantee can be less expensive than leasing. Some clients wish to start out leasing and then eventually buy plants a few years after the move.

The specification shown in Figure 10.1 requests two alternate quotations; one for leasing the plants with a maintenance and replacement guarantee, and one for purchase of the plants with a maintenance and replacement guarantee. This enables the client to compare the two quotations and determine which one is preferable.

Maintenance of Plants

Plants must be watered at least once a week. The amount is determined by a moisture meter inserted in the soil to check the moisture level. Plants must also be fertilized, sprayed, pruned, trimmed, rotated, and polished on a regular basis. In addition, the containers should be cleaned at least once a month.

Employee's own plants should be included in a comprehensive maintenance plan. These are frequently brought from home gardens where the environment is less controlled and, for this reason, often have bugs or diseases. It is possible to infest or infect many plants from one infested or infected plant. It is, therefore, advantageous to include inspection of employee plants in the maintenance contract. These will then be sprayed as needed to prevent the spread of a particular pest or disease.

Replacement of Unhealthy Plants

All plants should be inspected and inventoried quarterly. Any plants that look scruffy should be replaced. The plant contract should include replacement of unhealthy and unsightly plants (not just dead ones). Dead or unsightly plants are to be replaced with comparable plants. Sometimes another species is substituted for the original selection if there has been a continuing problem maintaining the original selection. Certain plants (i.e., Scheffleras, Pittisporums, and Ficus Benjaminas) are relatively difficult to maintain. Scheffleras tend to get spider mites and all three drop leaves and need particular care. Exotic plants such as Camelias or orange trees are also difficult to maintain. A Ficus Benjamina goes into shock and drops leaves any time it is moved. Other plants are much easier to maintain such as Warnecki, Janet Craig, Dracena Massangeana, Erumpens, Grape Ivy, Pothos, and Cissis. These varieties do not go into shock if they are somewhat neglected. They tend to last longer and look better longer than the others.

Planters

Most nurseries provide decorative containers for the client if desired. If the client doesn't want to make the investment up front for planters, it is usually possible to rent them along with the plants. In the long run, however, this can be more expensive than purchasing the planters initially.

Artificial Plants

Designers, in general, do not like anything artificial. Plastic plants have long been considered extremely tacky and are pet peeves of many designers. Dried flowers or other types of dried plants such as grasses and cat-o-nine tails can, however, be quite handsome. These arrangements work well in areas with no daylight and intermittent artificial light.

Silk flowers, when of good quality, bring out color accents in a space. They work well in a conference room or reception area. Silk flowers are a good alternative to cut flowers, which have to be changed each week and represent an on-going expense. Beaded flowers serve the same purpose.

Cut Flowers

Live flowers are wonderful on a reception desk or on tables in the executive dining room. They are seasonal and add sparkle, warmth, and beauty to a room. Arrangements can be made with a local florist to deliver flowers weekly. If the client is going to have live flowers, the designer should specify the vases. If there will be no live flowers, the designer does not have to include vases in his accessory package.

SPECIFICATIONS FOR INTERIOR PLANTING
FOR
(CLIENT)
(DATE)

I. Introduction

    A. It is the intent of ___(client)___ to install interior landscaping for its new facilitiy at _____ per the Plant Schedule dated _____.

    B. Delivery and installation is required on or about _____.

II. General Requirements

    A. The Contractor shall provide two alternate quotations: one for leasing the plants with a maintenance and replacement guarantee and one for purchase of the plants with a maintenance and replacement guarantee.

    B. Contractor's quotation for lease or purchase of the plants shall include:

        1. Conditioning and preparation

        2. Delivery and installation

        3. Labor and materials

    C. Contractor's quotations for maintenance and replacement guarantee shall include:

        1. All fertilizing, spraying, pruning, trimming, polishing, cleaning of containers and watering of plants.

        2. Inspection and replacement of any plants that are unhealthy or unsightly with comparable plants.

        3. Service of each plant as required, but no less than once a week. Contractor shall provide a maintenance schedule for approval by the Designer.

        4. Removal of any foreign particles from inside of containers.

        5. Addition of redwood bark where and when necessary.

        6. Rotation of plants to expose all sides to light.

        7. Application of pesticide, herbicide and fungicide to

Figure 10.1

any plant, including employees' personal plants to control possible spread of a particular disease.

8. Clean up of any area directly affected by the above listed services.

9. Plant care to commence immediately upon installation of plants.

D. The location of Contractor's growing and conditioning site shall be indicated and shall be open to inspection by representatives of the Designer. The Designer reserves the right to select, inspect and approve all plants prior to delivery and installation.

E. All of the plants purchased or leased by ___(client)___ shall be very healthy, in a vigorous growth condition, heavily branched and densely foliated.

F. Plant sizes and varieties shall be in accordance with the Plant Schedule dated _____.

G. All plants, including foliage, trunks, root systems and soil mass must be free of pests and pathogens.

H. All plants must be shade conditioned or climatized.

I. All plants shall be free of weeds.

J. Planters have been specified for purchase by __(client)__. Refer to Plant Schedule for sizes.

III. Plant Specifications

A. Plant Height

1. Overall height as specified in the plant schedule shall constitute a minimum requirement. Outstanding branches not visibly part of the foliage massing are to be discounted from the height measurement.

B. Plant Width

1. Overall plant width shall produce a bushy appearance. Outstanding branches not visibly part of the foliage massing shall be discounted from the width measurement.

C. Trunks, stems, branches or canes

1. All trunks or canes must be well formed, sturdy, well rooted and self supporting. Staking is unacceptable.

Figure 10.1 (*continued*)

    D. Foliage

        1. Must be rich green, turgid, substantially erect and
            free of blemishes.

        2. Must be substantially free of dust and residues from
            spraying.

    E. Root System

        1. Must be well developed.

        2. Must be well distributed throughout the container,
            such that the roots visibly extend on all sides to
            the inside face of the growing container.

        3. Must afford firm support and insure physical
            stability of the plant parts above the soil.

        4. Must support life systems required to produce
            vigorous healthy growth.

    F. Growing Medium

        1. Shall provide thorough drainage and satisfactory
            aeration of roots.

        2. Shall provide adequate mositure and nutrient
            retention as may be necessary to promote vigorous but
            controlled plant growth.

        3. Shall be of sufficient density to insure the
            stability of the plant.

        4. Shall be free of chemical residues which could be
            harmful to people.

        5. Soil level in the growing container shall be a
            minimum of 90% of the container height.

IV. <u>Planter Installation Procedure</u>

    A. All plants shall be installed in the plastic nursery
        container in which the plant was grown.

    B. Peat moss is to be placed on the bottom of the decorative
        planter and used as filler around the nursery container.
        The inner planter is to be supported so that its top is
        not more than 1-1/2" below the top of the decorative
        planter. Redwood bark shall be placed on the top surface
        to conceal the nursery container.

Figure 10.1 (*continued*)

216

V. <u>Installation of Plants</u>

    A. Contractor shall deliver all plants to the building and install according to the plans.

    B. It shall be the Contractor's responsibility to place all plants in their designated location according the plans.

    C. Contractor shall clean up all debris caused by the installation and shall be charged for any damage to the building or furnishings.

VI. <u>Client's Responsibility</u>

    A. Client agrees that plants will not be moved without the Contractor's consent; that the Contractor will not be responsible for damage to the plants by client's personnel, or resulting from extreme changes in temperature or prolonged absence of light.

    B. Client will provide a place with natural, adequate light, for storage of tools; soil, peat moss and bark chips in small amounts; extra planters; insecticides and sprayers; watering cans; and plants being nurtured back to health.

PLANTER SPECIFICATIONS

Planter Code	Size	Finish
MS-6	Smokador polyethylene #PL-1615 planter, size: 15.5"dx 14.5"h. clear	White
MS-7	Smokador Polyethylene #PL-1918P planter, size: 19"d x 18"h. clear	White
MS-8	Smokador #PL-8007A (MA) planter, size: 8"d x 7"h, lipless	Mirror Aluminum
MS-9	Smokador #PL-1414A (MA) planter, size: 14"d x 14"h, lipless	Mirror Aluminum
MS-10	Smokador #PL-1815A (MA) planter, size: 18"d x 15"h, lipless	Mirror Aluminum

Figure 10.1 (*continued*)

PLANT SCHEDULE
First Floor

Iden. No.	Area	Quantity	Height	Plant Type	Planter Code
1	Dir. Cable Cast	1	3'0"	Warnecki	MS-6
2	Cable Cast Open Area	1	3'6"	Janet Craig	"
3	" " " "	1	"	" "	"
4	Dir. Direct Sales	1	"	" "	"
5	Direct Sales Open Area	1	3'0"	Warnecki	"
6	" " " "	1	4'0"	"	"
7	West Reception Rm.	1	7'0"	Ficus Benjamina (Natural)	MS-10
8	" " "	1	5'0"	Marginata	MS-9
9	" " "	1	1'6"	Grape Ivy	MS-8
10	West Conf. Rm.	1	6'0"	Massangeana	MS-6
11	Outside West Conf. Rm.	1	3'0"	Janet Craig	"
12	Oustide West Toilets	1	3'0"	Warnecki	"
13	Bldg. Mgr. Clerk	1	3'6"	Janet Craig	"
14	Conf. Rm. #009	1	3'0"	Warnecki	"
15	Outside Training Mgr.	1	3'0"	Janet Craig	"
16	Computer Operations	1	5'0"	Massangeana	"
17	Commercial Insertion	1	5'0"	"	"
18	Cafeteria	1	5'0"	Eurumpens	"
19	"	1	3'6"	Janet Craig	"
20	"	1	4'0"	" "	"
21	Outside Personnel Mgr.	1	3'0"	Warnecki	"
22	Dir. Human Resources	1	3'0"	Janet Craig	"
23	East Reception Rm.	1	6'0"	Kentia Palm	MS-10
24	" " "	1	3'0"	Janet Craig	MS-9
25	" " "	1	1'6"	Pothos	MS-8
26	West Conf. Rm.	1	5'0"	Massengena	MS-6
27	Outside West Conf. Rm.	1	3'0"	Warnecki	"
28	Outside West Toilets	1	3'0"	Janet Craig	"
29	Customer Interview	1	5'0"	Eurumpens	"
30	Outside Cust. Interview	1	4'0"	Warnecki	"
31	Conf. Rm #022	1	5'0"	Eurumpens	"
32	Traffic	1	5'0"	Massangeana	"
33	PM/DM	1	5'0"	Kentia Palm	"
34	" "	1	4'0"	Warnecki	"
35	" "	1	3'0"	"	"
36	V.P. & Gen. Mgr.	1	6'0"	Ming Aralia	MS-10
37	" " "	1	3'0"	Janet Craig	MS-9
38	" " "	1	1'6"	Cissis	MS-8

Figure 10.1 (*continued*)

CHAPTER ELEVEN

ARTWORK

ARTWORK

Artwork adds the final, important touch to the design scheme. For this reason it is often the last thing selected for a project. This provides a more integrated interior when the project is finished. The artwork concept, however, should be determined early in the project. The actual selections are made later. Sometimes, for example, the designer has a concept of a logo wall or a supergraphics accent wall from the beginning of the project, but doesn't actually detail it until the project is well under way.

The most important space in a building or an office is the entrance/reception area. This area conveys a first impression of the office, which can influence how a visitor feels about the company and the rest of the space. In designing this area, the designer aims to captivate the visitor on his first glimpse of the offices and give him an idea of the firm's personality.

Selection of Artwork

Most artwork is selected from a pool of art available from local and well-known artists. The designer first chooses a theme for the art so that the space will have an integrated and coordinated appearance. This may mean a concentration on modern masters, impressionists, floral designs, or old English hunt scenes. These questions must next be answered.

- Who is going to locate and select the artwork?
- For what purpose is the art intended?
- What medium will be utilized?

Consultant/Select Own

Some clients prefer to select their own artwork. (Perhaps the chairman's wife is involved in local artistic circles and wants to be involved with the selection process.) Regardless of whether or not the client is involved, this is an extremely time consuming process. If the designer is being paid on an hourly rate, the fee can go up considerably—trips to galleries take a considerable amount of time.

It is often advantageous to hire a consultant who is familiar with the wide and varied market. The consultant usually knows where to locate specialized items, which can save countless frustrating hours spent by the designer who is not an expert in this field. An art consultant usually provides a quotation for all artwork framed. He frames the art if it is not already framed. He may also have a system where he has one price for a framed poster, and one for a framed print, instead of individual prices. This greatly simplifies budgeting and selection for the designer. Figure 11.1 is an example of an artwork proposal.

ART WORK PROPOSAL

Station: 16-1   Reception:
Artist: Hayslette   Size: see below   Medium: Lithograph/Dyptich
Title: "Night River One" Cato. No: L-73008   Value: $ see below
       (158/230)

                          with:
Artist: Hayslette   Size: 29 1/2"X80"**   Medium: Lithograph/Dyptich
Title: "Night River Two" Cato. No: L-43004   Value: $ 900.00 **
       (158/230)

Station: 16-2   Corridor:
Artist: Bleach   Size: 26 1/2"X22"*   Medium: Lithograph
Title: "Transient Park" Cato. No: L-42002   Value: $ 290.00 *
       (A/P)

Station: 16-3   Corridor:
Artist: Stritch   Size: 44"X30 1/4"*   Medium: Acrylic/Paper
Title: Untitled (Unique) Cato. No: AP-22006   Value: $ 375.00 *

Station: 16-4   Conference Room:
Artist: Bleach   Size: 29 1/2"X42"*   Medium: Lithograph
Title: Untitled (A/P)   Cato. No: L-75002   Value: $ 640.00 *

Station: 16-5   Corridor:
Artist: Stritch   Size: 44"x30 1/2"*   Medium: Acrylic/Paper
Title: Untitled (Unique) Cato. No: AP-22002   Value: $ 375.00 *

Station: 16-6   Corridor:
Artist: Stritch   Size: 44"X30 1/2"*   Medium: Acrylic/Paper
Title: Untitled (Unique) Cato. No: AP-22003   Value: $ 375.00 *

Station: 16-7   Executive Sec'y:
Artist: Pessic   Size: 29 1/2"X23"*   Medium: Lithograph (Unique)
Title: "Mountain Bends" Cato. No: L-72804   Value:$ 375.00 *
       (1/1)

Station: 16-8   Corridor:
Artist: Bleach   Size: 30"X22"*   Medium: Lithograph
Title: "Baltic Winds #1" Cato. No: L-43008   Value: $ 290.00 *
       (A/P)

Station: 16-9   Executive Sec'y:
Artist: Mala   Size: 32"x25 1/4"** Medium: Unique Collage
Title: Untitled   Cato. No: C-62704   Value: $ 375.00 *

Station: 16-10   Corridor:
Artist: Stritch   Size: 44"X30 1/4"*   Medium: Acrylic/Paper
Title: Untitled (Unique) Cato. No: AP-22001   Value: $ 375.00 *

Station: 16-11   Elevator Lobby:
Artist: Coignand   Size: 24"X19 1/2"** Medium: Lithograph
Title: Untitled/742/   Cato. No: L-43333   Value: $ 500.00 *(+)
       (26/75)

*   The sizes noted, and the values quoted, are for the works of art
     appropriately (*) mounted to art size; (**) tipped; (***) matted; and
     framed (*) in section-aluminum frames; *(+) – with security kits for
     security installation.

Figure 11.1

Purpose of Artwork

Quality art collections are escalating rapidly in value and are turning out to be sound investments. For this reason, more and more corporations are investing in original artwork. If the client is interested in an investment, a budget must first be established. It is easy to spend a great deal of money in this category. The designer should be careful to select enough art to fill the space before the budget is exhausted. Otherwise, the entire budget could easily be spent on four items, when twelve are actually needed.

Conversely, the client may want artwork to simply brighten and finish the space. In this case, posters, prints, and lithographs are specified. These are not as expensive as original art, and generally do not appreciate in value any faster than inflation.

Medium

There are many possible mediums for art from which to select. The designer may want sculpture in certain locations; for example, in an atrium planting area or reception area. Sculpture is usually placed on a pedestal unless it is tall enough to stand alone. There is usually special lighting to accent the work. Most other types of art hang on the wall.

For framed items, the designer must choose from oils, prints, lithographs, photographs, etchings, engravings, and posters. Collages also may be framed, but tend to be large. Tapestries are becoming increasingly popular and are usually commissioned. Stained glass is another popular accent. Artifacts from other civilizations can be quite dramatic (i.e., a Navajo rug or an African battle mask). Shells, rocks, and geodes can also add just the right decorative touch.

Buy, Rent, or Loan

The designer has the option to rent or borrow artwork instead of actually purchasing it. This means there is no initial investment, which may be preferable to some clients. With this option, it is possible to change the art every three to six months, which adds variation to the space. The client can always buy the artwork later when it fits in with his budget.

Dealers

Art dealers, consultants, and galleries are often willing to lease artwork to the client. They will put a presentation together from which the designer and the client may select. If the items chosen are unframed, the dealers usually frame them. The complexity of the service the client desires determines the monthly rental charge. If the artwork is rotated or changed every three months, the service will cost more than if the art is to be considered permanent.

Local Artists

Some corporations strongly support local galleries and artists. They will, accordingly, want to select art from local sources. Local art councils and consultants can assist in locating such people.

Local artists are more than happy to have their work displayed. If an artist is just starting out, he may be willing to loan the client some artwork in exchange for the publicity. The only problem arises when the artist has a show and needs some of the pieces from the client's office. For this reason, the rental agreement should stipulate that the artist will provide a substitute piece until the original work can be returned.

Museums

Often museums have extra artwork in their archives. They may be willing to loan the client the artwork in exchange for a contribution. The contribution comes out of a different financial "pocket" and may benefit the client as a tax deduction. A contribution is also beneficial to a firm's public relations. A community spirited corporation is often admired. Hereagain, the problem of removal for a show arises, and the agreement should call for replacement if a work is sold or needed for a show.

Corporate Art Program

The purchase of artwork for the client's new location often becomes the beginning of a corporate art program and the firm's investment in works of art. Such investments have proven to be lucrative and more and more corporations are beginning collections.

Inventory

All items should be cataloged by artist, name of the work, size of the piece framed, medium, date of the work, date acquired, purchase price, and present location. If the client has some existing pieces, they should be added to the inventory list. The existing work should be appraised in order to determine the value of the work. Numbering each piece is also a good idea in case some of the art is moved at a future date. The inventory number will provide permanent identification for insurance purposes and asset management.

Three Dimensional Accent Walls

There may be a large wall in the entrance or reception area which the designer wishes to treat with a special design accent or texture for greater impact. This can be constructed out of any material. Fabric and vinyl are most commonly used. The designer might, for example, want the client's logo in the center of the wall. This could be a three dimensional wrapped and padded form. Other wrapped and padded forms in another color could surround the logo as a textured background.

The designer might also want to construct a three dimensional wall with multilevels and different geometric shapes and then spray paint and lacquer it. Some research is often essential to determine an appropriate choice of materials.

Fabrication

Fabrication of three dimensional walls is complex. After the design concept has been determined, the interior project manager must engineer its implementation. A carpenter/cabinetmaker or a company specializing in stretched fabric walls may be of assistance in designing, specifying, and installing such a wall. The designer must first choose a material for use as a base for wrapping the fabric. Plywood and masonite are common bases. The interior project manager must ensure that the shapes in the design can be constructed in the material specified. Fabric will only wrap in certain directions simultaneously and will show frayed edges at outside cuts. The design must be appropriate for the medium. This is a practical, engineering issue. Designers often have concepts that are not practical. The interior project manager must work out a compromise that retains the designer's aesthetic intent but that is also possible to fabricate.

Attachment

After the fabrication is worked out, the attachment of the design to the wall is engineered. Whatever method of attachment is used, it must be concealed behind the artwork. Some sort of clip or cleat system is frequently utilized. Once the material, installation, and attachment is determined, a plan is detailed so that the installer will know exactly where to put each piece. This is a very detailed drawing that allows for clearance between the forms and overall "creep" due to the joining of many separate pieces.

Supergraphics

There may be a cafeteria or a long wide corridor where the designer would like to add some fun, colorful treatment. Supergraphics are ideal for this. They wrap around walls and help to unify a space. Supergraphics are scaled to the space and color coordinated with the interior. Here the designer is limited only by his imagination. After the design is complete, a detailed drawing is drafted for the painter. This drawing spells out exactly how to actually paint it on the wall; it must be exact or the finished product will not match the original concept. The interior project manager once again must ensure that the designer's concept gets translated into reality.

CHAPTER TWELVE

SIGNAGE

SIGNAGE

The purpose of signage is to direct the flow of traffic and to inform the visitor of his present location. Signs also tell the visitor how to get where he wants to go. Exterior signage is generally handled by the architect. The designer concentrates on the interior signage. This should coordinate with the exterior signage and with the interior design, if possible.

There are several different signage systems available and these are described in detail in this chapter. However, any system chosen should be flexible so that signs can be relocated as personnel move and the client renovates space. The system should also be one that any handyman can install so the client does not have to call in an expensive sign installer for minor changes. Adaptability for the future is an important consideration here.

Types

Each type of signage system has a unique appearance. Pin type raised letters are often used on entrance doors and large signs. They give a floating appearance and are favored by designers. The letters are usually attached from the rear by screws. Plastic and metal letters are frequently glued on to the door or sign. When the sign maker has to attach individual letters, the installation becomes more costly.

Other types of signs are printed, silk screened, or engraved. Printed and silk screened signs have a flat surface. Engraved signs are commonly made from color-layered plastic. They are formed by cutting through the top layer of color into a center core of a different color.

Numbers or Names

Many companies, especially those with a high turnover rate, prefer only room number signs on the doors. This is the least expensive method of identifying rooms. Room numbers are infinitely helpful to porters and other delivery people. They also proceed in a logical progression through the space and visitors have little difficulty finding a particular office. Figure 12.1 illustrates the layout of a typical numbered sign.

Some firms use room numbers and names. A slide out or otherwise removable plate is generally preferable for flexibility and turnover. In this way, only the nameplate is replaced instead of the entire mounting bracket. This is the best choice, but is costlier than numbers alone.

If a firm is small, a company may use only names on the office doors. However, this becomes unwieldy in a large company. If there is a medium to high turnover rate, changing the name plates is a costly nuisance.

Directory

A directory is usually placed in the lobby of a large building. If more than one company occupies the building, the directory may be placed near the elevator. A directory not only identified companies but can also identify where individuals and departments are located within each firm if space allows. Figure 12.2 is a typical directory sign. Depending on the size of the offices and the number of employees, the directory may specify a room number or only a floor. When only the floor is specified, the visitor may then be directed by more specific directories at each level.

Directional Signs

These signs are intended to direct people through the space. They have arrows which indicate, for example, that the accounting department is to the left and the purchasing department is to the right. Down the hall there will be another sign to direct visitors around a corner or to let them know where they are. Figure 12.3 is a typical directional sign.

Directional signs are particularly important when the space is designed with an open landscape system. There is a tendency to get lost in an open plan system since there are few walls and "you are here" signs. Exit signs are another type of directional sign, but are often part of the architectural contract because they are required by code and are not included here.

Room Number Sign

Figure 12.1

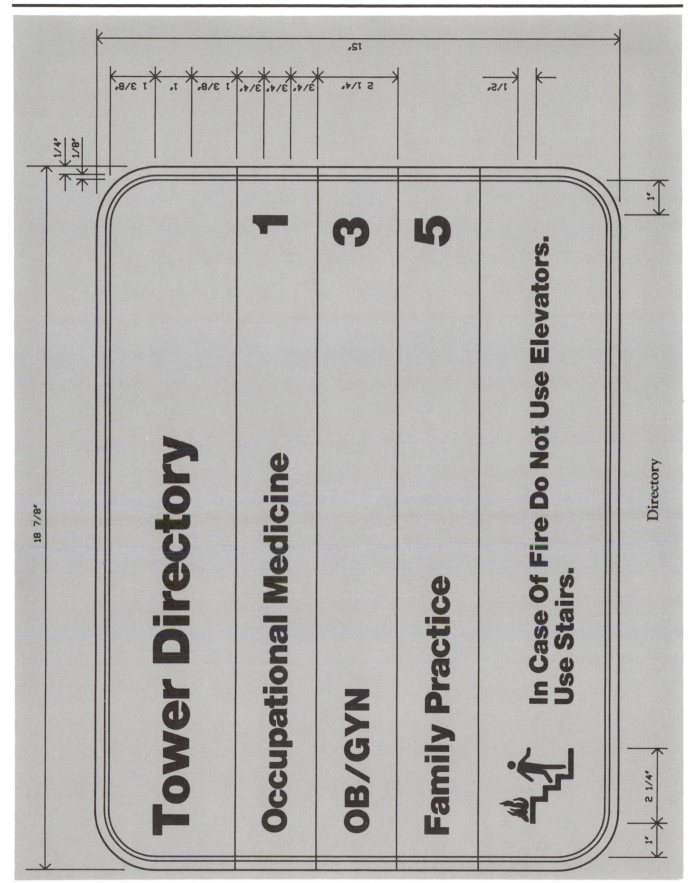

Figure 12.2

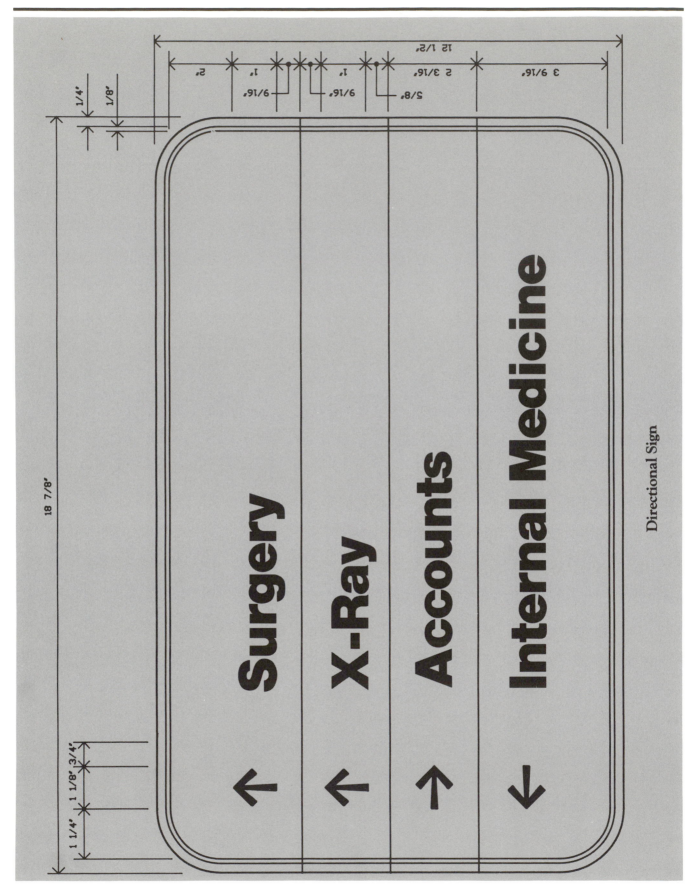

Directional Sign

Figure 12.3

General Information Signs

A client may want to label conference rooms, electric closets, telephone closets, janitor's room, toilets, etc. Toilets must be labeled as directed by the local building code. Either symbols and/or lettering can be utilized. It is helpful to have a conference room sign with a slide out "in-use" plate.

Some clients contend that the janitors know where the slop sink is and do not desire a sign on this door. The same holds true for telephone and electrical wiring closets.

Informational signs can indicate no re-entry floors in stairways, no smoking areas, parking, public telephones, fire extinguishers, and first aid. Figures 12.4 and 12.5 are informational fire protection signs. A system of internationally accepted symbols eliminate language barriers and readily communicate a universally understood graphic language.

Specifications

The sign specifications must include the catalog number, material to be used, lettering methods, type of holders, color of letters and background, type of letter, and mounting methods. Figure 12.6 is an example of a typical signage specification.

The designer should provide a location schedule or chart to ensure that the signs are installed in the exact locations specified. The room numbers indicated on the plans (which may not be the same as the final room number) should be cross referenced to the new numbers and signage on the schedule. Figure 12.7 is a schedule for room numbers and identification signs for a typical office floor.

Installation Methods

It is easiest to install signs with double faced tape. However, this method presents a maintenance problem. When the signs are removed, the tape can tear the paper surface of drywall. For this reason, a better quality installation is generally recommended. There are two basic types of signs with relatively permanent back plates and removable number and name plates. The first type is a slide-in bracket and the other uses either a magnet or velcro to attach the name plate.

All signs should be installed at the same height and general location for aesthetic as well as visual continuity. Figure 12.8 illustrates typical installation information for room number signs. Note that if the sign is installed on the door it is more difficult to read when the door is in an open position. Directional signs are often ceiling mounted in open areas so as to be seen above landscape panels.

Figure 12.4

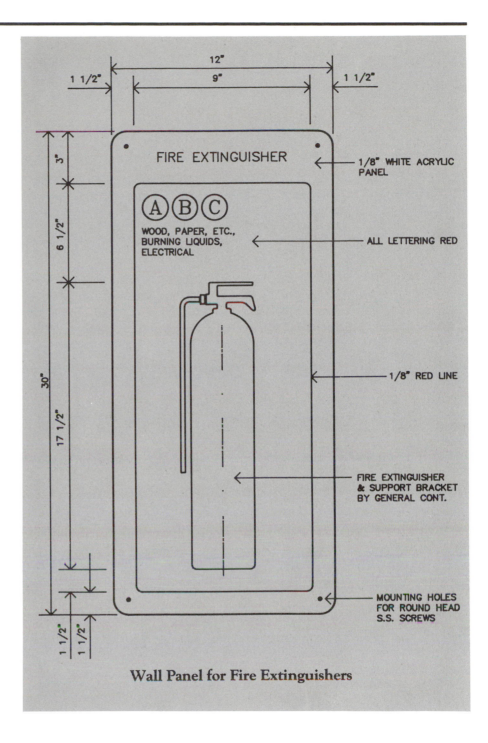

Wall Panel for Fire Extinguishers

Figure 12.5

SIGNAGE SPECIFICATIONS

Interior Signage for: _____(client)_____
Manufacturer (or approved equal): APCO Graphics Inc.
Signage System: IM System

1. The IM (Injection Molded) Sign Module shall be precision molded of high impact plastic, lightweight and strong. The module color shall be an integral part of the molded material.

2. The standard graphic application shall be accomplished by using a photographic screen printing technique whereby the image forms a chemical bond with the module surface. The material used shall be vinyl ink.

3. The IM System, while permanent in appearance, shall consist of interchangeable inserts and holders, available for wall, door and landscape partition mounting. The holder shall remain permanently affixed to the mounting surface wherever possible, while magnetically retained inserts are quickly and easily removed and replaced. Inserts will be mounted more permanently with double-sided vinyl tape wherever possible.

4. All signs shall be of the Radius Wall Holder (RH) series and shall have radius corners.

5. The background color for all holders and inserts shall be #43 putty.

6. The imprint color for all signs (except as specifically noted) shall be #6 Ginger.

7. All typography for all signs shall be Helvetica Medium, Initial Caps (HM, InC).

8. All arrows for directional signs and for directories shall be #A110, 3/4"H.

9. All panel clips shall be bent to accommodate a 2" thick landscape panel. The "C" dimension shall be 1".

Mounting Methods

1. All room number signs to be mounted with magnetic tape.

2. All identification signs to be mounted with vinyl tape.

3. All conference room signs to be mounted with vinyl tape.

4. All Directional sign holders to be screw mounted. All directional sign inserts to be mounted with magnetic tape.

5. All symbols signs to be mounted with vinyl tape.

6. All directory holders to be screw mounted. All directory inserts to be fastened with snap locks.

Figure 12.6

7. All identification signs to be utilized on landscape panels
    shall be mounted by panel clips.

Room Number Signs

Numbers shall be as specified on signage drawings and schedule.

Specifications:

    IM System Radius Insert #RI-154. Size: 1 1/2"H x 4"W. Copy
    size: 3/4".

Identification Signs

Nomenclature shall be as specified on signage drawings and
schedule. These signs are intended for room and department
identification.

Specifications:

    IM System Radius Insert #RI-158. Size 1 1/2"H x 8"W. Copy
    size: 1/2".
                Note: If the copy required on a particular sign
                        will not fit due to the length of the
                        nomenclature, the copy size shall be
                        reduced to 3/8" or 1/4" as required.

Conference Room Signs

Nomenclature shall be as specified on signage drawings and
schedule (i.e.: Conference Room, Training Room, Green Room).

Specifications:

    IM System Radius Insert #RI-66CSS with sliding strip
    feature to indicate "in use". Size 6"W x 6"H. Copy size:
    1/2".

Symbol Signs

Symbols shall be as specified on signage drawings and schedule.

Specifications:

    IM System Radius insert #RI-44. Size 4" x 4".

    Toilet Signs shall be Format #F-25 with Symbol #S-14 (Men)
    or Symbol #S-15 (Women) centered on the sign with the
    Nomenclature "Men" or "Women" in 3/8" copy.

    No Smoking Signs shall be Format #F-18 (Symbol only) with
    Symbol #S-1. Color of the circle with diagonal line shall
    be red.

    Handicapped Signs shall be Format #F-18 (Symbol only) with
    Symbol #S-3.

Figure 12.6 (*continued*)

SCHEDULE FOR
SIGNAGE SPECIFICATIONS

First Floor Room Number Signs

Drawing Room No.	Description	Room Number Signs Required
008	Director of Sales	110
125	Copier	112
005	Director Cable Casting	114
105	Freight Entry	116
141	Mechanical Equipment	117
151	Electrical Equipment	118
006	Building Maintenance Storage	119
007	Mail Room	120
139	Electrical Room	122
131	Conference Room	124
137	Mechanical Equipment	125
129	Janitor	126
135	Electrical Room	127
133	Elevator Equipment	128
009	Conference	130
010	Building Manager	131
011	Visitors Office	132
013	Training Manager	133
014	Interview	134
110	(2) Lunch Room	(2) 135
015	Training Manager	137
016	Personnel Manager	140
017	Personnel Director	142
018	Interview Room	143
019	Personnel Assistant	144
132	Storage	145
020	Cash Receipt	146
134	Storage	147
126	Copier	148
130	Janitor	149
138	Mechanical Equipment	150
Total Number Room Number Signs Required		32

Figure 12.7

First Floor Identification Signs

Drawing Room No.	Identification Signs Required	Building Room No./Location
007	Mail Room	120
113	Sales	(Panel hung)
115	Cable Casting	(Panel hung)
110	(2) Lunch Room	(2) 135
025	Traffic	152
023	Dispatch	166
159	(2) Tape Library	(2) 172
160	(2) Master Control	(2) 173
161	(2) Head End	(2) 174
158	Edit I	176
157	Edit II	177
156	Commercial Insertion	178
012	Computer Operations	180
149	Computer Room	184
154	Danger - Battery Room	187
002	Stair A	Stair A
001	Stair B	Stair B
004	Stair C	Stair C
003	Stair D	Stair D
103	Employees Only	Outside W. Entry
001	Employees Only	Outside N.W. Entry
004	Employees Only	Outside N.E. Entry
104	Employees Only	Outside E. Entry
–	Personnel	(Panel hung)
–	Demand Maintenance	(Panel hung)
–	Preventive Maintenance	(Panel hung)
–	Customer Repair	(Panel hung)

Total Number Identification Signs Required   31

First Floor Conference Room Signs

Drawing Room # CD/3	Identification Required	Room Number Required
127	Conference Room/In Use/Vacant	124
140	(2) Training Room/In Use/Vacant	138
128	Conference Room/In Use/Vacant	156

Total Number of Conference Room Signs Required   4

Figure 12.7 (*continued*)

First Floor Symbol Signs Required

Drawing Room # CD/3	Symbol Required	Building Location
147	(2) No Smoking	On Door Outside Each Corridor
149	No Smoking	184
153	No Smoking	186
156	No Smoking	
154	No Smoking	187
123	Men Handicapped (Symbol only)	Men's Restroom West
119	Women Handicapped (Symbol only)	Women's Restroom West
124	Men Handicapped (Symbol only)	Men's Restroom East
120	Women Handicapped (Symbol only)	Women's Restroom East
Total Symbol Signs Required		10

First Floor Fire Extinguisher Signs

Quantity Required	Drawing Room # CD/3	Room Description	Bldg. Rm. No. Location
3	160	Master Control	173
1	167	Equipment Maintenance	175
1	158	Edit I	176
1	157	Edit II	177
1	156	Commercial Insertion	178
1	148	Security	182
2	149	Computer Room	184
1	152	Telephone Room	185
2	159	Tape Library	172
1	139	Electrical Room	122
1	153	UPS	186
3	–	Headend Building	174
1	136	Electrical Room	158
1	166	Electrical Room	170
1	141	Mechanical Equipment	117
1	151	Electrical Equipment	118
Total Fire Extinguishers Required			22

Figure 12.7 (*continued*)

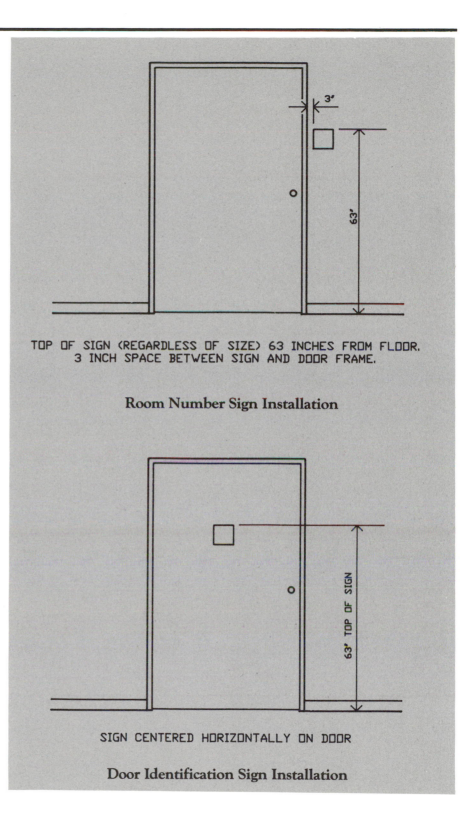

TOP OF SIGN (REGARDLESS OF SIZE) 63 INCHES FROM FLOOR.
3 INCH SPACE BETWEEN SIGN AND DOOR FRAME.

Room Number Sign Installation

SIGN CENTERED HORIZONTALLY ON DOOR

Door Identification Sign Installation

Figure 12.8

PROJECT MANAGEMENT AND DOCUMENTATION

CHAPTER THIRTEEN

PROJECT MANAGEMENT AND DOCUMENTATION

The most important thing to remember in supervising a project is to "get it in writing." Changes and problems invariably occur on every job and all of them should be committed to writing and approved with the signature of the client. This policy protects the designer from the possibility of unauthorized changes and provides an organized format for every change or problem that arises. This chapter contains descriptions of construction documents and procedures involved in an interiors project—those items to "get in writing"—with suggested methods for dealing with each one.

Contract and Retainer

A designer should never perform work on a handshake, even for a friend. This method of operation often results in confusion and disputes, and the designer frequently loses money, future work, and a friend. Before commencing work on a project, a designer and client *must* have a contract. Most firms have a standard contract or letter of agreement. This contract includes a detailed description of exactly what services the designer is expected to provide, his fee, and his required retainer. The retainer is advance money held by the designer in the event that the client cancels the contract. Each firm has its own policy with regard to determining retainers. The retainer is frequently ten percent of the contract, but may also be a fixed amount, such as $1000 or $1,500 for a small project.

The designer should not begin work until he has received the retainer and the signed contract. This indicates that the client is serious and protects the designer in the event that the client decides to terminate the agreement or unfairly withhold payments. The contract also protects the designer when the client makes major changes or requests additional services. With a signed contract spelling out every detail of the job, the designer can justify charging for the extra services requested.

For smaller projects, a letter of agreement is often used. This document should contain the same information as the contract. A sample letter of agreement is shown in Figure 13.1. Such documents have important legal implications. Those included in this book are for illustrative purposes only. For actual contracts or letters of agreement, an attorney should be consulted.

Documentation

The designer acts as his firm's representative and protector as well as agent for the client. Thus, it is his responsibility to document *everything* for any job. Every document must then be read and signed by the client. This includes every piece of paperwork from the contract to all changes in construction, furniture, furnishings, budgets, purchase orders, and deadlines. This process may appear to be tedious, but it eliminates future grief and potential legal problems.

Minutes of Meetings

A significant part of documentation involves recording the minutes of all meetings connected with the project. This is done whether the meetings are with the client, landlord, contractor, or vendor. Although it is time-consuming to record the minutes of every meeting concerning any given job, the importance of this policy cannot be overstressed. The minutes are a record (and sometimes the only record) of what was approved, changed, or discussed.

Copies of the minutes should be issued to all parties present at the meeting and any other individuals involved. If anyone disagrees with what is written, he notifies the designer so that the minutes can be revised. This procedure is a protective one for the designer—it corrects misunderstandings quickly and prevents disputes further down the road. Occasionally, a client says, "I never approved that," after something has been delivered and installed. If every meeting is recorded, the designer has the documentation needed to back up his actions.

Telephone Conversations

There are often more telephone conversations with the client than actual face to face meetings. It is good practice to record minutes of any telephone conversations in which the client has given a new directive or authorized a particular change. These documents should later be signed by the client. Even if these are only handwritten, they serve as memory joggers and, once again, serve to clarify details and prevent any problems which may arise later.

Memos

Memos are written for numerous reasons: to get information to various parties, document job progress, request samples or information on a particular product, expedite payment of an invoice, or share information. Memos or other correspondence requesting action by a third party (i.e., a vendor) should be kept in a "tickler" file. The file can be divided into categories such as sample requests, requests for delivery dates, information requested, action requested, and miscellaneous follow-up. The designer refers to the file once a week or so to see what information or samples have or have not been received. If necessary, the designer can then make a telephone call with complete knowledge of when and what was requested. Suppliers and vendors respond more rapidly to a written request than a verbal one, and a memo with specific details about a requisition avoids delays and misunderstandings.

LETTER OF AGREEMENT

Mr. Robert Smith
XYZ Company
333 West Street
Anytown, Anystate 10000

Re: 9th Floor - 333 West Street

Dear Mr. Smith:

It was a pleasure meeting with you. Confirming our conversation, we would be pleased to design your new 9th Floor offices. Our services include the following:

> Survey of client requirements
> Space planning and layout
> Renovation drawings after approval of space plans
> Interiors drawings after approval of layout
> Furniture and furnishings selections
> Budget
> Specifications
> Installation and move-in supervision.

All bidding, purchasing and expediting of orders will be done by your purchasing department.

Your 9th Floor is 10,000 square feet, per your lease agreement. Our customary fee is $2.25 per square foot for a not-to-exceed fee of $22,500. Any additional services or changes shall be billed at a rate of $60.00 per hour for principals, $40.00 per hour for professionals, $30.00 per hour for drafting, and $25.00 per hour for clerical work.

Any out-of-pocket expenses for blueprinting, travel, etc., shall be billed at cost. Our invoices are rendered monthly for work completed to date and are payable within ten (10) days.

We will proceed with work as soon as we receive a 10 percent retainer in the amount of $2,250 and your signed copy of this Letter of Agreement. This retainer will be deducted from our final bill.

We look forward to working with you.

Very truly yours,
DOE INTERIORS

Jane Doe

Approved by: _____

Date: _____

Figure 13.1

Frequently, the designer requests a sample or brochure from a supplier, initiated by the client. Copies of such requests should be given to all involved parties. The written document lets the client know that the designer followed up on his request. When the information is not forthcoming on a timely enough basis for the client, he at least knows that the delay is not the designer's fault.

Specifications

All specifications must be highly detailed. This enables the designer or client to bid out all the furniture, carpet, drapery, wall covering, etc., on a uniform basis. If the specifications are not complete, the bids will not be equivalent and thus not comparable, rendering the whole bidding process meaningless. (This subject is discussed in more detail in Chapter 7—"Specifications and Coding for Furniture".)

Purchase Orders

Purchase orders are written from the specifications. Therefore, if the specifications are not accurate, the purchase orders will not be correct. If an incorrect piece of furniture is delivered to the job site as the result of unclear specifications, the designer is responsible for replacement.

For large projects, there is usually a blanket purchase order covering the entire furniture order. Here the dealer is usually in such close contact with the designer that errors are prevented. For small jobs, however, the designer is often asked to write the purchase orders himself. In this case, he accepts total responsibility for the delivery of all necessary furnishing items. If the purchase order specifications are incorrect, the manufacturer usually calls to ask for additional information. This corrects the problem, but often results in delays. For this reason, every purchase order should be specific, detailed, and completely correct.

Change Orders

Change orders are forms used to change the scope of a previously authorized purchase order. They may be an addition, reduction, deletion, or may just be informational. Change orders are, unfortunately, almost always necessary on every project. Changes in quantity, color, or anything else should be documented on a change order to the vendor. Clients often think that they can cancel an item right up until the day it is to arrive on a job. It is usually possible to cancel or return items at a late date for a restocking charge, often as high as 25%, and freight charges both directions. Clients may also think that they can add three desks at the last minute and have them arrive with the original order when it can actually take 12–16 weeks or longer for delivery. Therefore, the client should be advised that after a certain point (i.e., after the furniture is started on the production line), an order can no longer be cancelled or changed without possible expense and/or delays.

Transmittals

The designer should keep a record of all parties receiving various documents and drawings and the dates they were sent. The simplest format for keeping track of this information is a transmittal form. (A sample transmittal form is shown in Figure 13.2.) Transmittals are usually three part documents. The original and a copy are sent out with the documents. The third part is retained by the designer. The party receiving the documents is supposed to sign his copy to indicate that he actually received the documents, and then return it to the designer. No drawings should ever be issued to a client, vendor, construction contractor, or anyone else without written verification in the designer's possession that they were sent. This protects the designer at a future date if he discovers people working with an outdated set of drawings. Documents such as specifications, budgets, or bidding documents often require a cover letter, but if they are sent for informational purposes, a transmittal will often suffice.

Inventory

The inventory of the client's existing furniture must be typed up (or computerized) in detail. The condition of each piece of furniture is listed on the inventory. (Chapter 5 contains a more detailed description of the inventory taking process.) The client can then make an informed decision as to which pieces to retain, sell, or donate to charity. If the existing furniture is to be reused, the inventory document is an invaluable tool for the movers. It can be used to tag the furniture in preparation for the physical move. The inventory is also used to check that the furniture is placed in the correct location after the move. If the existing furniture is for sale, the inventory is used by various buyers to provide quotations. This way a buyer can make an offer without spending much time taking his own inventory of the items. Similarly, the inventory can be used to itemize charitable donations.

Procedure Memorandum

The procedure memorandum is explicit and is sent to both the client and contractor and/or vendor. It explains how the job will proceed and exactly how any changes should be handled. A sample memo is shown in Figure 13.3, for furniture; however, it can be revised to handle contracts other than furniture. The procedure memorandum, in this case, assumes that the project is relatively large and that there is one furniture dealer for the majority of the furniture requirement.

Samples and Shop Drawings

All samples and shop drawings are submitted for the designer's approval. These are stamped with the designer's stamp and the appropriate action noted. Figure 13.4 illustrates a typical stamp. Drawings are stamped directly and must have the firm's name, designer's name, date, and any information about resubmission or correction. Since samples are frequently fabric and cannot be stamped directly, a 3″ × 5″ card stapled to the sample should be stamped and dated. Samples such as paint chips, tiles, VAT, are also accompanied by a 3″ × 5″ card attached to the sample in the best way possible. One copy of each drawing and/or sample should be retained by the designer, one of each is sent to the client, and one is returned to the vendor. If the delivered item does not match the approved sample, the vendor must correct the discrepancy. The stamp tells all concerned parties that the sample is approved, disapproved, or must be revised and re-submitted. The approval should also be dated.

Similarly, all drawings should be signed and dated by the client. The same approval stamp may be used to date the drawings. This is important because new drawings are often made when changes are processed.

Means Forms

**LETTER
OF TRANSMITTAL**

FROM:
_____
_____
_____
_____

DATE _____
PROJECT _____
LOCATION _____
ATTENTION _____
RE: _____
_____
_____
_____
_____

TO: _____
_____
_____
_____

Gentlemen:

WE ARE SENDING YOU ☐ HEREWITH ☐ DELIVERED BY HAND ☐ UNDER SEPARATE COVER

VIA _____ THE FOLLOWING ITEMS:

☐ PLANS ☐ PRINTS ☐ SHOP DRAWINGS ☐ SAMPLES ☐ SPECIFICATIONS

☐ ESTIMATES ☐ COPY OF LETTER ☐ _____

COPIES	DATE OR NO.	DESCRIPTION

THESE ARE TRANSMITTED AS INDICATED BELOW

☐ FOR YOUR USE   ☐ APPROVED AS NOTED   ☐ RETURN _____ CORRECTED PRINTS
☐ FOR APPROVAL   ☐ APPROVED FOR CONSTRUCTION   ☐ SUBMIT _____ COPIES FOR_____
☐ AS REQUESTED   ☐ RETURNED FOR CORRECTIONS   ☐ RESUBMIT_____ COPIES FOR_____
☐ FOR REVIEW AND COMMENT ☐ RETURNED AFTER LOAN TO US   ☐ FOR BIDS DUE_____
☐ _____

REMARKS: _____
_____
_____
_____
_____
_____
_____

IF ENCLOSURES ARE NOT AS INDICATED,
PLEASE NOTIFY US AT ONCE.

SIGNED: _____

Figure 13.2

PROCEDURE MEMORANDUM

I. <u>CONTRACTOR:</u> _____

   <u>JOB:</u> _____

   <u>INTERIORS CATEGORY:</u> _____

   <u>CONSTRUCTION CONTRACTOR:</u> _____

II. JOB PROCEDURE:

   A. <u>Correspondence</u>

      1. Official correspondence shall be primarily between the Designer and the Contractor. If other direct communication (for example, between the Designer and Subcontractor/ Supplier or between Manufacturer and Designer) is necessary, it <u>must</u> be with the full knowledge of the Contractor.

   B. <u>Shop Drawings</u>

      1. Shop drawings shall be submitted in triplicate and delivered to the Designer <u>only</u>.
      2. All shop drawings and submittals shall be accompanied by an explanatory letter of transmittal.
      3. Shop drawings in use on the job shall be dated and marked with the Designer's approved stamp.

   C. <u>Samples Submitted</u>

      1. Items 1, 2, and 3 in B above also apply.
      2. Contractor shall submit three (3) fabric samples and four (4) finish samples to Designer. Designer shall return one (1) fabric sample and two (2) finish samples to Contractor if approved. Disapproved samples shall be returned to Contractor only on request.
      3. Submittals shall be forwarded and all items marked in accordance with Designer's codes and tagging instructions.
      4. No materials, including those specified, shall be used in the work until such submittal has been made, and approval granted by the Designer.

   D. <u>Requests for Clarification and/or Inspections</u>

      1. All requests for clarifications of the Contract Documents, or additional instructions, shall come from the Contractor, through the Designer's Representative, to the Designer. If other requests or instructions are necessary, they shall be made or given directly (for example, from Manufacturer or Subcontractor to Designer) only with the full knowledge of

Figure 13.3

the Contractor. Instructions given without the Contractor's knowledge shall be ignored.

2. All requests for inspections by drapery, carpet contractor, etc., shall be made to the Designer.

E. <u>Changes Involving Adjustment in Contract Price</u>

1. <u>Quotation Request</u>: (See Exhibit A)
When a change is being considered, which involves an ADD or DEDUCT amount to the Maximum Cost, the Designer shall issue a Quotation Request. The Quotation Request is <u>not</u> authorization to proceed with the work.

2. <u>Change Order</u>: (See Exhibit B)
Upon receipt of the Quotation Request, the Contractor shall prepare his quotation of Maximum Cost or Credit for the change involved and submit his breakdown of cost to the Designer. If the Maximum Cost or Credit for the change is acceptable to the Designer and Owner, a Change Order (See Exhibit B) shall be issued changing the Maximum Cost of the total project. That part of the Quotation Request under "Scope," and the Maximum Cost for the Quotation Request, when approved, shall be transferred to the Change Order. The actual cost of all such changes shall then merge in the final cost of the work.

When additional drawings are required to explain the work in the Quotation Request, they shall be made part of the Quotation Request.

3. <u>Change Order</u>: A Change Order shall be issued by the Designer to change the Contract Documents and/or adjust the Maximum Cost.

F. <u>Changes NOT Involving Adjustment in Maximum Cost</u>

1. <u>Letter of Instruction</u>: (See Exhibit C)
When a change is required to effect clarifications or minor changes, which do not involve a change in the Maximum Cost, the Designer shall issue a Letter of Instruction. The Letter of Instruction <u>is</u> authorization to proceed with the work. When additional drawings are required, to explain the clarification or minor change in the Letter of Instruction, they shall be attached to the Letter of Instruction.

If the Contractor does not agree that a Letter of Instruction involves no price change, he shall give written notice to Designer, as per the procedure, for a Quotation Request.

Figure 13.3 (*continued*)

Exhibit A - Quotation Request
(Your Company's Name)

Mr. Walter Jones
General Dealer Co., Inc.
123 South Street
Anytown, Anystate   10000

Re: 333 West Street - 9th Floor
     Quotation Request No. 1

Dear Mr. Jones:

The following change is being considered for the subject project.

The work required under this change supersedes the original drawings
and specifications wherein it contradicts the same. All other
conditions remain unchanged.

The Contractor shall quote the maximum cost or credit for this work
and the change in the contract time.

     A. References:
         (List of drawings or category of specifications affected
             by the change.)

     B. Scope:
         (Description of the change.)

Very truly yours,

Jane Doe

cc: Architect
     Client

Figure 13.3 (*continued*)

Exhibit B - Change Order
(Your Company's Name)

Mr. Walter Jones
General Dealer Co., Inc.
123 South Street
Anytown, Anystate   10000

Re: 333 West Street - 9th Floor
      Change Order No. <u>3</u>

Dear Mr. Jones:

Under your Purchase Order No. <u>11211</u>, dated _____, with
<u>X Y Z Company</u>, we are authorized by the Owner, only when he has
affixed his signature to this instrument, to hereby direct you to:

Re: <u>Quotation Request No. 3</u>
      <u>(Description of change under "Scope.")</u>

Add four (4) C-5 chairs in fabric code D to Room 7.

And to change the Contract Maximum Cost, in accordance with the
Contract, as follows:

Add/XXXXXX <u>One thousand six hundred and 00/100</u> Dollars (<u>$1,600.00</u>)
Revised Contract Maximum Cost   <u>$94,750.00</u>

By reason of this modification, the contract time is hereby extended
by <u>no</u> working days.

APPROVED _____, 19

_____, Owner

ACCEPTED _____, 19

_____, Contractor

Very truly yours,
DOE INTERIORS

Jane Doe

cc: Architect
      Client

Figure 13.3 (continued)

Exhibit C - Letter of Instruction

General Dealer Co., Inc.
123 South Street
Anytown, Anystate   10000
Attn: Mr. Walter Jones

Re: <u>333 West Street - 9th Floor</u>
     Letter of Instruction No. <u>2</u>

Dear Mr. Jones:

The following instructions are issued for the purpose of
clarification. Contract is hereby authorized to incorporate
changes and proceed with the work. There shall be no cost or
credit for this item of work.

<u>Scope</u>:
Switch furniture in Room 11 with that in Room 5.

Very truly yours,
DOE INTERIORS

Jane Doe

cc: Architect
     Client

Figure 13.3 *(continued)*

Approvals, Acceptances, and Changes

All changes must be signed by the client and dated. This is the designer's record of the client's authorization to proceed. Occasionally, a client says he did not approve of a certain item after it is built or installed. The signed documents protect the designer from having to absorb any costs that may be associated with such a dispute. Any changes that a client requests must also be noted on a drawing and the client's signature obtained again. All of the parties should be notified of changes in writing. The following is a checklist of certain key items to be approved by the client.

- Preliminary space plan approval
- Final layout
- Design presentation: furniture, materials, and finishes
- Interiors drawings
- Working drawings
- Construction changes in the field
- Change orders
- Minutes of telephone conversations
- Special samples
- Bids
- Purchase orders

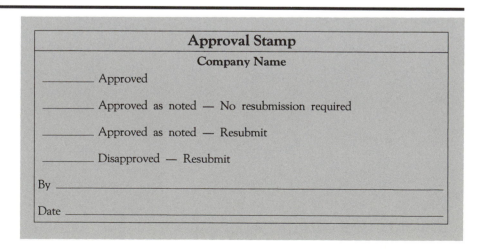

Approval Stamp

Company Name

_____ Approved

_____ Approved as noted — No resubmission required

_____ Approved as noted — Resubmit

_____ Disapproved — Resubmit

By _____

Date _____

Figure 13.4

Client Requirements

In the initial meeting with the client, his goals and objectives were discussed. In subsequent meetings, departmental and individual requirements were determined. These requirements tell the designer what furniture and furnishings are necessary in the space and how various departments relate to each other (for placement in the new office). Often, however, departmental or individual requests may not be feasible and are not approved. It is, therefore, important to document all the information and requests for final approval from the client before proceeding with space plans and furniture layouts.

Budget Approval and Revisions

Cost is always of prime concern to the client. Initially, a budget must be agreed upon that the client feels he can live with and the designer believes will be sufficient to fulfill the client's needs and aesthetic desires. This must be agreed to, in writing, at the beginning of a project. If, at any time during the course of a job, something occurs which will increase the project cost, the client must be notified in writing immediately. There are many reasons for potentially increased costs: the client wants to make changes, the demolition contractor finds an electrical conduit in the center of a new door opening, the designer leaves something out of the budget, etc. Some of these costs may be borne by the client. Requests for changes are often abandoned by the client after the costs are determined. More often though, when a client does request a change, he is willing to pay for it.

When establishing a budget, it is important to list all of the items or categories necessary to complete the job. Items not included in the designer's budget, such as sales tax, telephones, or computer equipment should be listed as excluded and noted as such. A contingency, usually ten to fifteen percent, is added to the budget to accommodate small changes and additions. The designer and the client must always remember that the budget is an estimate, or a "best guess" effort. The final costs will most likely vary somewhat from the budget, but the hope is that they will be lower, not higher, than the estimate.

Construction Progress

If the designer is performing a total interior renovation, he may be responsible for supervising the general contractor. Basically, this requires a daily check of the construction site to ensure that all specifications are being met, and a weekly job meeting with the general contractor and all his subcontractors. The client may also want to inspect the progress of the work and should be invited to the job meetings.

At all times, the designer must cooperate and communicate with the architect, general contractor, interiors contractors, and client. When there is a free flow of information, each party can do his job to the best of his ability. The designer is responsible for making sure that the construction is progressing according to schedule. The designer must notify the client and all interior vendors if the anticipated schedule is falling behind. This notice should be accompanied by an estimate of how far behind schedule the project is, with a new completion date.

Expedite Client Changes in the Field

The client frequently wants to make changes upon seeing in place what was before only a concept on paper. Since time is of the essence when the workmen are on the job and, ideally, they should only receive instructions from one source (to avoid confusion), the designer is often designated as the only one who can issue a field work order authorizing the changes. This procedure should already have been authorized by the client.

Figure 13.5 is a typical field work order. In this case the cost of the change is calculated subsequently by the general contractor and added to the cost of construction. *No* verbal changes, especially those involving additional cost, should ever be given to the contractor. Written documents are needed to later verify the contractor's invoices.

Maintain Project Schedule

In conjunction with the architect and general contractor, the designer must maintain a project schedule. Figure 13.6 is a form for tracking the project schedule. From this schedule, the designer gives monthly progress reports to the client. The actual work completed is compared to the scheduled work to be completed at the job meetings. With a well planned schedule, the designer is able to give vendors anticipated installation dates for furniture, carpet, wallcovering, etc. All vendors should be notified in writing whenever this schedule changes.

Schedule Delivery and Installation

The designer should coordinate the interiors installation with the architect and the general contractor. All interiors installers need some notice, in most cases two weeks, in order to schedule their work crews. This must be coordinated with the construction schedule and run smoothly with no time delays. For example, custom cabinetry is installed after the walls are painted and ceilings closed. Sometimes, however, it must be installed after the flooring contractor is finished. For large projects, there is often a phased installation and move-in. Frequently, two to three floors are occupied at a time. The scheduling procedure, in this case, is an ongoing function through two or more phases.

The designer should determine the required installation sequence, duration, and conditions of each interior vendor and fit these factors into the overall schedule. Carpet cannot be installed until the space is virtually complete and broom clean. However, the carpet installation can start on one floor if the construction on the next floor is to be completed in a few days. Window treatment, ideally, should be installed as soon as the carpet is complete. This is not always possible, depending on the timing of the move. It is preferable to install the window treatment before placing the furniture, so that the window treatment work crews will not move the furniture or climb on it. The furniture is scheduled next and should be placed only after the carpet installation is complete. The next items scheduled are plants, artwork, and accessories. All of the above should be complete prior to the actual move-in.

FIELD WORK ORDER

Mr. Walter Jones
General Dealer Co., Inc.
123 South Street
Anytown, Anystate 10000

Re: 333 West Street - 9th Floor

Dear Mr. Jones:

You are authorized to do the following work based upon unexpected field conditions or new client request. Please proceed with the work and submit cost estimate as soon as possible.

<u>Scope</u>: (Description of the work.)

If requested by client:

Approved by: _____
                      (client)

Date: _____

Very truly yours,
DOE INTERIORS

Jane Doe

cc: Architect
     Client

Figure 13.5

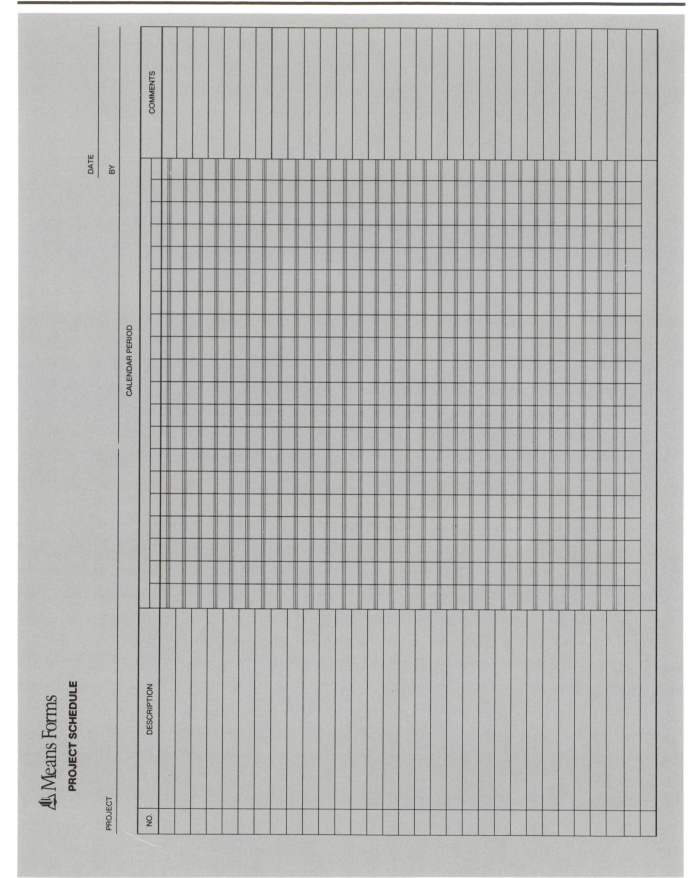

Figure 13.6

One of the problems the designer almost always faces is that construction is not completed on time. This compresses the designer's schedule and often results in a need for overtime if the client still wants to move in on the appointed date. The client must decide whether to delay the move-in or to pay for the overtime necessary to complete the project on time.

Installation Supervision

It is the designer's responsibility to supervise all the interiors contractors, inspect all items delivered and installed, and accept all items on the client's behalf. All items should be checked off on a master list of specifications or location charts. If there are any problems, the designer should correct them. Many things can go wrong at this phase of the project, but if the designer has kept accurate records and notified all vendors in writing of any material and schedule changes, problems should be kept to a minimum. It is virtually impossible to have a 100 percent perfect installation. There is always at least one piece of furniture delivered broken or in the wrong color. Sometimes things are not delivered as scheduled, or delivered items are stolen. As previously stated, the designer handles all of these problems. The client should be reminded that things invariably go wrong and that they will be remedied.

Loading Dock and Freight Elevator Scheduling

Building managers usually require the loading dock and freight elevators to be scheduled only before normal working hours (before 7:00 A.M.) or after hours (after 6:00 P.M.), or on Saturdays or Sundays. For the balance of the time, the dock and elevators may be unavailable or available on a first-come, first-served basis. This means that the installation supervisor may be on a job site waiting for a delivery for hours while the delivery truck circles the block waiting for loading dock space! For this reason, loading docks and elevators should be secured for one of these "off times", or possible delay due to waiting time should be anticipated.

Once actually in the dock, the potential for problems may not be over. The loading dock may be a long distance from the building freight elevators. Transportation of the furniture to the freight elevators may then be followed by a wait for the elevators. If there is a lot of traffic, the overall delivery can be frustratingly slow. During the day, freight elevators are also often on a first-come, first-served basis. For this reason, daytime deliveries are efficient only for fairly small deliveries. On the other hand, the building management may not permit any large deliveries during the day. All of these delays and considerations should be researched in advance. This avoids unanticipated delays and can affect scheduling of workers and the sequence of installation.

In order to deliver very large quantities of carpet, furniture, and other interiors items, it is necessary to schedule the use of freight elevators with the building manager. This should be done as early as possible by letter to the building manager. Deliveries made at night result in overtime installations. Nevertheless, night-time deliveries may actually be faster, and therefore, less costly. In addition, the building may allow deliveries directly through the lobby only after hours. This approach can avoid having to cart the furniture from the loading dock which may be farther away. Elevator schedules should be known very early in the job so that any overtime charges necessary can be included in the budget. The client, not the vendor, pays for any elevator and overtime installation charges.

Walkie-talkies

If the project is in a multi-story building, the designer may recommend that the client procure walkie-talkies for use during the installation. These may either be bought or rented. The use of walkie-talkies enables the designer to find an electrician, carpenter, furniture mover, or carpet installer quickly. This saves time otherwise spent running all over the building frantically looking for the individual needed. Although walkie-talkies are initially expensive, they can save time and prevent delays at critical times. The designer may even want to invest in walkie-talkies himself if he does a number of large jobs.

Troubleshooting

Problems inevitably arise concerning the size, location, quality, color, condition, delivery, or installation of furniture when dealing with large quantities. The designer should be prepared to deal with these as they occur.

On-Site Revisions

Sometimes on-site revisions are necessary. For example, a light switch is in the way, or something just does not fit in the space intended. A wall or floor may be crooked and the item cannot be adjusted to fit. A designer must be flexible in the face of such occurrences. He should first attempt to rearrange a few things so that the items required fit in the space. If this does not work, the item may be placed in an adjacent space. If all else fails, the item should be set aside until the designer and the client have time to deal with the situation properly.

Late Delivery

It is possible that some vital components may be missing from a shipment. The designer may arrange for loaned or rented furniture until the correct piece arrives if he is responsible for the oversight. If the items are not important, the client may elect to do without them until they arrive. If the items are late due to neglect or a mistake on the part of the furniture contractor, he should loan the client a comparable piece of furniture at no cost to the client. If the orders for furniture were placed late and the vendor has made every possible effort to have the furniture delivered on time, the client pays for any rental furniture. Occasionally, the manufacturer claims to have shipped an item though it has not yet arrived on the job. In this case, tracers are usually put on the shipment and a search is made of the furniture contractor's warehouse. In all cases, the furniture contractor is responsible for providing the item. The furniture does not belong to the client until it is on the job and accepted by the designer.

Incorrect Items

When an item arrives in the incorrect finish, color, or fabric, the designer should find out why this has occurred. This can be done by double-checking the orders and specifications. If the mistake is the furniture contractor's or manufacturer's fault, it is replaced at no cost to the client. If the incorrect item represents a glaring mistake that cannot remain on the job, the furniture contractor provides a suitable replacement to use until the correct item is delivered.

Improper Installation

If items are improperly installed, the contractor or dealer should come back and correct the situation. Unfortunately, this is not always easy. The contractor feels he has completed the majority of the project and now wants to go on to other jobs. Getting repairmen back to fix a few minor items may become quite a struggle. The only recourse the designer has in this situation is not to authorize final payment until all such corrective work is done.

Damaged Goods

If a damaged item is delivered to the job site, the designer decides whether it can be repaired acceptably on the job or if it is damaged beyond repair. If the item cannot be repaired, the designer does not accept it at the time of delivery. The damaged item is sent back on the truck in which it arrived. The contractor determines who damaged the piece and who has to pay for the replacement. The client never pays for this type of repair or replacement.

Security

Depending on the job site and the location, the designer may recommend security arrangements. As soon as any items are delivered to the job site, security becomes very important. During construction, the general contractor is responsible for security. As soon as the space is turned over to the client, it becomes his responsibility. Security guards should, in general, be present during the furniture installation and move-in. After all workmen are off the premises, all locks should be changed. This is the client's responsibility, but the designer should remind him so that this important item can be arranged in advance.

Small Projects

Small projects invariably mean fewer changes, fewer meetings, fewer problems, and, happily, less paperwork! A small project may be 1,500 square feet of space as opposed to nine floors of 10,000 feet each. Not even the smallest of projects is fail-safe, however, and the designer should be prepared for problems. When the client finally gets into the space, someone always decides he doesn't like the layout of his office and rearranges the furniture. The designer may not like it, but that is how the individual wants to live with it. This happens on large jobs too, and the designer must always grin and bear it. In the end, it is the client who is paying the bill and it is he and his employees who must be happy with the end result.

THE ACTUAL MOVE

THE ACTUAL MOVE

With the appropriate planning, the actual move may be smoother than anticipated. However, the move is the most important event because it is the most visible phase of the project. Anything wrong at this stage gets magnified ten-fold, no matter how capable the designer's performance has been until now.

Specifications and Bidding Documents

As with other categories of interior work, the physical move must be specified in detail to obtain competitive prices from movers. The specifications for moving explain the scope of the project and enumerate the requirements for inspection, protection, labor and installation, packing and unpacking, furniture placement, mover's drawings, tagging, and supervision. The specifications should also cover all the information that the movers are required to submit and the terms and conditions of the contract. Typical moving specifications are shown in Figure 14.1 (shown at the end of this chapter). This example is for illustrative purposes only. As with any other specifications, they should be tailored to fit the client's unique circumstances.

After the specifications are complete, an Invitation to Bid letter is written. Figure 14.2 is sample Invitation to Bid for the move (shown at the end of this chapter). This letter is more specific than the previous bid letters for other categories. It allows the move specifications to be used, unchanged for each project. The details can be enumerated in the Invitation to Bid, thus saving on future paperwork.

A proposal form is shown in Figure 14.3 (shown at the end of this chapter). When properly filled in by the bidders, the designer should be able to compare proposals from movers with a great deal of accuracy. A note of caution: movers often underestimate the cost of a move in order to get the job. A clause in the specifications that the final payment for the move will not vary more than 15% in either direction from the quoted price can prevent this kind of misrepresentation from occurring. The actual bill at the end of the job is based on the number of hours worked by a certain number of men, and can frequently be much higher than the estimate. If the 15% clause is included, the bidders will be more likely to produce a more accurate bid.

Preparing the Client

There are two phases involved in preparing the client for a move. The first is to advise the client of various things that can go wrong. The second is to prepare all the personnel involved for the physical move. The former serves to keep the client calm in the event that something actually does go wrong. The latter educates the personnel so they know what to expect and what is expected of them.

As previously stated, alerting the client to possible disasters can be helpful. The designer may relay stories of other jobs, saying something like, "look at all the things that went wrong, but when the president arrived Monday morning, everything was under control." The most confidential file of the president's is always in the one carton that is lost; the flood is always in the chairman's office; the broken desk chair is always the executive vice presidents', etc. If forewarned, however, the client is more likely to shrug his shoulders in the face of a problem and say, "you told me something like this would happen". The designer's control of the situation is paramount. If he can keep the pandemonium to a minimum, almost any problem will eventually be solved.

Brochures

If the move is a large one, the client should issue a move brochure elaborating the special features of the new building. The brochure, or employee kit, shows plans of the space and department locations, and explains new telephone, parking, and office procedures to be followed in the new facility. Such a brochure, or employee kit, is shown in Figure 14.4, at the end of this chapter (floor plans, not shown here, would normally be included). Special notes can be added by the president and/or chairman of the board for a more personal touch. The brochure answers numerous questions that employees may have about the new building. Producing a move brochure allows the designer to concentrate on other things besides answering questions. The brochure also serves as a handbook for building use after the move. It should be distributed about a week before the move.

Moving Plans

The mover should prepare color coded moving plans for use during the move. These are mounted on foam core board. The mover usually utilizes his own numbering system, but will use the architectural numbers if asked to do so and if the numbering system is not confusing to his workers. These plans indicate the room numbers and the individual office layouts.

If a move is large, it is subdivided into zones. Each zone will have a different color tag. This enables the mover to direct all the items with orange tags, for example, to one elevator or truck and all the items with a green tag to another. This way, if something is in the wrong zone, it is easy to spot. This system makes the move more efficient, less costly, and more organized.

The mover labels the items in each space on the plan with piece numbers. When the tagging is done, each item is marked with the new room number and the piece number in the room. A layout of the space indicating all the piece numbers is posted on the entrance door to each space. When this is done, the movers know exactly where to place each item without requiring the presence of a supervisor to direct them.

The move plans serve as the main reference during the actual move. They are generally kept by a supervisor near the elevator or entrance to the building or in the mover's field office.

Tagging

About two weeks prior to the move, the mover starts preparing the tags to be utilized. Using his move plans as a guide, he writes up tags for employee's desk contents boxes and each item to be moved. As previously stated, these tags show the new space number and the piece number in the space.

About a week before the move, the mover physically tags everything to be moved. Contents tags are left with individuals to be affixed to the cartons as they are packed. The mover works with the existing furniture inventory and acts as a final check that the plans match the information in the inventory. It is much easier to correct an inconsistency at this point than to do so while the mover is in the hallway with a desk on end on a dolly with other items backing up behind him down the corridor. Anything that is not being moved can be tagged with a red "do not move" tag. These are easy to spot and hard to confuse with other tags.

Scheduling

Proper scheduling is essential to a smooth move. It is the project manager's responsibility to remember everything that has to be set up and all the people who must be notified. Much coordination is necessary between the building manager and the mover, i.e., elevator scheduling for materials deliveries, in addition to the actual move. Arrangements have to be made for security, walkie-talkies, and a locksmith.

Coordinate with Building Manager

As discussed in Chapter 13, the building manager should be consulted for after hours access to the building, elevators, elevator operators and elevator protection, collapsing revolving doors, security, after hours heat or air conditioning, etc. The building manager should be notified as soon as the moving date is known. The arrangements should be stipulated in writing to avoid confusion.

Deliver Materials

Cartons and bins are delivered to the present offices about a week ahead of time so that some packing can be done in advance. Masonite is also delivered to the present site, where it will be laid in the corridors and taped together to enable the dollies to roll more easily than over carpet. If the floors are vinyl tile, it is not necessary to put down masonite. Masonite or another type of floor and wall protection are delivered to the new location at the same time. The field office, if one is necessary, is set up at this time and stocked with move plans, extra tags, tape, markers, screwdrivers, extension cords, etc. If there is no field office, these items are delivered to a predesignated location.

Packing

The majority of the packing is not usually done until just before the move. Archives, "dead files", or relatively unused store rooms can be packed in advance by the mover. In general, the rest of the packing is started a week to three days before the move. Employees usually pack their desks, credenzas, and any personal effects they may have. The movers pack files, bookcases, store rooms, and any equipment. Employees should be asked, whenever possible, to take their personal effects home until after the move is complete.

Security

During the move, the designer should arrange for extra security guards. With all the activity, it is easy for typewriters, televisions, and stereos to mysteriously disappear. Guard service is needed in the present location as well as the new location, until all items are out of the old space and into the new.

Walkie-talkies

As previously discussed, walkie-talkies are invaluable during a move. These should be obtained three to five days in advance for a large move, and one day in advance or the same day for a small move. A place should be provided for the walkie-talkies to be secured and recharged during the move.

Locksmith

It is a great headache saver to have a locksmith present the day of the move. Keys are almost invariably lost and the desks or files are locked. Nothing can be unpacked until the item in question is opened. Locks get jammed or keys broken off in locks and all progress stops until the problem is corrected. A locksmith can take down the key codes from the lock cylinder and deliver the new keys the next day. A locksmith is not inexpensive, but if the move is a large one, the cost will be justified.

Iron Workers

Depending on union regulations, iron workers may have to be scheduled a few days in advance of the move to unbolt files and shelving. This should be done as late in the move as possible to avoid dangerous situations. The ironworkers are then scheduled to re-bolt the files in the new space. Files should be moved first so that they can be bolted while the rest of the move is proceeding. Then, when the physical move is complete, they should be refinished (if planned).

Supervising the Move

The designer manages the overall move and supervises the mover's personnel. Spot checks that all is going according to schedule are all that should be necessary if a good mover has been selected and properly instructed.

Protection

Building management does not traditionally allow a move to take place without the proper protection to the building's public spaces. This includes placing masonite or other protective material over floors, cardboard over walls, and pads in the elevators.

Most important to the client is the new space. It is helpful to survey any wall and floor damage prior to installation of any protection. If the space is found to be in good condition at the time of the pre-move survey, and damage is detected after the protection is removed, that damage can most likely be attributed to the mover. The mover will have to pay to have it repaired. A pre-move survey is especially helpful if there is a lot of damage done in the move. If the building is not inspected prior to the move, the client may have to pick up the tab for all the repairs.

Protection is usually installed in the office space during the week of the move. Nothing can be installed in the public spaces until the evening of the move so this is the last thing done before the actual start of the move. The designer should inspect the protection to ensure adequate coverage.

Room Numbers and Directional Signs

The designer should make sure the mover has put up all the necessary signs in the correct locations in the new space. When the movers come off an elevator, these directional signs tell them which way to turn. Directional signs are necessary at all intersections.

Signs should be attached by masking tape to door frames or vinyl wallcovering. They should never be attached to painted drywall with scotch tape as the tape can rip the surface when removed. The mover should also attach the individual room plans to the door of the room.

The Move

If a company is moving from many locations to one, the movers will start in one or two locations depending on how many moving crews are hired. Each initial location is completed before moving on to the next site. The designer should check the space to make sure that everything that was supposed to be moved has actually been moved from the space. The movers should not be permitted to leave any location until this inspection is complete. Initially, in the new space, the mover places each item according to the plan, but does not take time to align things or measure clearances. This is done after all of the items are in the building.

Unpacking

If the employees come in on Saturday or Sunday to unpack, the space is in much better shape by Monday morning. Generally, the movers unpack what they packed; store rooms, files, special equipment. The employees unpack their desks, credenzas, and personnel effects.

Some of the movers should be assigned to fold the boxes flat and store them in bins for removal from the premises. Cartons can usually be reused for two to three additional in-house moves, so it is beneficial to save those that are in good condition. Sometimes, the mover takes the boxes back and gives the client a credit on the final invoice.

The designer still needs some movers for the day(s) after the move to continue unpacking, as it never happens that all employees come in over the weekend to unpack. This would be a much reduced crew from the main move crew.

Furniture Set-up

After the move, the designer with a crew of three men could set each item in its exact location according to the moving plans and the design concept. This takes a lot of time, but gives the space a much more orderly look. At this time any unpacked cartons are put on top of desks and credenzas to enable the cleaning crew to clean underneath the furniture.

It is at this time that problems are corrected and areas rearranged as necessary. For example, if a file will not fit in the spot indicated on the drawing, but the file is essential to the occupant, the space must be rearranged to somehow fit all the items. This stage, however, cannot begin until the main move is complete.

Remove Protection

After the main move and the minor shifts are complete, the floor and wall protection is removed. The visual quality of the space improves dramatically when this is accomplished. Now it starts to take on character. If the protection is taken down before the employees come to unpack, there is a better immediate acceptance of the new space.

Inspect for Damage

After the protection is removed, the designer should tour the building with the mover to determine any new damages from the move. The damages are marked on two sets of plans: one for the mover and one for the designer. If the inspection is performed early, the mover cannot attribute the damage to someone else, and will have to take responsibility for correcting any damages.

Missing Item Search

Now is the time to scout out the missing carton with the president's confidential files, or the favorite painting that is the personal property of the chairman. (It is *never* merely a clerk's file carton that is lost.) The missing items turn up 99.9% of the time. Usually, they are buried under other boxes in the wrong office, or were inadvertently left untagged and are in an area of other unmarked items to be identified.

Clean-up

When the mover leaves the premises on Saturday or Sunday, the protection is gone, all empty cartons are disposed of, all furniture is placed and aligned, all files and shelving bolted, and all unpacked cartons are on top of desks and credenzas. The cleaning crew should come in on Sunday afternoon or evening and give the offices a special cleaning. Any tags still remaining on the furniture should be removed by the cleaning people. When the offices open for business Monday, they will look presentable and workable.

MOVING SPECIFICATIONS
for
<u>   (client)   </u>

A. <u>SCOPE OF WORK</u>

1. Furnish all necessary vans, drivers equipment and helpers required to perform the move; including the packing, loading, unloading, placing, installing, unpacking and removing of cartons as specified and indicated on the enclosed drawings and documents.

2. Furnish all necessary tags, cartons, boxes, bins and crates as required to move office contents per a physical tour of the present location(s).

3. Provide all necessary protective coverings for floors, walls, doors, and elevators both in present location(s) and new location(s).

4. Provide moving drawings indicating moving room numbers and zones.

5. Tag all furniture, equipment, and contents per the moving room numbers and zones.

6. Provide qualified supervision throughout the move at all locations.

B. <u>GENERAL REQUIREMENTS</u>

1. INSPECTION

A. The Moving Contractor shall tour the present location(s) and estimate the number of cartons, boxes, crates and tags required for the move.

B. After such tour the Moving Contractor shall visit and inspect the new location(s) in the presence of a company representative, and should familiarize himself with all field and operating conditions before submitting an estimate.

C. The Moving Contractor should estimate the number of men and hours required to complete the move as specified, based on elevator restrictions, stairs, number of locations, or other conditions inherent to the facilities.

2. PROTECTIVE COVERINGS

A. Provide adequate protection for the walls, building, equipment, and furniture. Install protective coverings on all vinyl, glass, marble and special wood finishes adjacent to moving traffic area. Protect elevator cabs by padding the walls and install protective covering around door jams. Provide ramps as required. Upon completion of the move, remove all coverings and other similar items from the site.

Figure 14.1

B. Provide, deliver, lay and tape an adequate amount of 4'-0" X 8'-0" masonite sheets to protect lobby areas and carpeted corridors from dolly wheels. Masonite shall be removed at the completion of the move. Any tape marks remaining on the carpet after removal of the masonite must be cleaned off.

3. LABOR AND INSTALLATION

A. Movers shall use only such personnel with proper union jurisdiction.

B. The Contractor is to provide labor to unbolt all file and storage cabinets from the wall or each other on the day of the move. Provide labor the next morning at the new location(s) to level, shim and bolt these cabinets back together. This is necessary for safety reasons, and the Contractor will be held responsible for any damage or injuries resulting from improperly fastened cabinets. All files and overfiles must be aligned with a leveling tool so all joints match.

C. Contractor shall disconnect all desk returns the afternoon of the move and reconnect in the new facility (facilities).

D. Contractor shall disassemble and reassemble in the proper configuration all landscape furniture in the new location(s). A storage area shall be assigned for any spare parts.

E. Provide labor, as required, to assist in packing items prior to the move. Provide labor, as required, to assist in unpacking items on the day after the move.

F. The Moving Contractor shall have one person designated as supervisor, who will assist in the labeling of cartons and equipment and will ensure that the move is complete in accordance with plans and specifications.

4. PACKING AND UNPACKING

A. Moving cartons shall be distributed three days prior to the move.

B. Two and three drawer high file cabinets shall be moved if they are going to the same person in the new location. Otherwise, mover's personnel shall assist in unloading, packaging and properly tagging the contents, and unpacking at new location(s).

C. Items located on shelving in storage rooms shall be placed in cartons by movers and unpacked at designated location(s) in the new facility (facilities).

Figure 14.1 (*continued*)

274

D. Typewriters, dictating and transcribing units, calculators, adding machines and time stamps should be packed by movers and moved in special padded bins, which are specially manufactured for this purpose.

E. Company personnel are expected to pack their own personal effects, their desks and their credenzas.

F. Empty cartons are to be folded flat and removed from the premises by the Contractor as soon as possible.

5. FURNITURE PLACEMENT

A. All furniture and equipment shall be neatly positioned at final location(s) and in strict accordance with the drawings.

B. All items to be moved should be left in a neat and orderly fashion at the new location(s). Cartons containing personal effects and other items should be neatly stacked on top of desk and credenza if possible or in one corner of an office or room allowing occupants full access to space and equipment.

C. All files shall be level with matching heights.

6   MOVERS' DRAWINGS

A. Mover shall provide moving plans indicating room numbers of all areas. These numbers shall be physically placed in each area in the new location prior to the move and shall be removed at the completion of the move.

B. Jobs of over 10,000 square feet shall be formulated on a zone concept using different color tags for different zones, blocks of space, or floors.

C. Each existing item of furniture or equipment shall be numbered on the movers' plans. The room plan with these item numbers shall be placed on the door to each space in the new facility (facilities) to assist the moving crews in specific placement of items.

7. TAGS

A. Mover's tags shall be colored with the zone color and numbered with the room number and item number to correspond with the movers' drawings.

B. Blank tags should be left with appropriate instructions with department heads in case they are needed.

C. Movers' personnel shall tag all furniture and equipment per the drawings.

Figure 14.1 (*continued*)

D. Tags which cannot be attached to items until just before moving time should be filled in to correspond to the numbers on plans and left by mover for attaching by others.

8. FIELD OFFICE

A. On a large move the moving contractor shall be provided a field office in the new premises to avoid a lag in communications or operations.

9. ELEVATORS

A. Moving Contractor shall assist in making necessary arrangements for elevator service at buildings involved. The Mover will not be responsible for charges incurred for elevator operators, mechanics and security guards.

10. SUPERVISION

A. The Moving Contractor shall provide supervision at the present location(s) to assist the moving crews in properly locating all items to be moved.

B. The Moving Contractor shall provide appropriate dispatchers to check loading operations.

C. The Moving Contractor shall provide supervision at the new location(s) to assist the moving crews in the proper placement of all contents and equipment. If zones are used one supervisor should be provided per zone.

D. The Movers' supervisory personnel shall be responsible to the Moving Coordinator as designated by the Company.

C. MOVER QUALIFICATIONS

1. Moving Contractor shall submit the following information with his estimate:

A. Location of carrier.

B. Applicable tariffs.

C. Number of full-time employees.

D. Average length of service of employees.

E. Experience of supervisory personnel.

F. Number of trucks owned (or long-time leased) by type.

Figure 14.1 (continued)

G. Other types of equipment available.

H. Description of warehouse facilities - size, location and physical features.

I. Insurance coverage and moving company coverage.

J. Number of men to be used on the job.

K. Number and description of all vehicles and other equipment to be used on the job.

L. List of other moves of similar magnitude.

M. Dun and Bradstreet report.

N. Union Affiliations.

O. Advise which hours and days represent straight time and overtime.

D. TERMS AND CONDITIONS

1. DEFINITIONS

A. The "Client" shall be _____ or any of its divisions.

B. The "Contractor" shall be the selected moving contractor.

2. GENERAL CONDITIONS

A. The Contractor shall be retained as an independent contractor during the term of the Agreement to perform the services called for herein.

B. The Contractor shall not be the agent or local representative of the Client for any purpose whatsoever other than the services provided for in this Agreement.

C. The Contractor shall provide the necessary facilities, trucks, typing and clerical work, supplies and labor required to accomplish the work called for herein.

D. The Contractor shall preserve and maintain Client's contents and equipment in as good condition as same was received by him.

Figure 14.1 (*continued*)

E. Contractor shall comply with all applicable laws, ordinances, codes, rules and regulations in performing the services called for herein.

F. Contractor shall have the responsibility of insuring that the materials to be moved are properly loaded and secured to prevent damage to materials, person and property en route.

G. The Contractor shall be liable for all loss and damage to Client's property caused by the move.

H. Contractor shall be liable for damages to buildings, building fixtures and grounds caused by men or equipment under the Contractor's control.

I. In the event that Contractor leaves a vehicle loaded or partially loaded overnight or over a weekend or holiday period, Contractor shall lock, seal, obtain written approval from Client and leave vehicle in a security area.

J. All goods and equipment in the care of the Contractor under the Agreement shall remain the property of the Client and title to said property shall not pass to the Contractor under any circumstances.

3. TERMS

A. The Client agrees to reimburse the Contractor for all services and work performed under the Agreement in accordance with the plans and documents at the agreed amount. For services and work not covered by Client's specifications Client shall pay the Contractor such compensation as the parties shall have mutually agreed in writing.

B. Contractor shall maintain complete and accurate accounting and payroll records, to substantiate all charges hereunder.

C. In the event the Contractor defaults in the performance of the Agreement, the Client shall have the right to terminate the Agreement immediately upon written notice to the Contractor.

1. Upon the termination of the Agreement, Contractor agrees to return any property or records of the Client remaining in his possession.

D. Invoices for services rendered are to be forwarded in accordance with Client's instructions.

E. Contractor agrees to hold the Client and its personnel harmless and to indemnify them against any and all claims for all loss, expenses, liability or damage arising out of or in connection with the performance of work under the Agreement.

Figure 14.1 (*continued*)

MOVE BID LETTER

___(vendor)___   ___(date)___
___(address)___
_____

RE: ___(project)___

Dear _____:

You are invited to submit an estimate to relocate our offices from ___
(list multiple addresses if appropriate)   to (list multiple
addresses if appropriate)   per the enclosed drawings, inventory and
specifications.

We anticipate a weekend move commencing Friday, ___(date)___ with all
contents, furniture and equipment being moved into the new
location(s) on Friday night. On Saturday, ___(date)___ we anticipate
the exact positioning of furniture and equipment and the unpacking of
contents into files and storage rooms. Sunday, ___(date)___ would be
clean-up day with the removal of empty cartons and masonite.

Please provide your estimate on the attached proposal form. All
proposals must reflect the attached Specifications and Conditions.

We reserve the right to accept or reject any or all proposals
submitted in part or in their entirety. We also retain the option of
negotiating further with the Mover submitting the most favorable
proposal.

We anticipate moving ___(number)___ people with their contents. We
also anticipate moving approximately ___(number)___ desks, _(number)_
files, ___(number)___ chairs, ___(number)___ credenzas and cabinets, __
(number)__ sofas, and ___(number)___ tables. These quantities are
estimates only and are not to be considered as a commitment unless
otherwise specified.

Proposals must be received no later than 12:00 Noon on ___(date)___ .
There will be no extension dates for proposals. Your proposal should
be sent in a sealed envelope to:

                    (Person and Address)

Any questions should be addressed to ___(name)___ at ___(telephone
number)___ . All questions will be answered in writing and will be sent
to all bidders.

Very truly yours,

cc: Owner
     Designer

encl.

Figure 14.2

MOVE PROPOSAL FORM
FOR
(client)

Estimated Hours to Complete the Move _____

Description	Number	Unit Measure	Unit Cost	Total Cost
Trucks Required	_____	Per Hour	$_____	$_____
Estimated Tally Loads	_____		_____	_____
Helpers	_____	Straight Time	_____	_____
"	_____	Overtime	_____	_____
Drivers	_____	Straight Time	_____	_____
"	_____	Overtime	_____	_____
Supervisors	_____	Straight Time	_____	_____
"	_____	Overtime	_____	_____
Cartons	_____	Each	_____	_____
Bins	_____	Each	_____	_____
Crates	_____	Each	_____	_____

Estimated packing charges   _____
Estimated unpacking charges   _____
Estimated leveling, shimming and bolting   _____
Special Containers   _____
Other:(Itemize)

_____ _____
_____ _____
_____ _____
_____ _____

Total Estimated Cost $_____

Moving Contractor _____
Date   _____
Accepted By   _____
Date   _____
Approved By   _____
For   _____
Date   _____

Figure 14.3

EMPLOYEE KIT

XYZ COMPANY
New National Headquarters

<u>Basic Data</u>:

(A) Seven-and-one-half (7-1/2) story office building.
     1. Four (4) floors of office space above ground.
     2. Three-and-a-half (3-1/2) floors of parking space below
         ground.

<u>1st Floor</u>

Lobby, lunch room, main conference room, building manager,
audiovisual workshop, visitor parking.

<u>2nd Floor</u>

International, Administration, International Home Video,
West Coast A&R, Data Processing, Accounting, Royalties,
Financial Planning.

<u>3rd Floor</u>

Domestic, Data Processing, Accounting, Payroll, Personnel,
Financial Planning, Operations, Word Processing.

<u>4th Floor</u>

Domestic, Marketing, Sales, Advertising, Credit,
Administration, Executive.

<u>Move-Related Problems</u>:

It's quite possible that the air conditioning and lighting will not
function properly for several months, or your wastebasket is the wrong
color, or the draperies do not properly shield the sun from your eyes.
It will take time to effectively balance the flow of hot and cold air,
and to clear up all the other "bugs" which usually crop up in a newly
built facility.

If you are plagued by any problem which requires corrective action,
please try to be kind, considerate, understanding, and patient. The
people who have been assigned to act on your behalf as friendly "bug"
killers may be besieged, bothered and bewildered for many months.

If you have a legitimate problem, please contact _____. But,
remember, we're counting on you to be considerate, understanding and
patient. With your cooperation, we look forward to making our move
satisfying, harmonious and productive. It is helpful if you divide
your problems into the categories of: construction related,
telephones, furniture, keys and other.

Figure 14.4

AUTO ENTRY TO BUILDING: On Montgomery Way while traveling SOUTH
                               ONLY:

                               Auto gate will be up daily from . . .

                                   7:45 a.m. to 9:15 a.m.

                                          and

                                   4:30 p.m. to 6:00 p.m.

                               Card keys used all other times . . .

                               Visitor parking by reservation only . . .

                               RIGHT TURN ONLY WHEN EXITING EITHER LOT.

BUILDING ACCESS

A.   During regular business hours, employees may enter the
        building through the main pedestrian doors or via a vehicle
        through the parking garage. (Pedestrian traffic is not
        permitted through the garage entrance at anytime.)

        (Walking from one parking level to another via the drive ramps
        is not permitted at anytime.)

B.   Entry to the building after normal business hours can be
        achieved in the following manner:

        1.   You must be on an approved list.
        2.   Entry through the main lobby door by ringing door bell.
        3.   Entry through the security garage by use of a card key.

        (All persons entering the building after hours must sign in,
        and present acceptable identification.)

        If you should enter through the security guarded garage, the
        elevator must be taken to the main floor to sign in before
        proceeding to your destination. Those persons who are not on
        the approved list for entry after hours will not be admitted.

GARAGE ACCESS

A.   Each employee will be assigned a permanent parking location.
        All parking stalls are numbered.

        1.   Should an employee who does not own an auto be assigned a
              parking space, the employee's supervisor should be
              advised so that the space can be reassigned.

Figure 14.4 (*continued*)

    2.   Should an employee join the XYZ Company after the initial assignment of spaces, the employee will be assigned the most convenient space available at that time.

    3.   Should no parking space be available, the employee's name will be placed on a chronologically sequenced waiting list and assigned the first space made available.

B.   All employees who are assigned parking spaces will be issued card keys which will be electronically read when inserted into the garage card key unit. The card keys will operate the parking gate arm and the overhead metal security gate. Both will operate simultaneously and will allow only one car to enter (clearance height: 7' 0").

Should an employee forget his or her card, the employee must park on the street until a new card can be obtained.

Card keys must be used at all times when security gates are down. (Report card loss to supervisor. Replacements of lost card keys will be made by the Building Manager at the employee's expense.)

C.   The building is located at a very busy intersection. Therefore, during peak traffic hours, the auto gate and security gates will be locked in an open position to expedite the entry of employees into the parking garage. Each authorized car will bear an XYZ Company logo which will identify the car to the guard who will be stationed at the entry of the garage ramp. Any car that enters the garage during the peak hours without a logo will be advised to proceed to the first level, turn around and exit. Refusal to do so may result in the car being towed away by the police.

Logos may be lost due to trading or changing of cars. Lost logos can be replaced though the Personnel Department. For more than one car, please request additional logos.

D.   There are three (3) elevators in the building that travel from the lower level of the garage to the top floor.

Each elevator has a floor restriction feature, and can be locked off to bypass any floor, or to stop at any floor (i.e.: when coming into the building on off hours via the garage, the elevator will be programmed to stop first at the security checkpoint before proceeding to the designated floor.) Elevator activity will be monitored at the lobby level.

VISITOR PARKING

A.   When it is known that vendors and visitors are expected in advance, a reserved parking space can be made available by calling the main floor reception desk. Visitor parking entry

Figure 14.4 (*continued*)

is electronically controlled by the reception desk. Anyone without a reservation will be denied entry to the visitor parking area.

B.   All visitors must be received at the elevator lobby on each floor either by a secretary or the person they are visiting. All maintenance service personnel must first report to the Building Manager's office. All visitors and service personnel must sign the visitor's register.

LUNCH ROOM AND VENDING AREAS

A.   The lunch room and vending areas are provided solely for the use of the employees. Helping to keep these areas clean will be the responsibility of all employees who use the areas.

EMPLOYEE WORK AREAS (RESTRICTED ACCESS)

Employees are requested to remain in their general work areas, unless their duties carry them to other areas.

A.   MARKETING/CREDIT/ADMINISTRATION: Only those people who have been authorized will be permitted on the floor after regular business hours.

B.   COMPUTER ROOMS: 2nd and 3rd Floors.

C.   CONFERENCE ROOMS: 1st, 2nd, 3rd and 4th Floors. To reserve a conference room, please call Personnel.

D.   Subterranean and tower stairs are emergency exits, and should not be used at any time other than an emergency. (Exception: Fire drills.) All subterranean stairways servicing all parking levels terminate on the ground level. The tower stairway services all floors above ground up to the roof. All exits into the areas are locked and equipped with panic hardware. Even though the doors are locked, they will open, but a horn will sound. The doors can only be reset with the Building Manager's key.

TELEPHONE USAGE

The telephone system is a centrex: an outside call can be dialed directly into your extension, or an outside call to the main floor can be connected to your extension. Transfer and tie lines to the Los Angeles Branch and to the Studio are also included in the system. (Complete usage instructions will be covered under separate cover.)

Figure 14.4 (*continued*)

A.   Restricted usage of the phone will be effected in various
        parts and stations in the building. Local and ___, ___,
        and ___ area codes will be unrestricted.

B.   WATS USAGE: There will be WATS lines for use on long distance
        calls within the continental United States. Access to a WATS
        line can be obtained by dialing the building Operator (O).
        Guidelines for usage and acceptable time periods will be
        covered under separate cover.

C.   Each parking level will have "call down phones" for emergency
        use. Simply lift the receiver and the phone will self dial the
        building Operator. These phones have no other use.

D.   EMERGENCY: Most of the telephone instruments will have red or
        black buttons on the face near the touch tone pad. These
        buttons are to be used when there is a power failure in order
        to secure a dial tone.

SUPPLY REQUISITION

All supplies will be kept in the mail room, which is the first level
below the lobby. Servicing of office supply needs will be done by
the mail clerks.

A.   Supplies are no longer self service. They must be
        requisitioned on a supply requisition form and hand delivered
        or mailed to the mail room on the second garage level. (Please
        see the copy below detailing the new "Supply Requisition"
        procedure.)

B.   Stock requisitions must be completed and placed in the
        outgoing mail basket for required supplies. The supplies will
        be delivered with the next delivery of mail. (Mail delivery
        and pick up - twice daily.) Urgent requests for supplies can
        be phoned to the mail room, but must be followed up by hard
        copy. The stock requisitions will aid in establishing separate
        inventory controls for international and domestic.

C.   Supply Requisition Procedure - Supplies are stored in the mail
        room. Servicing of office supply needs is an exclusive
        responsibility of the mail room. In order to obtain supplies,
        a "Requisition for Supplies" form must be filled out and
        submitted by your department. All relevant details must be
        furnished, (i.e.: quantity, catalog number, size and
        description). The department and the individual requesting
        supplies must be identified by name.

        The requisition may either be mailed or brought directly to
        the mail room. All requisitions will be filled only by mail
        room employees. A list of stocked office supplies is available
        from the mail room upon request. If there is an item you need

Figure 14.4 (continued)

that is not stocked, please contact the mail room for assistance.

ARCHIVE STORAGE PROCEDURE

Archive Storage, located in a room adjacent to the lowest level of parking, has been set up with storage racks to accommodate 600 legal size transfer files. The storage slots in the racks are numbered. Each legal size transfer file will be assigned a slot or transfer number. Nothing can be placed in storage unless it is in a legal size transfer file and has an assigned transfer number. All boxes sent to this area must be coordinated with _____.

To use the basement storage facility, please observe the following procedure:

1.   Place items to be stored in a legal size transfer file.

2.   Request a transfer file number from the mail room.

3.   Affix the "Document Transfer Label" to the front of the transfer file. Indicate the department, the date and the transfer number assigned by the mail room. Do not fill in the "Assigned Whse. Box No." box.

4.   Complete the "Warehouse Storage Box Inventory Sheet"; retain the second copy (yellow). The original and third copy (pink) will be picked up along with the transfer file.

5.   The "Warehouse Storage Box Inventory Sheet" is to be used by each department in order to maintain accurate records of what is in storage. Mail room personnel will retrieve transfer files by transfer number only.

(If you have any questions in regard to this procedure, please contact _____.)

TWX, TELEX, QUIP

There will be two TWX machines available for domestic. One will be reserved for sending, and the other for receiving. The sending machine will be located in Word Processing on the third floor, and the receiving machine will be located in the mail room. There will also be two machines on the International floor for sending and receiving.

A.   Outgoing TWXs will be typed on a TWX communication form and submitted to Word Processing for transmission. Verifying copies of the TWX will be attached to your transcript and returned to you. Incoming TWXs will be delivered upon receipt.

Figure 14.4 (*continued*)

B.   International will be responsible for sending and receiving
        their own telexes.

C.   The Quip machine will be located on the third floor in Word
        Processing. If you expect to receive a document via Quip,
        please notify Word Processing, so that your document can be
        routed to you immediately after receipt. For sending documents
        via Quip, simply deliver it to the Word Processing Center and
        it will be processed as soon as possible.

SECURITY

The building will be secured both by manpower and electronic
equipment. There will be 24-hour uniformed guard service. Closed
circuit cameras will be positioned at strategic points for viewing
motorized and pedestrian traffic. The garage will be secured 24
hours a day with a metal overhead gate.

A.   Aside from the cleaning service, there will be a handyman on
        the premises during the regular business hours. The handyman
        will perform such duties as picture hanging, furniture
        movement and adjustments, replacement of light bulbs, etc. The
        handyman may be reached through the Building Manager.

        Note: Only picture hooks are to be used when hanging items on
        the wall. The handyman will supply what is needed upon
        request.

B.   KEY REPLACEMENT: The Building Manager will have a complete set
        of duplicate keys for all offices, files and desk drawers.
        Replacements for lost keys can be obtained from his office.

FIRE EXITS

If you're located in the red blocked area, follow the arrows for the
nearest exit to the outside. There is a stairwell in the center of
the building and at the back (West side) of the building. In case of
fire or emergency, use these exits - not the elevators. In the
garage, there are stairways on the West side and South side which
are to be used in case of fire or emergency.

FIRE SAFETY PROCEDURE

1.   There are fire exit maps located at each work station and in
        all common areas that indicate your location and emergency
        exits.

2.   In case of fire or emergency, the building is to be vacated in
        an orderly manner by the nearest available exit. Do not use
        the elevators.

Figure 14.4 (*continued*)

287

Each floor will have a fire safety leader and alternate. These people will be in charge during a fire or emergency and will insure that the floor is completely vacated.

4.   Fire extinguisher locations are indicated on the fire exit maps.

5.   Periodically, there will be fire drills at which time all employees will vacate the building as described in paragraph #2.

FIRST AID STATIONS

There are first aid kits located on the top three floors in the coffee areas. In the event of a major injury requiring first aid treatment, please contact the Building Manager on extension ____. He has more sophisticated first aid material available for nonprofessional treatment.

PARKING STRUCTURE

Locate level by the painted columns and parking slot by number. Head in parking only . . . please!

Figure 14.4 (*continued*)

DEPARTMENT LOCATIONS

Department	Location

<u>DOMESTIC</u>

Department	Location
Accounting	3rd floor, southwest
Audio/Visual	1st floor, north
Building Manager	1st floor, west
Credit	4th floor, northwest
Data Processing	3rd floor, west
Administration	4th floor, west
Financial Planning	3rd floor, south
Lunch Room	1st floor, north
Main Conference Room	1st floor, southwest
Marketing	4th floor, west
Operations	3rd floor, north
Payroll	3rd floor, south
Personnel	3rd floor, south
Sales	4th floor, southwest
Telecopier, TWX	3rd floor, west
Traffic	3rd floor, north
Travel	4th floor, west
Word Processing	3rd floor, west
Executive	4th floor, west

<u>INTERNATIONAL</u>

Department	Location
Accounting/Finance	2nd floor, north
A&R	2nd floor, southwest
Data Processing	2nd floor, northwest
Administration	2nd floor, southeast
Video	2nd floor, southwest

Figure 14.4 (*continued*)

Requisition for Supplies

To Purchasing Agent   Date   No.

Please furnish the following   To Be Used For

Quantity	Part or Cat. No.	Size	Full Description	

When Wanted

Deliver To   Dept.   Charge to   Acct. No.

Source of Supply   P.O. No.

Make this form in duplicate.
Retain one for references.   Signed   Approved
Use a separate sheet for each kind of goods.   For Dept.

Figure 14.4 (*continued*)

POST-MOVE
ADMINISTRATIVE
DUTIES

CHAPTER FIFTEEN

POST-MOVE ADMINISTRATIVE DUTIES

Now the designer/project manager must attend to all of the minor details and resolve leftover problems. This is often a thankless task, but it is a necessary one. In addition, all invoices should be checked and approved and maintenance specifications provided for the client and his employees.

Punch List

A punch list is a detailed itemization of everything that still needs to be finished or corrected near the end of the project. It is often developed during a tour of the offices with the client and/or major contractors. Sometimes the punch list is broken down by category or trade. Frequently, it is compiled by room number. The list is occasionally used to bargain with a vendor and then to settle for a credit instead of getting every last scratch repaired.

Getting punch list items corrected can be a very difficult task. The vendors do not want to waste their time with minor, time-consuming, non-compensated details. It takes a great deal of perseverence to get all the details resolved satisfactorily. Unfortunately, the designer has not finished the project if the punch list items are not resolved.

Missing items that were delayed in production or shipping, or returned as unacceptable or incorrect, need to be delivered. Expediting these deliveries is never easy and can be time consuming and frustrating.

Maintenance Specifications

The space looks better longer if proper maintenance procedures are established and implemented. It is to the designer's benefit to assist the client in setting up a quality maintenance program for his new offices.

Many vendors provide specifications on the maintenance of their product if this information is requested. Sometimes the information is not available, in which case the designer should research and provide it for the client. Figure 15.1 (shown at the end of this chapter) shows a General Maintenance Schedule for furniture, upholstery, drapery and curtains, carpet and rugs, wood flooring, vinyl flooring, plastic laminate, vinyl wallcovering, grasscloth, marble, painted walls, and ceramic tile.

Final Invoices

Each invoice must be checked against the purchase order and receiving reports for accuracy. Price and quantity delivered in good condition are verified. The designer should check the math for freight, delivery, installation, and taxes. Warehousing charges are another item to verify. Any extra charges are checked against the contract to ensure that they are accepted add-on costs.

If a vendor is billing the client in total, but there is punch list work to be done on a few of the items, the designer should advise making a partial payment. Remember that as long payment is withheld, the designer and client have the bargaining power to get the corrective work done. If this power is relinquished by full payment, it may be more difficult to get corrective work done by the vendor.

After an invoice is approved, it is given to the client for actual payment. It can be difficult to get invoices paid in a timely fashion, therefore the designer should keep reminding the client of payment requirements. Unfortunately, the vendor calls the designer (with whom he has worked and is familiar), and not the client, to inquire when he will be paid. The designer can always refer the vendor to the company's accounting department, but should continue to expedite the payments until they are forthcoming.

Accurate records should be kept of what has been approved for payment. Sometimes things are double billed and the client certainly does not want to pay for something twice.

Post Occupancy Evaluation

After the client has moved in and has been working in the new space for a period of time, it is useful to perform a post occupancy evaluation, or "POE". This gives the designer insight as to the success of this project and better information for future projects. No matter how good a designer is, there is always room for improvement.

A POE is conducted via a questionnaire given to the occupants of the space. An example is shown in Figure 15.2 (shown at the end of this chapter). It requests information such as the employee level of satisfaction with the new work place in terms of privacy, acoustics, lighting, personal comfort, aesthetics, function, efficiency, etc. The questionnaire should be customized for each project and should revolve around the design concepts and project goals. An example of how to present a POE is shown at the end of this chapter in Figure 15.3. Figures 15.2 and 15.3 are derived from "How to Develop an In-House POE", by Gere Picasso in *Facilities Design and Management*, November/December 1987.

This phase of a project is often ignored and regrettably so. The designer needs feedback to see if his concepts are correct. If they are, all well and good. If not, modifications, if possible, should be made. If the space as designed does not function properly for the occupants, it is not serving its purpose. If the designer does not retrofit to correct the problem, the occupants will do their own retrofitting, often to the detriment of the designer's reputation or the aesthetics of the space. Many strange looking solutions can result.

A POE will pinpoint problem areas before they become critical so various solutions can be studied and developed. If employees know a problem is being worked on, they are much more tolerant of the situation than if they think the problems are being ignored.

Many POE's are done with the idea that they will show an increase in efficiency, productivity, and effectiveness, and they often do indicate substantial increases in morale and motivation. A lot of research is being conducted in these areas. Other surveys can be developed around effectiveness criteria to check the results. If positive results are confirmed, it means the planner did his homework diligently and designed the space properly for the functions being housed there. It would be wonderful if this was always the end result, but, more likely, the designer will always find room for improvement, especially in light of continually evolving technological advances.

After Project Completion

A designer who is self-employed or working for a design/architectural firm, a furniture dealer, or a developer, will go on to the next assignment upon completion of a project. However, if the designer/project planner is a planner or facility manager employed by a corporation, building owner, bank, or government agency, chances are that he will be involved with some ongoing maintenance of the space and also with retrofitting the space over time as the organization grows and changes.

A facility manager/director often hires a designer/planner to handle an interiors project or a relocation for him. In order for the facility manager/director to properly supervise the designer, he should be familiar with all the phases and processes of an interiors project, as detailed in this book.

All who are involved in interiors projects will find this book tremendously helpful as it spells out the necessary steps to be followed and takes the guesswork out of supervising and managing the project. The forms shown in the book illustrate "hands-on" methods and can be used over and over for future projects and become part of an interiors project record management system.

GENERAL MAINTENANCE SCHEDULE

FURNITURE

Wood, Lacquer Finish:

To clean, use a soft clean cloth and sparingly apply lemon oil or a good furniture wax. WIPE DRY.

Wood Secretarial Desk Stations:

Clean finish using a soft clean cloth; sparingly apply liquid or paste wax as directed on container. Buff dry; be sure all excess wax is removed. DO NOT USE OIL.

Aluminum:

To clean: Use steam, MILD soap or detergents. WIPE DRY WITH CLEAN CLOTH.

Bronze:

Use a soft clean cloth and wipe down. Occasionally, wipe down with lemon oil sparingly applied to a soft cloth. WIPE DRY. NEVER USE WATER, SOAP, DETERGENT OR SCOURING AGENT.

Marble tops:

Care and Maintenance: Wipe with a clean damp cloth. Once a month, wash top and apply a thin film of a good "marble wax" as directed. Remove excess from surface.

Fabric Upholstery:

Vacuum regularly to remove loose dust. If need for cleaning the upholstery is due to general soiling accumulated over a period of month or years, the following alternatives are possible:

Solvent Cleaners: You may use "Carbona" "Renuzit" or some other dry cleaner of this nature according to the manufacturer's instructions. Wipe gently with a cloth in a sweeping motion. If the fabric is mounted on foam rubber, use special care so the solution does not come in contact with the rubber.

Foam Cleaners: Cover a small area of the fabric at a time with foam, according to the manufacturer's instructions. Avoid soaking. Wipe or sponge off the foam and then wipe again with a damp sponge or cloth so that no traces of the cleaning agent remain. Do not rub.

Figure 15.1

Commercial Dry Cleaning: Fabrics treated with "Scotchgard" Stain Repellent may be safely and successfully cleaned by commercial dry cleaning firms utilizing recognized dry cleaning procedures.

Dry Cleaners: Sprinkle cleaning material - such as "Glamorene" for instance - freely over the fabric according to the manufacturer's instructions. Remove it completely with a vacuum cleaner.

Everyday Stains: This may fall into two categories: (1) Stains which remain surfaced on the fabric and (2) Stains which have been forced between the fibers.

Stains Which Stay Surfaced: Spilled liquids, water, soft drinks, coffee, party drinks, salad oils, etc., should be "lifted off" the surface of the fabric with a folded tissue or cloth. When most of the liquid has been "lifted off", the residue should be gently blotted with a clean surface of the cleaning cloth until the stain disappears. (Important note: Gently blot. Do not rub.)

Stains Which Are Forced Between The Fibers: In the case of stains which are forced between the fibers, two methods are possible depending on whether the spilled liquid is water or oil-based. (In removing these stains, you will encounter one of the major advantages of "Scotchgard" Stain Repellent. When you have completed the stain removal, no solvent ring remains.)

To clean forced-in stains, choose one of these methods:

For Watery Stains: Soft drinks, coffee, party drinks, tea, milk, etc. Use diluted ammonia or a detergent solution. Apply to stained area without soaking the fabric. Dab lightly with a sponge or cloth. Do not rub.

For Oily Stains: Moisten a cloth with any household solvent and dab the soiled area gently. Blot with a dry tissue. Repeat this procedure until the stain is gone. (Important note: Gently blot. Do not rub.) If the fabric is on a foam rubber base, avoid the use of excessive solvent to prevent damage to the foam rubber base.

Stubborn Stains: Certain materials such as shoe polish, lipstick, rouge, etc., will form stains because of the dyestuffs or pigments deposited on the fabric. These cannot be easily removed from treated or untreated fabrics. Recommended cleaning procedure is to sponge with carbon

Figure 15.1 (*continued*)

tetrachloride followed by patting with a dry absorbent cloth.
Repeat the process until the stain is removed. If a trace of
color persists, bleach with diluted hydrogen peroxide.
(Caution: First test bleach on an obscure portion of the
fabric to see if the colors are affected.)

<u>Leather</u>:

To clean: Use a MILD soap (Ivory, etc.) Work up good suds,
rinse clean with clear water, RUB DRY to bring up luster. DO
NOT use any commercial products, such as saddle soap to "oil"
or "feed" the leather. These products attack stitching and
then discolor the leather from the underside. This leather
will not dry out.

<u>DRAPERY AND CASEMENT CURTAINS</u>

<u>Lined Draperies</u>:

DO NOT LAUNDER. Send to a reputable dry cleaning
establishment. Top headings may require occasional careful
dusting with soft brush attachment to electric vacuum or
feather duster.

<u>Casement Curtains of Rovana, Verel and/or Rayon Fibers</u>:

Draperies of Rovana, Verel-modacrylic, and rayon, which have
been satisfactorily processed and properly finished, may be
washed, dry-cleaned, or wet-cleaned, resulting in good
dimensional stability. For best results, decorative designs
such as resin bonded colored prints should be wet-cleaned if
the lining and heading permit.

Rovana and Verel yarns are thermoplastics, hence care should
be exercised in home ironing and commercial pressing to avoid
shrinkage, glazing, or discoloration which may occur with the
use of too high a temperature.

The following procedures are recommended:

<u>Home Laundering</u>:

<u>Hand Wash</u> - Warm water (105 degrees F.) with soap or
detergent - drip dry.* Because of the inherent soil resistant
properties of the Rovana yarn, this procedure may be used if
convenient.

<u>Machine Wash</u> - Synthetic setting or low temperatures wash
(105 to 120 degrees F.) with soap or detergent - drip dry* or
tumble dry* at low temperature setting. As with any ease of

Figure 15.1 (continued)

298

care fabric if tumbled dry, it is important that the drapery be removed from the dryer as soon as the cycle is completed, since wrinkling is apt to occur if the drapery remains folded in the tumbler. Drying is usually effected quite rapidly and the draperies should be re-hung as soon as possible after drying for best appearance since fabrics containing thermoplastic materials, if allowed to cool while wrinkled, usually result in objectionable appearance.

<u>Ironing</u>:

If touch-up ironing is needed, press on the face of the fabric using one of the following procedures:

1. Iron with low temperature - synthetic or rayon setting (275 to 300 degrees F.) - a damp pressing cloth is recommended to minimize sticking.

2. Iron with steam using the rayon or steam setting (not to exceed 300 degrees F.) a dry pressing cloth is recommended.

<u>Commercial Laundering and Dry Cleaning</u>:

<u>Laundering</u>: Using a low titre soap, suds for five (5) minutes at 90 to 105 degrees F. Repeat sudsing for an additional ten (10) minutes, rinse twice for three (3) minutes each with water at 90 to 105 degrees F. Scour for fie (5) minutes at 90 to 105 degrees F. at a pH of 5.0.

High water levels should be used throughout this procedure to avoid crowding. The machine should be stopped during draining and refilling. The drapery may be extracted provided the extractor is cut off immediately after reaching top speed (less than 15 seconds). This will minimize wrinkling and allow less pressing.

Tumble dry* up to 140 degrees F. for as short a cycle as practicable (usually 10-15 minutes) and remove drapery from dryer immediately after drying. Drapery should be hung as soon as possible for best results.

<u>Drycleaning</u> - The following procedures, using petroleum solvent or synthetic solvent, have resulted in satisfactory dimensional stability. A short cycle (2-5 minutes) with little or no moisture present and a high solvent level should be used. Avoid crowding, extract lightly and air dry to minimize shrinkage. Tumble drying for 10-20 minutes, not exceeding 140 degrees F. yields acceptable results, but caution must be exercised since undue shrinkage may result if the temperature in tumbling exceeds 140 degrees F.

Figure 15.1 (*continued*)

      Wet cleaning - Wet clean in warm water (105 degrees F.) and
      soap or synthetic detergent. Rinse thoroughly in clear water
      at the same temperature as the first bath. Extract very
      lightly to avoid wrinkling. Air or cabinet dry not to exceed
      140 degrees F. If tumble dried*, use low heat setting (140
      degrees F. Maximum).

Finishing:

      Since Rovana and Verel yarns are heat sensitive and
      shrinkage, glazing or discoloration may occur with the use of
      too high a temperature in finishing with steam, the following
      procedure is suggested:

1. Steam the drapery heading on a sleever - pat with pad to
    remove wrinkles.

2. Steam the body of the drapery on the bed of a padded
    press. Use the minimum amount of steam possible. Do not
    lower the head of the press. Use bottom steam only.

3. Flat surfaced fabrics can be pressed on a flat bed press
    operating at 55 p.s.i. steam (275 degrees F. maximum) as
    follows:

    a. Lay the drapery on the buck with face or right side
       up - smooth and spread by hand.

    b. Spray lightly with a fine mist of water.

    c. Close head for two to three seconds.

    d. Open head and vacuum (if available) or allow fabric
       to cool.

4. If hand finishing any portion of the drapery is
    necessary, use the synthetic or rayon setting on the iron
    (275 to 300 degrees F.) with a damp pressing cloth.

* Open constructions, such as mesh or diffusion cloth, should be pin
  framed during drying for maximum dimensional stability.

CARPET CARE

Wall-to-Wall:

      To clean: Daily vacuum cleaning. If a loop occurs, clip at
      surface with scissors. Use a professional cleaner for
      cleaning rugs.

Figure 15.1 (continued)

<u>Area Rugs</u>:

To clean: Daily vacuum cleaning. If a loop occurs, clip at surface with scissors. Use a professional cleaner for cleaning rugs. TURN RUGS EVERY SIX MONTHS IF POSSIBLE.

<u>For removal of specific spots and stains</u>:

<u>Oily Materials</u>:   (butter, grease, oil, hand cream and ball point pen ink)

Remove excess material, apply a drycleaning fluid, dry the carpet; repeat application if necessary, dry carpet and gently brush pile.

<u>Oily Foodstuffs</u>:   (coffee, tea, milk, gravy, chocolate, blood, salad dressings, ice cream, sauces, eggs.)

Remove excess material, absorbing liquids and scraping semi-solids, apply detergent-vinegar-water solution*, dry the carpet, apply dry-cleaning solvent, dry carpet and gently brush pile.

<u>Stains</u>:   (fruit stains, washable ink, urine)

Same as above except do not apply dry cleaning solvent; apply second application of detergent-vinegar-water solution if necessary; dry rug and gently brush pile.

<u>Heavy grease, gum</u>: (Paint, tar, lipstick, crayon)

Remove excess material, apply a dry cleaning fluid; apply detergent vinegar water solution, reapply a dry cleaning fluid, dry carpet and gently brush pile.

<u>Cigarette Burns</u>:   Cigarette damage cannot be completely remedied except by reweaving. However, an area of carpet charred in a superficial manner can be improved by this procedure.

1.   Carefully clip off blackened ends of tufts using small, sharp scissors.

2.   Follow this with an application of the detergent vinegar water solution as described in the general procedure for spot removal.

Figure 15.1 (*continued*)

301

* Add one teaspoonful of a neutral detergent, such as those used for fine fabrics, to a quart of warm water. To this add one teaspoonful of white vinegar which is a weak acid and will serve to neutralize any alkaline materials.

WOOD FLOORING

Sweep daily with soft cloth dust mop or soft brush attachment to vacuum. DO NOT USE ANY OIL-BASED SWEEPING COMPOUNDS.

Periodically apply thin coats of fine pastewax with a lambswool applicator. (Drying time as indicated on container.) Buff with soft cloth or electric buffer. NEVER USE WATER, SOAP, DETERGENT OR SCOURING AGENT.

VINYL FLOORING

Daily:

Sweep daily with a soft fibre or hair broom to remove surface dirt. Do not use oil-based sweeping compounds as they tend to leave a film which will repel wax or may even have a damaging effect on some types of flooring.

Light Cleaning - Weekly Basis:

If floor is swept daily, a light weekly washing will be effective. Damp mopping with cool water may be all that is necessary (no detergent or cleaner.) Heel marks or smudges may require extra attention. In this case light rubbing with fine steel wool (O or OO) and detergent are effective. These spots should then receive a light application of wax. It is important to use a clean mop and to change the rinse water frequently.

Major Cleaning and Wax Removal:

Depending on traffic, a major cleaning may be done on a monthly, quarterly, or even at longer intervals. Use only liquid detergents. Soaps tend to leave scum or metallic deposits particularly when used in hard water areas. A strong detergent may be used, if necessary, on vinyl tile. Avoid scouring cleansers as they leave deposits which are difficult to rinse off. Annually remove wax by utilizing a scrubbing machine with fine steel wool pads.

Rinse Procedure:

Never flood a floor with rinse water as it may loosen the

Figure 15.1 (continued)

adhesive bond under the flooring. Remove wash water with a
clean mop or sponge. Rinse with a minimum amount of clear,
cool water. Allow the floor to dry thoroughly before applying
finish.

Application of the Finish:

Apply a thin coat of wax with a clean string mop or lambswool
applicator. Allow to dry for 20 to 30 minutes, longer on
humid days, before applying the second coat.

PLASTIC LAMINATE WALLS OR SURFACE TOPS

To clean, use a damp cloth with warm soapy water. Rinse with
clear water and wipe dry.

VINYL WALLCOVERING

To clean, use a damp cloth with warm soapy water. Rinse with
clear water and wipe dry.

GRASSCLOTH

Stains:

Use a mild detergent mixed in cool water with a dampened
cheesecloth. Lightly wipe up and down over the spot. Be sure
not to soak the paper to any degree as it will then peel off
the wall. Removal of the stain will probably take many
applications and quite a long time. Bleed out the wet area to
avoid a water stain and let the spot dry. If there is grease
in the spot, it will be necessary to repeat the entire
process using denatured alcohol instead of soapy water.

CORK (Bulletin Board)

General Cleaning:

Wipe with a damp cloth using mild soapy water.

For Stains:

Use a scrap piece of cork board of the same type and rub
lightly over the surface to be cleaned.

Figure 15.1 (*continued*)

MARBLE WALL PANELING

Wipe down with a clean damp cloth. DO NOT USE SOAPS OR DETERGENTS. Periodically wash and then apply a thin film of a good "marble wax" as directed. Be sure all excess wax is removed from the surface.

PAINTED WALLS

Smudges and fingerprints can be removed with warm water and mild detergent (specified for all paint finishes) using soft cloths. Rinse with clear warm water and soft cloths, wipe dry. DO NOT SOAK, - DO NOT USE ANY SCOURING AGENTS.

CERAMIC TILE WALLS OR FLOORS

Any ceramic tile can be cleaned with detergent or soap and warm water. Harsh abrasives, particularly on glazed tile, should be avoided. Finishes of any kind, waxes or polishes, should be avoided.

The least impervious surface in any tile installation is the grouting which is somewhat porous. This can be cleaned with a brush and warm soapy water (soaking should be avoided) though it will usually darken somewhat with age. AVOID FLOODING THE FLOOR SURFACE.

Figure 15.1 (*continued*)

POST OCCUPANCY EVALUATION
QUESTIONNAIRE

Please indicate your answers to the questions below about the new office environment and return this questionnaire to the Facility Management Department.

Please use the following answers:

1   Strongly agree
2   Moderately agree
3   Neutral
4   Moderately disagree
5   Strongly disagree

Questions: Responses:

1. My work area lighting is sufficiently bright.   _____

2. My work area lighting is sufficently adjustable.   _____

3. I have sufficient work surface and desk top area.   _____

4. My work surfaces are at the correct height.   _____

5. I have sufficient file storage.   _____

6. I have sufficient book storage.   _____

7. My work area is aesthetically pleasing.   _____

8. I have sufficient acoustical privacy in my work area. _____

9. I have sufficient visual privacy in my work area.   _____

10. My work area is appropriate for my status.   _____

11. My desk chair is sufficiently adjustable.   _____

12. The ambient temperature is sufficiently adjustable. _____

Figure 15.2

Post Occupancy Evaluation Results							
		Strongly Disagree					
Environmental		Moderately Disagree					
		Neutral					
Item From		Moderately Agree					
		Strongly Agree					
Questionnaire		Post-Move Mean					
		Pre-Move Mean					
		N=3 ●	N=3 ■	1	2	3	4	5
My work area lighting is sufficient		2.3	2.7				
I have sufficient work and desk-top area		3.4	1.3				
I have sufficient privacy in my work area		4.3	2.7				
My work area is commensurate with my status		4.0	2.5				

Figure 15.3

INDEX

INDEX